C
Mana
Atrial Fibrillation

First Edition

Peter R. Kowey, MD

Main Line Health and Lankenau Medical Center
Professor of Medicine and Clinical Pharmacology
Jefferson Medical College
Philadelphia, PA

Adam Mohmand-Borkowski, MD

Cleveland Clinic
Cleveland, OH

James F. Burke, MD

Program Director,
Fellowship in Cardiovascular Disease,
Lankenau Medical Center;
Clinical Associate Professor of Medicine,
Jefferson Medical College

PROFESSIONAL
COMMUNICATIONS, INC.

Provided as an educational service by:

Boehringer
Ingelheim

Professional Communications, Inc.

A Medical Publishing and Communications Company

400 Center Bay Drive
West Islip, NY 11795
(t) 631/661-2852
(f) 631/661-2167

PO Box 10
Caddo, OK 74729-0010
(t) 580/367-9838
(f) 580/367-9989

For orders only, please call
1-800-337-9838
or visit our Web site at
www.pcibooks.com

ISBN: 978-1-932610-49-9

Printed in the United States of America
First Printing: February 2011
Second Printing: April 2012

DISCLAIMER

The opinions expressed in this publication reflect those of the authors. However, the authors make no warranty regarding the contents of the publication. The protocols described herein are general and may not apply to a specific patient. Any product mentioned in this publication should be taken in accordance with the prescribing information provided by the manufacturer.

This text is printed on recycled paper.

DEDICATION

To my beloved grandmother, Maria Kowalska, who
suffers from atrial fibrillation and its complications.

— AMB

ACKNOWLEDGMENT

I would like to gratefully acknowledge the generous philantropic support that the Main Line Health Heart Center has received in support of our educational and research endeavors. Special thanks to: Adolph and Rose Levis Foundation/Barbara and Harvey Brodsky, Albert M. Greenfield Foundation, Bob and Ronna Hall, and Annette and Chuck Pennoni. If not for their support, this publication would not have been possible.

— PRK

I would like to acknowledge the editorial assistance of Terry Burke and Phyllis Freeny.

— JFB

TABLE OF CONTENTS

TABLES

FIGURES

1 Introduction: Definition and Classification

Definition

Atrial fibrillation (AF) is the most common sustained cardiac arrhythmia. This rhythm disturbance continues to increase in prevalence (see *Chapter 2*) and is associated with a mortality rate almost twice that in patients with normal sinus rhythm (NSR).

AF is a supraventricular tachyarrhythmia characterized by disorganized atrial electrical activation without effective atrial contraction, leading to:

- A wide spectrum of clinical symptoms (eg, palpitations, shortness of breath, lightheadedness)
- Deterioration of hemodynamics (eg, fall in atrial mechanical function and reduction in cardiac output)
- A risk of atrial thrombus formation that may cause systemic embolization.

AF is a clinical syndrome, rather than a single entity, since there are several electrophysiologic mechanisms leading to AF, no obligatory association with structural heart disease, and multiple reversible causes that may trigger AF. There is no single optimal therapy for all patients, and there are different treatment strategies that may be applied to treat AF.

Electrocardiographic Diagnosis

Regardless of all potential mechanisms and causes, AF has a common appearance on the electrocardiogram (ECG) characterized by:

- Absence of P waves—physiologic action potential initiated by a sinoatrial (SA) nodal cells depolarizing atrial wall (P wave) is replaced by uncoordinated atrial depolarization

- Presence of fibrillatory (f) waves at a rate between 400 and 700/minute that vary in morphology, amplitude, and timing:
  - f waves do not represent total atrial activity but only the larger vectors generated by the multiple waves of depolarization
  - f waves may be invisible on surface ECG (especially in long-standing AF) and they are best seen in the inferior and right precordial leads—extracardiac artifacts (eg, muscle tremor) may falsely suggest presence of f waves
- Irregularly irregular QRS complex (R-R interval):
  - R-R interval may be regular in AF in the presence of complete heart block when junctional or ventricular pacemaker takes control of the ventricles
  - AF with a very rapid or very slow ventricular response may appear to be regular on surface ECG
- Ventricular rate, which usually ranges from 100 to 160 beats per minute (BPM):
  - AF with ventricular rate <60 BPM suggests coexisting atrioventricular (AV) nodal disease, effect of AV nodal drugs, or high vagal tone
  - AF with ventricular rate >200 BPM suggests conduction via accessory tract that bypasses the AV node (pre-excitation syndrome), catecholamine excess, or parasympathetic withdrawal
- Usually narrow QRS complexes:
  - AF with wide QRS complex (>120 ms) may be due to pre-excitation with ventricular activation via an accessory pathway, preexisting bundle branch, or abnormal AV conduction due to rate-related aberration.

An example of fibrillation on ECG is shown in **Figure 1.1**.

■ **ECG Dilemma in Diagnosis of AF**
- A very rapid (ie, >200 BPM), irregularly irregular, wide–QRS-complex tachycardia suggests AF with conduction via an accessory pathway, but

FIGURE 1.1 — Electrocardiographic Features of AF

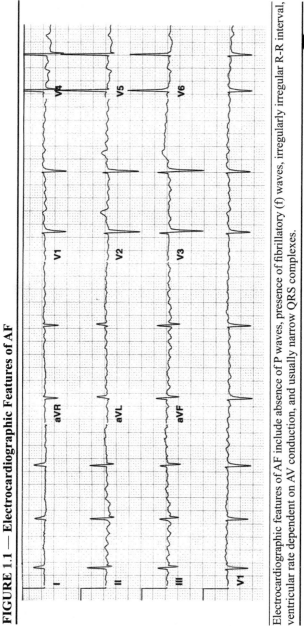

Electrocardiographic features of AF include absence of P waves, presence of fibrillatory (f) waves, irregularly irregular R-R interval, ventricular rate dependent on AV conduction, and usually narrow QRS complexes.

presence of criteria for ventricular tachycardia should always be considered, particularly if the ventricular rhythm is regular
- In patients with AF and pre-excitation syndrome, the ventricular rate can exceed 300 BPM and lead to ventricular fibrillation
- Electrocardiographic diagnosis of AF in patients with implanted pacemakers may be difficult and require temporary inhibition of the pacemaker to reveal underlying AF
- Differential diagnosis of AF includes:
  - Multifocal atrial premature beats
  - Multifocal atrial tachycardia (ventricular rate >100)
  - Wandering atrial pacemaker (ventricular rate <100)
  - Atrial tachycardia or atrial flutter with varying AV block.

Related Arrhythmias

AF may occur in association with other arrhythmias, most often atrial flutter or atrial tachycardia (**Figure 1.2**). These arrhythmias are closely related and may coexist in the same patient.

Atrial flutter arises most often via reentrant mechanism in the right atrium and is characterized by:
- A saw-tooth pattern of regular atrial activity (flutter waves), particularly visible in ECG leads II, III, aVF, and V1
- Absence of isoelectric line between flutter waves
- Atrial rate typically from 240 to 320 BPM
- Common association with 2:1 AV block, resulting in a regular or irregular ventricular rate, characteristically 150 BPM
- Inverted flutter waves in leads II, III, and aVF and upright in lead V1 (typical or counterclockwise atrial flutter)
- Flutter waves upright in leads II, III, and aVF and inverted in lead V1, due to reversed direction of activation in the right atrium (RA) (atypical or clockwise atrial flutter).

FIGURE 1.2 — AF Family of Tachyarrhythmias

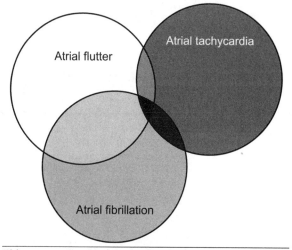

This group of tachyarrhythmias shares much in common, including pathophysiology arising from atrial tissue, often involving critical areas near where veins (pulmonary veins, coronary sinus, vena cava) enter the atria.

Wyse DG, Gersh BJ. *Circulation*. 2004;109(25):3089-3095.

Approximately 75% of all patients with atrial flutter will, at some time, present with AF. Conversely, atrial flutter may arise during treatment with AADs prescribed to prevent recurrent AF or following extensive ablation of AF. Especially with coarse fibrillatory waves in lead V1, AF is often misdiagnosed as atrial flutter.

Atrial tachycardia, AV reentrant tachycardia, and AV nodal reentrant tachycardia may also trigger AF. A typical ECG with atrial flutter is shown in **Figure 1.3**.

Classification of AF

Historically, various classification systems have been used to describe AF. The 2006 American College of Cardiology (ACC)/American Heart Association (AHA)/European Society of Cardiology (ESC) Guidelines organized these classifications. These guidelines describe the

FIGURE 1.3 — Electrocardiographic Features of Atrial Flutter

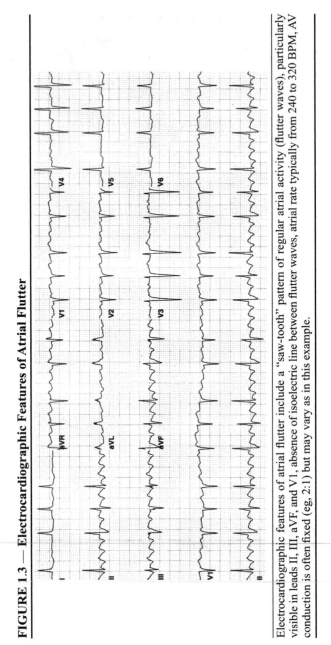

Electrocardiographic features of atrial flutter include a "saw-tooth" pattern of regular atrial activity (flutter waves), particularly visible in leads II, III, aVF, and V1, absence of isoelectric line between flutter waves, atrial rate typically from 240 to 320 BPM, AV conduction is often fixed (eg, 2:1) but may vary as in this example.

character of arrhythmia at a given moment, and all AF labels used in this document have specific therapeutic implications. Initially, AF should be characterized as a *first-detected* episode (either symptomatic or asymptomatic) or *recurrent* episode (two or more documented episodes). This division influences the patient's evaluation, management, and prognosis. The following labels are used to describe the subsequent course of the disease:

- *Paroxysmal AF*—arrhythmia terminates spontaneously (without pharmacologic or electric cardioversion) in <7 days (usually <24 hours)
- *Persistent AF*—episode fails to self-terminate within 7 days but AF eventually terminates spontaneously or is terminated by cardioversion
- *Permanent AF*—arrhythmia lasts for >1 year and cardioversion either has not been attempted or has failed.

After termination of first-detected episode, AF can be classified as paroxysmal or persistent or become permanent. Recurrent AF is either paroxysmal or persistent (**Figure 1.4**).

Additionally, the new 2010 ESC Guidelines define a new category, *long-standing persistent AF*, which is defined as AF lasting >1 year when it is decided to adopt a rhythm-control strategy. This category distinguishes a population of AF patients who should be considered for possible ablation therapy *(see below)*.

The pattern of AF may change during the natural course of the disease or in response to treatment. A patient may have frequent episodes of paroxysmal AF and occasional persistent AF, or persistent AF may become paroxysmal during therapy with AADs.

The above classification of AF applies only to episodes:

- Lasting >30 seconds
- Without a reversible cause.

Episodes of AF shorter than 30 seconds do not meet criteria for paroxysmal AF but may be clinically relevant in certain situations (eg, patients with symptomatic AF), in the assessment of the effectiveness of therapeutic

FIGURE 1.4 — Patterns of AF

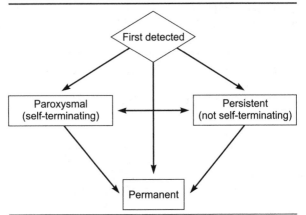

1) Episodes that generally last ≤7 days (most <24 hours); 2) episodes that usually last >7 days; 3) cardioversion failed or not attempted; and 4) both paroxysmal and persistent AF may be recurrent.

Fuster V, et al. *Circulation*. 2006;114:e257-e354.

interventions, and in the presence of an accessory AV nodal bypass pathway.

Episodes of AF secondary to myocardial infarction (MI), pericarditis, cardiac surgery, pulmonary embolism (PE), pulmonary disease, hyperthyroidism, or other reversible causes are considered separately and the foregoing classification should not be applied. AF that occurs in these settings may require treatment of the underlying acute process to terminate the arrhythmia.

The frequently used term "lone AF" generally defines a subset of patients with a favorable prognosis with respect to thromboembolism and mortality. There is no standard definition for lone AF. The ACC/AHA/ESC guidelines apply this term to patients who are <60 years of age with paroxysmal, persistent, or permanent AF without clinical or echocardiographic evidence of cardiopulmonary disease (including hypertension) (see *Chapter 13*). Conversely, in some validated models of AF, diabetes is considered a risk factor for thromboembolism but by conventional definitions, such patients could still be considered to have lone AF.

SUGGESTED READING

Arnsdorf M. Electrocardiographic and electrophysiologic features of atrial fibrillation. In: Basow DS, ed. *UpToDate*. Waltham, MA: UpToDate; 2010.

European Heart Rhythm Association; European Association for Cardio-Thoracic Surgery, Camm AJ, Kirchhof P, Lip GY, et al. Guidelines for the management of atrial fibrillation: the Task Force for the Management of Atrial Fibrillation of the European Society of Cardiology (ESC). *Eur Heart J*. 2010;31(19):2369-429.

Fuster V, Rydén LE, Cannom DS, et al; American College of Cardiology/American Heart Association Task Force on Practice Guidelines; European Society of Cardiology Committee for Practice Guidelines; European Heart Rhythm Association; Heart Rhythm Society. ACC/AHA/ESC 2006 Guidelines for the Management of Patients with Atrial Fibrillation: a report of the American College of Cardiology/American Heart Association Task Force on Practice Guidelines and the European Society of Cardiology Committee for Practice Guidelines (Writing Committee to Revise the 2001 Guidelines for the Management of Patients With Atrial Fibrillation): developed in collaboration with the European Heart Rhythm Association and the Heart Rhythm Society. *Circulation*. 2006;114(7):e257-e354.

Prystowsky EN. The history of atrial fibrillation: the last 100 years. *J Cardiovasc Electrophysiol*. 2008;19(6):575-582.

Prystowsky EN, Waldo A. Atrial fibrillation, atrial flutter, and atrial tachycardia. In: Fuster V, O'Rourke R, Walsh R, Poole-Wilson P, eds. *Hurst's The Heart*. 12th ed. New York, NY: McGraw-Hill Professional; 2008:953-982.

Savelieva I, Camm J. Update on atrial fibrillation: part I. *Clin Cardiol*. 2008;31(2):55-62.

2 Epidemiology

Atrial fibrillation is the most common cardiac arrhythmia treated in clinical practice. It has dramatically increased in prevalence over the decades, and is now an epidemic in the developed world. Epidemiologic studies on AF, such as the Cardiovascular Health Study (CHS), the Framingham Study, the Rochester Epidemiologic Project, the Anticoagulation and Risk Factors in Atrial Fibrillation (ATRIA) study, and the Rotterdam Study, have shown consistent results in the United States and Europe that document an increasing burden of AF.

Prevalence and Incidence

It is estimated that AF affects 1.0% to 1.5% of population in the developed world, with >3 million cases in the United States and 4.5 million in Europe. This may not represent the true burden of the disease since the overall prevalence of AF in the United States and Europe varies from 1% to 5.5 % in epidemiologic studies.

AF is a disease of older adults (mostly with cardiovascular [CV] disease). Prevalence of AF is low at ages <55 years (0.1% to 0.2%) but then sharply rises after age 60, reaching 5% at age 70 and approximately 10% by age 80.

Like the prevalence, the incidence of AF increases with age and the presence of CV disease. The incidence ranges from <1 per 1000 patient-years in those <50 years of age, rising to approximately 19 per 1000 patient-years in those between 65 and 74 years of age and >30 per 1000 patient-years in those age 80 years or older (**Figure 2.1**).

Trends in Prevalence

- The prevalence of AF has increased over the past few decades and is projected to increase dramatically in the coming decades.

FIGURE 2.1 — Age-Specific AF Incidence in
Various Epidemiologic Studies

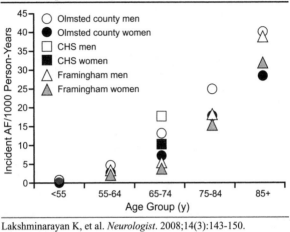

Lakshminarayan K, et al. *Neurologist.* 2008;14(3):143-150.

- The ATRIA study estimated 2.3 million cases of
  AF in the year 2000 in the United States and projected a 2.5-fold increase in the number of patients
  with AF over the next 50 years (5.6 million cases
  by year 2050).
- A recent Mayo Clinic analysis also projected an
  increase in prevalence of AF by 2050. Assuming
  a continued increase in AF incidence, the number
  of patients with AF in the United States by 2050
  will reach 15.9 million (a 3-fold increase from an
  estimated 5.1 million AF cases in 2000). If there is
  no further increase in AF incidence, the projected
  number of adults with AF will be approximately
  12.1 million by 2050 (**Figure 2.2**).
- Approximately one third of patients with AF
  are >80 years old. It is estimated that by 2050,
  approximately 50% of patients with AF will be
  >80 years old.
- There are conflicting data as to the gender effect
  on increasing incidence and prevalence.
- A few trends present in developed counties are
  hypothesized to be responsible for the increased
  burden of AF:

FIGURE 2.2 — Projected Number of Persons With AF in the United States Between 2000 and 2050

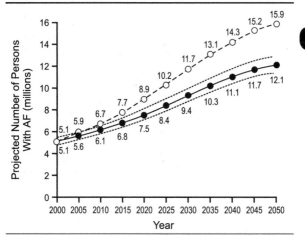

Assuming no further increase in age-adjusted AF incidence *(solid curve)* and assuming a continued increase in incidence rate as evident in 1980 to 2000 *(dotted curve).*

Miyasaka Y, et al. *Circulation.* 2006;114(2):119-125.

- Growth of the elderly population, which has higher prevalence of risk factors for AF
- Advances in treatment of CV conditions (eg, MI, heart failure [HF]), followed by increased survival of patients being at risk for developing AF
- Improved detection of CV disease and monitoring of patients
- Growth in cardiac surgery procedures frequently associated with AF in the postoperative period
- Epidemic of other chronic medical conditions predisposing to AF, such as diabetes, obesity, metabolic syndrome, and sleep apnea.
- Known risk factors and trends incompletely explain the dramatic increase in the prevalence of AF:
  - New-onset AF doubles with each decade of life, independent of the prevalence of known risk factors.

- The Rochester Epidemiology Project indicates that the modest increase in prevalence of known risk factors does not explain the increase in prevalence of AF in the last 30 years.
- Results of the Framingham Heart Study suggest that even after age adjustment, prevalence of AF is increasing.
- Both Rochester and Framingham studies indicate that the increase in prevalence of AF is not merely related to the increased use of the ECG in the community with improved detection of AF.
- Other possible factors that may influence increased AF prevalence in developed countries include:
  - Increase in prevalence of chronic inflammatory conditions
  - Psychosocial factors (eg, frequent changes in lifestyle, stress, anger/hostility)
  - Increase in coffee consumption (although not well established as a risk factor for AF, a recent study from Italy shows higher risk of developing AF with a high intake of coffee).

Lifetime Risk

- Based on Framingham data, men and women at the age of 40 have a lifetime risk of 1 in 4 of developing AF.
- Lifetime risk of AF at age of 40 is still high (1 in 6), even in the absence of predisposing conditions, such as MI and HF.
- Lifetime risk remains the same for elderly patients (accelerated increase in risk of AF is balanced by shortening of life span).

Demographics

- Median age of patients who have AF is approximately 75 years, with approximately 70% between ages 65 and 85 years.

- AF is more common in men than in women, but overall prevalence of AF patients may be the same in both genders since there are more elderly women.
- AF is more prevalent in Caucasians than in African Americans, even if HF is present. Despite the fact that many of the known AF risk factors (eg, hypertension) are more common in African Americans, there is a lower prevalence of AF in African Americans that is perplexing.
- AF prevalence in Asians may be similar to that in Caucasians. An epidemiologic study from Japan assessed the prevalence of AF in patients >40 years of age at 1.3%. A health survey of the elderly population in Hong Kong also reported a prevalence of AF of 1.3%. The first epidemiologic study of AF in China assessed the AF prevalence in that country to be 0.77%.
- Most patients with AF have evidence of structural heart disease. This is particularly true of patients with permanent AF—>80% have a known underlying cause. In contrast, in most patients with paroxysmal AF, there is no clear etiology.

Consequences and Prognosis of AF

Although embolic stroke and impaired hemodynamics (especially in patients with HF) are the most prominent complications of AF, this arrhythmia also significantly increases all-cause mortality and affects quality of life (QoL).

■ Thromboembolism

AF is an independent risk factor for stroke. It is associated with a 5-fold increase in embolic stroke risk. An analysis of pooled data from randomized controlled trials indicates that risk of stroke is similar for paroxysmal and permanent AF. An increased risk of stroke is most prominent in AF patients with rheumatic valve disease, reaching a 17-fold increase in the absence of anticoagulation. Stroke risk also greatly increases with advancing age. In the Framingham study, the attributable risk of stroke ranged from 1.5 % in patients aged 50 to 59 years to 23.5% in patients 80 to 89 years old. The Copenhagen Stroke Study investigators reported that the presence of AF was also associated with greater stroke severity as assessed by increased neurologic deficits, longer hospitalizations, and higher mortality.

AF may induce a hypercoagulable state, leading to systemic emboli and subclinical cerebral emboli even in the absence of stroke. A recent study from Germany in stroke-free patients with AF indicates that AF is a risk factor for reduced cognitive function and hippocampal atrophy. Dementia was approximately twice as common in AF patients as in patients without AF in the Rotterdam study.

Patients with AF are also at higher risk for peripheral emboli. In a study from Denmark that examined the risk of peripheral thromboembolism in patients discharged from the hospital with a diagnosis of AF, the relative risk (RR) of peripheral thromboembolism was 4.0 in men and 5.7 in women with AF compared with a non-AF control group. The most common sites of peripheral emboli were extremities, followed by mesentery, pelvis, and kidney.

■ Impaired Hemodynamics

AF with an uncontrolled ventricular response may also lead to tachycardia-induced cardiomyopathy in a previously normal ventricle. This is best documented in patients with HF. Strong epidemiologic evidence suggests that AF is an independent risk factor for progressive left ventricular (LV) dysfunction, exacerbation of HF symptoms, and increased mortality in patients with underlying heart failure. In the Framingham study, the development of AF in HF patients was associated with 2.7-fold increased risk of death in women and a 1.6-fold higher risk in men. In the Studies Of Left Ventricular Dysfunction (SOLVD) Treatment and Prevention trial, investigators reported 1.34-fold increased risk of all-cause death in congestive heart failure (CHF) patients with AF. In the Danish Investigations of Arrhythmia and Mortality on Dofetilide (DIAMOND) study, AF was associated with a lower survival in patients with CHF (25% greater risk of death) and increased risk of LV dysfunction and MI. In the Digitalis Investigation Group (DIG) study, the development of atrial tachyarrhythmias in HF patients was associated with 2.5-fold increased mortality and a 3-fold greater risk of hospitalizations for HF. In the recently published results of the EuroHeart Failure Survey, new-onset AF was an independent predictor of in-hospital mortality and was associated with longer intensive care unit (ICU) and hospital stays in patients with HF. Interestingly, in-hospital mortality was not increased in HF patients with a previous history of AF (whether paroxysmal, persistent, or permanent).

■ Mortality

Several trials have shown increased mortality in patients with AF. The RR of overall mortality ranges from 1.4 in the Manitoba Study to 2.3 times control in the Whitehall study. This increased mortality is mostly caused by stroke. Increased mortality was more pronounced in women and was not limited to patients with other CV conditions. In the Framingham Study, AF conferred a 2-fold increased mortality risk independent of concomitant CV disease. In AF patients, the subsequent development of HF is associated with a pronounced increase in RR of mortality (3.1 in women, 2.7 in men). The development of AF is also a risk factor for sudden cardiac death and increased mortality in patients with hypertrophic and restrictive cardiomyopathies.

■ Hospitalizations and Costs of AF

The cost impact of the increasing prevalence of AF is significant. Based on The National Hospital Discharge Survey Analysis, hospitalizations for AF increased 2- to 3-fold in the United States between 1985 and 1999 (**Figure 2.3**). The rise in the rate of hospitalizations was most prominent in elderly patients with AF (patients >75 years of age were responsible for >50% of total number of hospitalizations). Annual cost of treatment of AF in the United States in 2005 dollars was estimated at $6.65 billion (including nearly $3 billion due to the cost of

FIGURE 2.3 — Age-Specific Prevalence (per 10,000 Population) of Hospitalizations for AF Among Adults ≥35 Years of Age by Year, 1985 to 1999

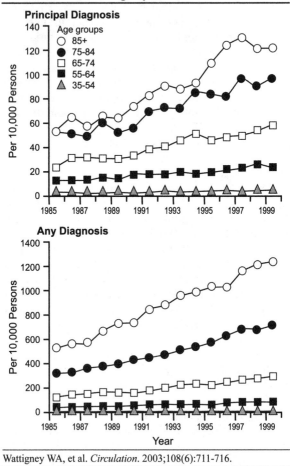

Wattigney WA, et al. *Circulation.* 2003;108(6):711-716.

hospitalization). In Great Britain and France, treatment of AF accounts for 1% of the health care budget.

■ Reduced Quality of Life

AF and its complications are associated not only with increased morbidity and mortality but also negatively impact on QoL. There is no clear relationship between a patient's symptoms and the presence of the arrhythmia. Specifically, patients with symptomatic AF have a high incidence of asymptomatic AF episodes, and patients with asymptomatic AF seem to have poorer functional capacity and global life satisfaction. Therefore, symptoms and QoL are generally used as secondary outcome parameters in clinical trials. Most often, a self-administered questionnaire has been used to measure QoL in AF patients. The majority of studies on the QoL focused on symptomatic patients undergoing interventional treatment (AV nodal ablation and pacing, the MAZE operative procedure and pulmonary vein isolation). Most of these studies show improved QoL with interventional treatment compared with pharmacologic therapy or placebo. This seems to be particularly true in highly symptomatic patients.

QoL has also been studied in major trials comparing rhythm- vs rate-control pharmacologic strategy. No significant QoL benefits were observed with rhythm-control strategies. It has been suggested that patients with well-controlled heart rates and a more predictable clinical course have better QoL. However, a recent analysis of the Atrial Fibrillation Follow-up Investigation of Rhythm Management (AFFIRM) study did not show any significant relationship between QoL and heart rate, either at rest or during exercise. Failure of current antiarrhythmics to keep patients in sinus rhythm (SR) and a more predictable disease in rate-controlled patients may be responsible for nonsuperiority of the rhythm-control strategy. Whether more effective rhythm-control strategies will improve QoL is unclear.

SUGGESTED READING

Go AS, Hylek EM, Phillips KA, et al. Prevalence of diagnosed atrial fibrillation in adults: national implications for rhythm management and stroke prevention: the AnTicoagulation and Risk Factors in Atrial Fibrillation (ATRIA) Study. *JAMA*. 2001;285(18):2370-2375.

Heeringa J, van der Kuip DA, Hofman A, et al. Prevalence, incidence and lifetime risk of atrial fibrillation: the Rotterdam study. *Eur Heart J*. 2006;27(8):949-953.

Kannel WB, Benjamin EJ. Status of the epidemiology of atrial fibrillation. *Med Clin North Am*. 2008;92(1):17-40.

Lakshminarayan K, Anderson DC, Herzog CA, Qureshi AI. Clinical epidemiology of atrial fibrillation and related cerebrovascular events in the United States. *Neurologist*. 2008;14(3):143-150.

Lloyd-Jones DM, Wang TJ, Leip EP, et al. Lifetime risk for development of atrial fibrillation: the Framingham Heart Study. *Circulation*. 2004;110(9):1042-1046.

Miyasaka Y, Barnes ME, Gersh BJ, et al. Secular trends in incidence of atrial fibrillation in Olmsted County, Minnesota, 1980 to 2000, and implications on the projections for future prevalence. *Circulation*. 2006;114(2):119-125.

Wang T, Benjamin E. The epidemiology of atrial fibrillation. In: Kowey PR, Naccarelli GV, eds. *Atrial Fibrillation*. New York, NY: Informa HealthCare; 2005:1-26.

Wattigney WA, Mensah GA, Croft JB. Increasing trends in hospitalization for atrial fibrillation in the United States, 1985 through 1999: implications for primary prevention. *Circulation*. 2003;108(6):711-716.

3 Pathophysiology

Mechanism of Atrial Fibrillation

The development of AF is an end point of numerous disease states that cause structural alterations in the LA and abnormalities in the electrical system of the heart. The underlying mechanism of AF is complex and remains incompletely understood. The conceptual model of this arrhythmia has significantly evolved over the years with a better understanding of molecular, electrophysiologic, and atrial remodeling. The initiation and maintenance of AF requires the presence of the following (**Figure 3.1**):

- Triggering event
- Anatomic substrate
- Factors that perpetuate the arrhythmia.

■ Initiating Event

AF is characterized by the presence of multiple activation wavelets within the atria, which are then conducted to the ventricle in disorganized fashion. The underlying mechanism through which multiple wave fronts occur is still controversial. No single factor has been identified as the sole cause of this arrhythmia. Principal theories include single-focus and multiple-sources hypotheses.

The single-focus theory states that a single rapidly firing focus is the root cause. Wave fronts from the primary focus cross through areas of varying refractoriness, which leads to irregular global atrial activity characterizing AF. Fibrillatory conduction is produced as a regular, but very rapid, rate of firing from a single focus that cannot be conducted to the rest of the atrial tissue in a 1:1 ratio.

Foci of rapidly firing atrial myocytes extending into the pulmonary veins (PVs) have been shown to be associated with many episodes of paroxysmal AF. These foci demonstrate delayed afterpotentials and triggered activity in response to catecholamines, rapid atrial pacing. or

FIGURE 3.1 — The Basic Scientist's Box

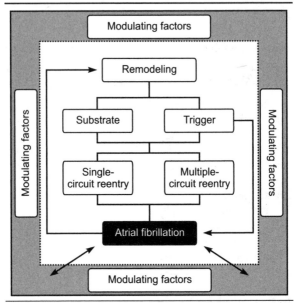

A substrate and trigger are the basic elements for mechanisms that invoke reentry. However, the model also provides for a rapidly firing focus (trigger) to lead directly to AF via fibrillatory conduction. It is not always possible in current models to distinguish between a rapidly firing focus and a single, small reentrant circuit. AF itself leads to remodeling that tends to perpetuate the process. Modulating factors contribute to AF initiation and perpetuation, and AF can produce modulating factors that further perpetuate it or produce manifestations of AF.

Wyse DG, Gersh BJ. *Circulation*. 2004;109(25):3089-3095.

mechanical stretch. The PVs of patients with paroxysmal AF demonstrate a markedly reduced effective refractory period and progressive conduction delay in response to rapid pacing. Conduction block between the PV and the LA is often present. These electrophysiologic features make pulmonary vein foci especially prone to initiate and propagate AF. Less-common sites of initiating foci have been found in the superior vena cava, ligament of Marshall (left atrial epicardial neuromuscular bundle), left posterior free wall, crista terminalis, and coronary sinus.

The multiple-source hypothesis posits that the mechanism of AF involves multiple reentrant circuits within the atria. These produce multiple wavelets and results in fractionation of wave fronts propagating through the atria into self-perpetuating "daughter" wavelets. These wavelets continuously perpetuate themselves and initiate each other. Based on this model of AF mechanism, the number of wavelets at any moment depends on the refractory period, conduction velocity, and anatomic structure of the atria. Short refractory periods and delayed conduction increase the number of wavelets. Also, a certain atrial mass is required to keep a minimal number of circuits for perpetuation of arrhythmia.

Both the focal and multiple reentrant wavelet mechanisms may coexist in some patients (**Figure 3.2**). Automatic foci are not necessary to initiate AF. In the presence of an anatomic substrate, other electrophysiologic mechanisms may lead to AF.

■ Arrhythmia Substrate

It is not clear whether structural atrial changes precede or follow the development of AF, but strong evidence exists that fibrosis and increased atrial size/volume may independently trigger the arrhythmia.

Areas of fibrosis within the atria may produce heterogeneity of conduction within the atria, leading to conduction block and the development of reentry circuits. The conduction system may also be affected by fibrosis, leading to sinus node dysfunction and AV block. Atrial fibrosis may be caused by inflammation, autoimmune disorders, or gene mutations affecting the structure of the extracellular matrix. Fibrosis can also be caused by atrial dilation secondary to associated underlying CV disease (eg, valvular disease, coronary artery disease [CAD], hypertension, HF). Less-common causes of abnormal atrial structure leading to AF include hemochromatosis, amyloidosis, and cardiac sarcoidosis.

Inflammation as a substrate for AF may be caused by a primary infectious process. Histologic changes consistent with myocarditis were reported in 66% of atrial biopsy specimens from patients with lone AF. An inflammatory state, reflected by an elevated C-reactive protein

FIGURE 3.2 — Posterior View of Principal Electrophysiologic Mechanisms of AF

A. Focal Activation

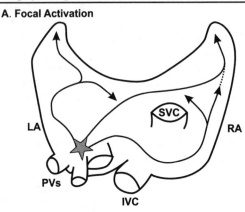

B. Multiple Wavelets

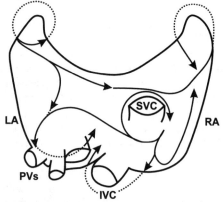

Focal Activation *(A)*—The initiating focus *(indicated by the star)* often lies within the region of the PVs. The resulting wavelets represent fibrillatory conduction, as in multiple-wavelet reentry.

Multiple-Wavelet Reentry *(B)*—Wavelets (indicated by arrows) randomly reenter tissue previously activated by the same or another wavelet. The routes the wavelets travel vary.

Konings KT, et al. *Circulation.* 1994;89(4):1665-1680.

(CRP), may induce AF via disruption of membrane structure in conditions such as ischemia and oxidative stress. These changes in turn may lead to tissue damage followed by loss of atrial muscle mass and interstitial fibrosis.

An autoimmune process in AF is suggested by high serum levels of antibodies against myosin heavy chains, antimuscarinic receptor M_2 autoantibody, and antiheat shock protein antibody in some patients. The strongest correlation exists for antimuscarinic antibody. The presence of this antibody is an independent predictor of AF.

An increased left atrial volume as measured by echocardiography is thought to be an independent determinant of CV events, including AF. A restrictive transmitral Doppler flow pattern (evidence of diastolic dysfunction) is an even stronger predictor of the development of AF. This led to the conclusion that myocardial stretch is an important mechanism of AF, especially in the elderly.

More recently, the reservoir function of the LA, which represents the filling of the LA during ventricular systole and depends on atrial compliance, was showed to be superior and incremental to maximum LA volume alone. LA reservoir function estimated noninvasively using the LA emptying fraction ([maximum-minimum LA volume]/maximum LA volume) was found to be a robust, independent predictor of first AF or flutter in patients older than 65 years.

Although the presence of an anatomic substrate (atrial abnormalities) plays an important role in development of AF, isolation of the PVs will prevent AF in many patients with paroxysmal AF, even in the presence of abnormal atrial structure.

■ "AF Begets AF"

Strong evidence exists that AF alters atrial electrical and structural properties such that atrial tissue becomes more susceptible to maintain and perpetuate this arrhythmia.

Structural changes in the atria involve both atrial cardiomyocytes and components of the extracellular matrix (ECM). AF can cause atrial dilation secondary to loss of contractility and increased compliance of atrial cardiomyocytes. Loss of sarcomeres and decreased contractility are most likely a protective response against the high stress associated with rapid atrial rates. Stretch-related induction of growth mechanisms increases the ECM and fibrosis. Atrial stretch increases local synthesis of angiotensin II, and subsequent angiotensin II type 1 receptor activation, followed by atrial hypertrophy, increased synthesis of collagen, and apoptosis. Interstitial fibrosis contributes to conduction delay, causing the electrical impulse to spread through alternative pathways, increasing the number of reentrant circuits.

Additional changes at the atrial cellular level involve remodeling of gap junctions with reduction in the expression of connexins, which are proteins in the intercellular channels between the myocytes that allow transport of small molecules and ions. There is also an increased metalloproteinase activity that contributes to atrial dilation in AF.

AF also leads to electrical remodeling that perpetuates the arrhythmia. The rapid atrial rate increases cellular calcium loading that may lead to cell injury. As a defense mechanism to minimize calcium loading, alterations in gene expression take place to down-regulate the L-type calcium current. This leads to a shorter action potential duration and a shortened atrial refractory period. Paradoxically, these changes make AF more persistent. Thus a protective mechanism to prevent cellular injury may actually promote AF. On the ionic level, repolarization and refractoriness of atrial tissue are dependent on both the inward Ca^{2+} and outward K^+ currents and their densities. As such, early activating K channels may also be implicated in electrical remodeling in patients with AF.

AF causes a variety of alterations in the atrial structure and function of the electrical system that can lead to maintenance of arrhythmia. Remodeling explains why paroxysmal AF often becomes chronic and why longstanding AF is more resistant to treatment.

■ Modulating Factors

The exact mechanisms through which arrhythmogenic foci are triggered and how existing arrhythmia is modulated remain incompletely understood. These are likely multifactorial processes, but emerging data suggest that the autonomic nervous system and inflammation play important roles in the initiation and maintenance of AF.

Changes in autonomic tone, involving both the sympathetic and parasympathetic nervous systems, are implicated in initiating paroxysmal AF. In an experimental model of AF, simultaneous stimulation of the parasympathetic (acetylcholine) and sympathetic (isoproterenol) nervous systems was a stronger inductor of AF than either of them separately. This explains the observation that in many patients with pulmonary vein foci, a primary increase in adrenergic tone followed by a marked vagal predominance is present prior to the onset of paroxysmal AF.

Different types of autonomic stimulation trigger AF as a function of arrhythmia substrate. Pure autonomic initiation of AF is rare. Paroxysmal AF is mostly vagally dependent in young patients with lone AF and in those who have nocturnal episodes of arrhythmia. AF associated with increased sympathetic tone has been observed in those with underlying organic heart disease, paroxysmal AF episodes before the onset of atrial flutter, or episodes of paroxysmal AF in the postoperative period. Persistent AF is also associated with high sympathetic tone.

Inflammation may trigger and modulate AF via different mechanisms, such as cellular degeneration, apoptosis, and atrial fibrosis. Evidence for a profibrillatory effect of inflammation is strengthened by the observed increased rate of AF after cardiac surgery (known to induce systemic inflammatory response), the arrhythmogenic effect of inflammatory molecules in experimental models of AF, as well as the benefit of anti-inflammatory medications in patients with AF.

Hemodynamic Effects

The hemodynamic effects of AF may be responsible for patients' symptoms and influence therapeutic strategies. Adverse hemodynamic effects of AF include rapid heart rate, irregular ventricular rhythm, loss of atrial contraction, impaired coronary blood flow, and neurohormonal activation.

■ Rapid Heart Rate

AF with a rapid ventricular rate limits the time of diastolic ventricular filling. In patients with LV dysfunction, a rapid heart rate may have deleterious effect on the cardiac output. AF with a rapid ventricular rate can also lead to hemodynamic failure in patients with valvular lesions (eg, mitral stenosis [shorter diastole decreases filling time of the left ventricle across the stenotic valve] and mitral regurgitation).

Uncontrolled tachycardia can impair LV function and produce a dilated cardiomyopathy (eg, tachycardia-induced cardiomyopathy). This diagnosis is most common in patients with clinically silent AF with a rapid ventricular response (>120 BPM) for a sustained period of time. Because of the lack of clinical symptoms of AF, such patients often present with new-onset HF secondary to cardiomyopathy rather than AF. Control of ventricular rate may reverse this type of LV dysfunction within a few weeks.

In animal models of tachycardia-induced cardiomyopathy, an initial drop in cardiac output may occur within 24 hours and then progress over 5 weeks. The severity of the cardiomyopathy is a function of the rate and duration of pacing. Cessation of pacing leads to left ventricular ejection fraction (LVEF) improvement in 24 hours and a return to control levels within weeks (**Figure 3.3**).

■ Irregular Ventricular Rate

The irregular ventricular rhythm has negative hemodynamic consequences independent of the ventricular rate. Compared with patients with a regularly paced rhythm at the same ventricular rate, patients with AF have significantly reduced cardiac output, elevated central venous pressure, increased sympathetic activity, and decreased coronary blood flow. The adverse hemodynamic effect of an irregular rhythm may be multifactorial. Variation in ventricular filling leads to a beat-to-beat decrease in myocardial contractility and abnormal ventricular mechanics. Patients treated with AV nodal ablation and insertion of a ventricular pacemaker with regular pacing may improve functional capacity, LV function, and QoL.

FIGURE 3.3 — Several Proposed Mechanisms of Tachycardia-Induced Cardiomyopathy and the Evidence Supporting Them

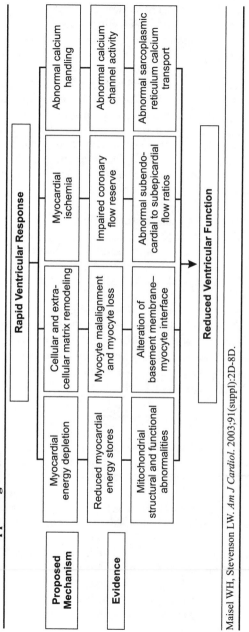

Maisel WH, Stevenson LW. *Am J Cardiol.* 2003;91(suppl):2D-8D.

■ Loss of Atrial Contraction

The loss of atrial contraction causes an increase in LV end diastolic pressure (LVEDP) and reductions in LV contractility and stroke volume. This has particular hemodynamic significance in patients with reduced ventricular compliance associated with hypertensive heart disease, aortic stenosis, hypertrophic cardiomyopathy, and restrictive cardiomyopathy. In such patients, early passive LV filling is decreased and stroke-volume dependence on atrial contraction is magnified. Also, patients with decreased LV filling, such as those with mitral stenosis and right ventricular failure, are more prone to hemodynamic deterioration with AF.

■ Impaired Coronary Blood Flow

Coronary blood flow occurs in diastole and depends on the difference between aortic diastolic pressure and LVEDP. AF with a rapid ventricular response and shortened diastole leads to increased LVEDP and impaired coronary flow. Coronary vascular resistance also increases, mediated by activation of α-adrenergic receptors. These alterations may explain chest pain during AF, even in those without CAD. In patients with underlying CAD, decreased coronary flow reserve during AF can be especially important in this scenario since compensatory coronary vasodilatation is limited.

■ Neurohormonal Activation

AF increases levels of atrial natriuretic peptide (ANP), a reflection of altered systemic hemodynamics. ANP levels decrease as soon as 24 hours after successful cardioversion, suggesting rapid normalization of endocrine activation when NSR is restored. Although brain natriuretic peptide (BNP) levels are not usually increased in patients with new-onset AF (unless concomitant HF is present), a study (mean follow-up 2.6 years) of patients with episodic AF who converted to normal sinus rhythm showed elevated levels of Nt-proANP and Nt-proBNP and, to a lesser extent, aldosterone. These data suggest that AF-induced LV remodeling and dysfunction may be present before an echocardiographic or a clinical diagnosis is made.

AF with a rapid ventricular response causing a fall in cardiac output leads to a compensatory release of neurohormonal vasoconstrictors (angiotensin II and norepinephrine) that helps to maintain blood pressure (BP) but that also increases afterload.

Thromboembolism

The pathogenesis of thromboembolism in AF (in particular, stroke) and prevention strategies will be discussed in *Chapter 13*.

SUGGESTED READING

Abhayaratna WP, Fatema K, Barnes ME, et al. Left atrial reservoir function as a potent marker for first atrial fibrillation or flutter in persons ≥65 years of age. *Am J Cardiol*. 2008;101(11):1626-1629.

Arnsdorf M, Lip G. Hemodynamic consequences of atrial fibrillation and cardioversion to sinus rhythm. In: Basow DS, ed. *UpToDate*. Waltham, MA: UpToDate; 2010.

Baba A, Fu M. Autoantibodies in atrial fibrillation: actor, biomaker or bystander? *Autoimmunity*. 2008;41(6):470-472.

Burstein B, Nattel S. Atrial fibrosis: mechanism and clinical relevance in atrial fibrillation. *J Am Coll Cardiol*. 2008;51(8):802-809.

Chou CC, Chen PS. New concepts in atrial fibrillation: neural mechanisms and calcium dynamics. *Cardiol Clin*. 2009;27(1):35-43.

Fuster V, Rydén LE, Cannom DS, et al; American College of Cardiology/American Heart Association Task Force on Practice Guidelines; European Society of Cardiology Committee for Practice Guidelines; European Heart Rhythm Association; Heart Rhythm Society. ACC/AHA/ESC 2006 Guidelines for the Management of Patients with Atrial Fibrillation: a report of the American College of Cardiology/American Heart Association Task Force on Practice Guidelines and the European Society of Cardiology Committee for Practice Guidelines (Writing Committee to Revise the 2001 Guidelines for the Management of Patients With Atrial Fibrillation): developed in collaboration with the European Heart Rhythm Association and the Heart Rhythm Society. *Circulation*. 2006;114(7):e257-e354.

Issac TT, Dokainish H, Lakkis NM. Role of inflammation in initiation and perpetuation of atrial fibrillation: a systematic review of the published data. *J Am Coll Cardiol*. 2007;50(21):2021-2028.

Kourliouros A, Savelieva I, Kiotsekoglou A, Jahangiri M, Camm J. Current concepts in the pathogenesis of atrial fibrillation. *Am Heart J*. 2009;157(2):243-252.

Prystowsky EN, Waldo A. Atrial fibrillation, atrial flutter, and atrial tachycardia. In: Fuster V, O'Rourke R, Walsh R, Poole-Wilson P, eds. *Hurst's The Heart*. 12th ed. New York, NY: McGraw-Hill Professional; 2008:953-982.

Wyse DG, Gersh BJ. Atrial fibrillation: a perspective: thinking inside and outside the box. *Circulation*. 2004;109(25):3089-3095.

4
Risk Factors

Introduction

The association between AF and numerous cardiac and noncardiac conditions suggests that multiple alternative pathways may lead to this arrhythmia. Cardiac conditions that elevate left atrial pressure and result in left atrial dilatation are more likely to induce AF. Examples of structural heart disease that may cause such elevation and dilatation include hypertensive heart disease, HF, coronary disease with a history of an MI, and valvular heart disease.

Associated noncardiac conditions, such as obesity, hyperthyroidism, acute stroke, postoperative state, infections, and alcohol abuse, as well as changes in autonomic nervous system may lead to AF, even in the absence of underlying heart disease. A strong family history of AF suggests a genetic etiology. Others with paroxysmal, persistent, or permanent AF have no history of heart disease or other identifiable precipitating factors at the time of initial presentation (lone AF).

AF etiologies and risk factors are presented in **Table 4.1**.

Idiopathic AF, Physiologic Factors, and Genetic Factors

■ Lone AF

In the subset of patients with AF, the etiology remains unknown. Lone AF refers to patients <60 years of age with paroxysmal, persistent, or permanent AF without any clinical or echocardiographic evidence of cardiopulmonary disease (including hypertension). This subset of patients with AF has a favorable prognosis regarding thromboembolism and mortality. At the time of initial presentation, 10% to 30% of patients with AF

TABLE 4.1 — AF Etiologies and Risk Factors

- Idiopathic (lone AF)
- Genetic AF
- Age-induced atrial changes
- Atrial dilatation or pressure elevation:
  - HTN and LVH
  - Systolic or diastolic HF
  - Valvular heart disease (mitral, tricuspid) and RHD
  - Cardiomyopathy leading to systolic or diastolic dysfunction
  - Pulmonary HTN (PE, OSA, COPD)
  - Hemodynamic disturbances (increased pulse pressure)
  - Congenital heart disease
  - Intracardiac thrombus or mass
- Atrial ischemia:
  - Acute MI
- Inflammatory or infiltrative atrial disease:
  - Pericarditis
  - Amyloidosis
  - Myocarditis
- Atrial arrhythmias:
  - Sick sinus syndrome
  - SVTs (particularly WPW)
- Noncardiac conditions:
  - Obesity
  - Metabolic syndrome
  - Alcohol intoxication
  - Hyperthyroidism
  - Neurogenic (hemorrhagic or large ischemic stroke)
  - Infections (pneumococcal pneumonia)
- Postoperative:
  - Post–CABG and valve surgery (most common)
  - Post–cardiac transplantation
  - Post–noncardiac surgery (especially intrathoracic)
- Changes in autonomic tone:
  - Increased parasympathetic tone (sleep, digoxin)
  - Increased sympathetic tone (anxiety, stress, caffeine, sympathomimetic medications)
- Endurance sport practice

have no obvious etiology and can be classified as lone AF. However, with time, underlying heart disease may be discovered using more sensitive techniques for the diagnosis of underlying heart disease. The use of these more sensitive techniques may be responsible for a much lower prevalence of lone AF as shown in the long-term follow-up data from the Mayo Clinic and Framingham studies (only 2% to 5%). The discrepancy may also reflect sampling sites—more lone AF in the office than in the hospital.

Lone AF is felt to be related to electrophysiologic triggers in structurally normal atria. Genetic factors and some newly emerging risk factors may explain these phenomena. For example, in one study, accumulated lifetime physical activity, height, and left atrial size were the risk factors for lone AF in otherwise healthy middle-aged individuals.

■ Atrial Changes With Aging

The presence of AF rises sharply as age increases, reaching approximately 10% by age 80. Although this increased risk is mostly related to a higher prevalence of traditional risk factors in the elderly, atrial changes resulting from normal aging may also contribute to the increased risk. Fibrosis with aging may occur in the sinus or AV node or nerves supplying these structures or the atrial myocardium (including amyloid deposition), and may lead to atrial dilatation.

■ Genetic AF

A growing amount of data suggests a genetic predisposition to AF. The Framingham Heart Study showed that the RR of developing AF is increased by 85% if at least one parent has a history of this arrhythmia. Hereditary factors may explain some cases of lone AF and the lack of this arrhythmia in certain patients with severe structural heart disease. This genetic susceptibility to AF may be divided into two categories: monogenic with a Mendelian hereditary pattern and polygenic.

In monogenic AF, both autosomal dominant and recessive inheritance patterns have been reported. Most often, monogenic inheritance is association with mutated genes in potassium channels (*KCNQ1, KCNE2, KCNJ2,* and *KCNH2* genes). Autosomal dominant AF also has been linked with loci at 10q22-q24 region (unknown gene). AF occurs in association with other inherited structural heart diseases. Mutations in SCN5 (cardiac sodium channel gene) have been associated with an autosomal dominant form of AF, usually in association with a dilated cardiomyopathy.

Genetic susceptibility to AF is most commonly polygenic. Although previously referred to as nonfamilial AF, polygenic AF most likely possesses a hereditary component. This form of AF occurs through the interaction of different genes and environmental factors and is frequently associated with underlying heart disease. This form of inheritance can explain a modest increase in the RR of AF in first- and second-degree relatives. Polygenic AF has been associated with abnormalities in the following genes: potassium channel, sodium channel, sarcoplasmic reticulum calcium ATPase (SERCA2) regulatory, renin-angiotensin system, connexin-40, and genes related to inflammation.

Our knowledge of AF genetics is growing rapidly with the progress of genetic testing and the availability of genome-wide single-nucleotide polymorphism (SNP) markers. Recently, researchers from Iceland performed genome-wide association scans looking for an association with AF or atrial flutter. They identified a strong association between two sequence variants on chromosome 4q25 (near gene PITX2) and AF. At least 35% of European-descent individuals have at least one of these variants, which increases the risk of AF by 1.39 to 1.72. The association between variants on chromosome 4q25 with AF was even stronger in the Chinese population, where it is carried by 75% of individuals. These variants are adjacent to gene PITX2, which plays a key role in heart development by directing left-right asymmetry of the heart. Researchers reported a new genetic variant (linked with an increased risk of AF) in the ZFHX3 gene on chromosome 16q22. This association is found only in patients of European descent. More than one third of this population carries a copy of the variant in the ZFHX3 gene. The presence of this variant increases the risk of AF (odds ratio [OR] = 1.21), ischemic stroke (OR = 1.11), and cardioembolic stroke (OR = 1.22). The ZFHX3 gene variant does not correlate with the presence of other risk factors for AF, such as obesity, hypertension, or CAD.

The risk of AF associated with the variant on 16q22 chromosome is lower than for the two variants on chromosome 4q25 (20% vs 72% and 39%, respectively). The risk doubles for individuals who carry two copies of these variants. Both genes, PITX2 and ZFHX3, may work via the same pathway, and their genetic variants may confer independent and additive risk.

As with many diseases, we anticipate that in any individual patient, there is a complex interaction between genetics and extrinsic factors that ultimately results in AF. A better understanding of the genetics of this condition is essential to understanding this interplay.

■ Endurance Sports Exercise

Although the benefit of regular moderate exercise in controlling CV risk factors has been well documented, the correlation between excessive sports practice and a higher prevalence of AF has also been noted. Results of small studies in competitive athletes demonstrate that the probability of AF is two to 10 times higher after adjusting for other risk factors. These data reveal the need for larger epidemiologic studies to clarify the association and set limits on the intensity of exercise for the prevention of AF in select individuals without losing the CV benefits.

Several possible mechanisms for an increased prevalence of AF in athletes exist. An increase in LV mass and left atrial diameter (as an adaptation to excessive exercise) is common in competitive athletes. A higher frequency of premature atrial contractions and hypovolemia leading to alternations in BP may also contribute to the increased incidence. Additionally, increased vagal tone may also play a role. Aerobic exercise may induce esophageal acid reflux, which has been shown to stimulate vagal reflexes and AF (**Figure 4.1**).

Cardiac and Noncardiac Conditions Associated With AF

■ Hypertension

Hypertensive heart disease is the most common underlying disease in patients with AF. In the Manitoba

FIGURE 4.1 — Possible Etiopathogenic Factors Influencing the Development of AF in Athletes

Triggers

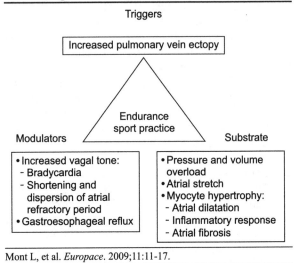

Increased pulmonary vein ectopy

Endurance sport practice

Modulators

- Increased vagal tone:
  - Bradycardia
  - Shortening and dispersion of atrial refractory period
- Gastroesophageal reflux

Substrate

- Pressure and volume overload
- Atrial stretch
- Myocyte hypertrophy:
  - Atrial dilatation
  - Inflammatory response
  - Atrial fibrosis

Mont L, et al. *Europace.* 2009;11:11-17.

follow-up study, a history of hypertension increased the risk of AF by 1.42-fold. While this is a relatively mild increase in risk, the high prevalence of hypertension in the population (53% in the mentioned study) makes hypertension the most common risk factor for AF in the developed world.

High arterial pressure may induce left ventricular hypertrophy (LVH), with a subsequent volume load of the LA leading to atrial remodeling.

■ Heart Failure

In the report from the Framingham Heart Study, the incidence of AF in patients with HF was 5.4 % per year. It increases from <10% in those with new New York Heart Association (NYHA) class I to 50% in those with NYHA class IV. Furthermore, the Epidemiology, Practice, Outcomes, and Costs of Heart Failure (EPOCH) study, which examined racial variation in the presence of AF among patients with HF, showed that blacks with HF have a lower prevalence of AF than whites (20% vs 38%). Both systolic dysfunction and diastolic dysfunction increase the risk of AF. The development of AF in HF appears to predict death independent of other factors and regardless of LV systolic function. However, the pathophysiologic mechanism that leads to AF in patients with HF is complex. Atrial dilatation and remodeling, leading to changes in neurohormonal and electrical activity, may create an environment in which HF leads to AF and AF decompensates HF.

■ Coronary Artery Disease and Acute MI

CAD is a rare cause of AF, unless acute complications are present such as decompensated HF. Although AF as a presenting rhythm of an acute MI is uncommon, it occurs transiently in 6% to 13% of patients in the peri-infarct period. Possible mechanisms include atrial stretch secondary to LV dysfunction and atrial ischemia. The widespread use of interventional coronary revascularization (percutaneous coronary intervention [PCI]) for treatment of acute MI has been associated with a notable decline in the incidence of AF in CAD. The incidence of AF in patients with chronic CAD (without other associated risk factors) is low. However, AF is an independent predictor of increased mortality in patients with CAD.

■ Valvular Heart Disease

Rheumatic heart disease (RHD) is seen in conjunction with AF, but due to a decreasing occurrence of RHD in the developed world, it has decreased as a risk factor AF. The presence of AF is 50% in combined mitral regurgitation and stenosis and rises to 70% if tricuspid regurgitation is also present.

AF is common in other nonrheumatic mitral regurgitant processes such as myxomatous mitral valve or annular calcification. AF is less common in aortic valve disease but may be seen as a late complication of aortic stenosis or regurgitation.

Isolated right heart valvular disease is an infrequent cause of AF.

■ Pericarditis

Pericarditis complicating cardiac surgery likely contributes to postoperative AF. However, a direct causative relationship has not been proven. Transient AF is more common in acute pericarditis than myocarditis (in contradistinction to ventricular arrhythmias). Long-standing pericarditis is commonly associated with AF. A causative relationship between pericarditis and AF is best documented in constrictive pericarditis. In an analysis of a series of patients with constrictive pericarditis, 22% had AF. The presence of pericardial calcification appears to increase the risk of AF.

■ Hypertrophic Cardiomyopathy (HCM)

The incidence of AF in patients with HCM is four to six times higher than in the general population (approximately 2% per year). Some contributing factors for AF development in HCM include LVH, restrictive LV filling, atrial dilatation, and mitral regurgitation. The presence and severity of an outflow tract gradient has not been shown to increase the risk of AF. Additionally, although the development of AF in HCM can lead to rapid hemodynamic failure, the impact on mortality has not been fully elucidated.

■ Congenital Heart Disease

AF frequently complicates congenital heart defects. For instance, it occurs in approximately 20% of adults with atrial septal defect (ASD). The incidence of AF in ASD is age related with as many as 60% of patients >60 years of age having both conditions. Furthermore, other forms of congenital heart disease that affect the atria, or the effect of surgical correction of other congenital defects, may result in AF.

■ Pulmonary Vascular and Pulmonary Disease

AF occurs in approximately 10% of patients with documented PE and sometimes is the only sign of acute PE. Therefore, a PE must be considered in the differential diagnosis of new-onset AF.

AF may complicate the course of chronic obstructive pulmonary disease (COPD). COPD may lead to atrial arrhythmias including AF through multiple mechanisms, including hypoxia with elevated catecholamine levels, respiratory acidosis, and right ventricular failure. The side effects of therapy, such as β-agonists, theophylline, or digoxin, also result in AF. Multifocal atrial tachycardia (MAT) may mimic AF on physical examination, and it may be difficult to distinguish between MAT and AF on ECG.

The incidence of AF is significantly increased in patients with obstructive sleep apnea (OSA), even in the absence of underlying heart disease. The risk of post–coronary artery bypass graft (CABG) AF is notably higher in patients with an abnormal preoperative sleep study. The impact of OSA therapy with continuous positive airway pressure (CPAP) on AF is unclear.

AF occurs occasionally in a host of other pulmonary and pulmonary vascular conditions. Possible causes include hemodynamic changes resulting in increased left and/or right atrial pressure, hypoxia, respiratory acidosis and/or alkalosis with associated electrolyte shifts, increased circulating catecholamines, right ventricular failure, and effects of medications used to treat the underlying condition.

■ Obesity

Obesity is an epidemic in the western world. When compared with people with a normal body mass index (BMI) (<25 kg/m^2), obese individuals (BMI >30 kg/m^2) are significantly more likely to develop AF, and the risk of a new onset of AF is 3% to 8% higher with each unit increase in BMI.

Obesity may lead to AF through multiple mechanisms: increased left atrial size (due to diastolic dysfunction, increased plasma volume, and neurohormonal activation), autonomic dysfunction, and sleep apnea, all of which commonly occur in obese patients.

■ The Metabolic Syndrome

The metabolic syndrome, defined as the constellation of abdominal obesity, hypertension, hypertriglyceridemia, impaired glucose tolerance, and low high-density lipoprotein (HDL) cholesterol, is a well-established CV risk factor. The Niigata Preventive Medicine Study of

28,499 patients in Japan showed that the risk of developing AF is significantly greater in those with the metabolic syndrome.

■ Hyperthyroidism

AF is the most common CV complication of hyperthyroidism. Overall, the incidence in patients with hyperthyroidism varies from 8% to 15%. Although more common in men and in patients with triiodothyronine (T_3) toxicosis, the incidence in patients with hyperthyroidism also increases with advancing age. AF occurs in <1% of patients under the age of 40 years and up to 25% above the age of 60 years.

Subclinical hyperthyroidism (defined as a low level of thyroid-stimulating hormone [TSH] and normal level of thyroid hormone) is as strong a risk factor for AF as is clinical hyperthyroidism. There is a 5-fold increased risk that correlates strongly with the TSH level. Although new-onset AF is caused by clinical hyperthyroidism in <1% of cases, serum TSH should still be measured in all patients with new-onset AF in order to exclude subclinical thyroid disease. Identification of hyperthyroidism as an etiology of AF is crucial because within 6 weeks of becoming euthyroid, 60% of patients have a spontaneous conversion to NSR. Hyperthyroidism leads to AF via direct effect of thyroxine on the myocardium and the conduction system (increased automaticity, shortening of action potential and refractory period), hypercatecholamine state, and increased cardiac sensitivity to catecholamines. The management of hyperthyroidism requires direct treatment of the excessive thyroid state. β-Blocker therapy alone is inadequate but is used effectively to control the ventricular response.

■ Alcohol and Other Toxins

AF frequently occurs after binge drinking (the holiday heart syndrome). While even a small amount of alcohol can trigger AF in susceptible patients, chronic moderate alcohol consumption does not appear to increase the risk in the vast majority of patients. Chronic heavy alcohol use is associated with an increased incidence of AF in men. In the Framingham Study, the risk of developing AF was increased by 34% when the amount of alcohol consumed was more than three drinks per day. Several proposed mechanisms involving alcohol consumption may lead to AF, including toxic effect on cardiomyocytes, hyperadrenergic state, impaired vagal tone, and increased intra-atrial conduction time.

Regular consumption of caffeine was not found to be associated with increased risk of AF in the Woman's Health Study and the Danish Diet, Cancer, and Health Study. However, data from a retrospective study from Italy suggest that increased coffee consumption in non-habitual drinkers results in a greater risk.

The results of the prospective, population-based Rotterdam Study demonstrated that current and former cigarette smokers have an increased risk of AF compared with nonsmokers (RR 1.51, 95% CI 1.07-2.12, RR 1.49, 95% CI 1.14-1.97, respectively). The results of this study suggested that former smoking constitutes an equally strong risk factor as current smoking.

■ **Medications**

Inhaled or systemic sympathomimetic drugs (eg, albuterol, theophylline, and medications that increase vagal tone, such as digoxin) may contribute to the development of AF. AF and other arrhythmias occur in critically ill patients being treated with positively inotropic agents, such as dobutamine or milrinone.

The use of adenosine to treat supraventricular tachycardia (SVT) may result in AF. Although adenosine terminates SVT in 99% of patients, it may lead to AF in 12% of recipients by transient shortening of atrial refractoriness. Notably, in patients with underlying pre-excitation syndrome, it can result in a very rapid ventricular rate because of conduction via an accessory pathway.

■ **Cardiac Surgery**

AF is a common complication of post–cardiac surgery. AF may occur in up to 40% of patients after CABG, up to 50% after valve surgery, and up to 60% after CABG and valve replacement. In the majority of cases, AF occurs in the early postoperative period (day 2 to 4). AF may complicate cardiac transplantation in up to one fourth of patients, most often in the absence of transplanted heart rejection. AF is much less likely to develop after noncardiac surgery, with the highest risk after intrathoracic surgery. It is a self-limited condition in most instances, although it may persist in a few patients.

■ **Other Supraventricular Arrhythmias**

Atrial flutter can exist as a pure entity or transition into AF. AF may also develop in patients with other forms of SVT, particularly in up to one third of patients with Wolff-Parkinson-White (WPW) syndrome. Furthermore, AF may be a consequence of sick sinus syndrome, which may present as intermittent tachycardia and bradycardia.

Controversies on the Reversible Risk Factors for AF

Traditionally, AF secondary to reversible causes was believed to have little impact on a patient's long-term prognosis (eg, AF in hyperthyroid patients or in critically ill patients in the ICU). However, developing evidence suggests that AF in the context of some reversible causes does not necessarily have a benign outcome.

Physicians commonly overlook transient AF during acute MI, and no evidence-based guidelines exist for long-term antithrombotic and antiarrhythmic therapy in patients with acute MI and AF. However, AF during acute MI is an independent predictor of mortality rates after multivariate analysis. In a study of patients >65 years of age with acute MI, the presence of AF carried a poor prognosis, including higher in-hospital (25.3% vs 16.0%), 30-day (29.3% vs 19.1%), and 1-year (48.3% vs 32.7%) mortality. Interestingly, patients who develop AF during hospitalization had a worse prognosis than patients who initially present with AF.

The presence of AF during hospitalization for acute MI is particularly detrimental to patients with depressed LV systolic function and/or CHF. An episode of AF in the setting of acute MI increases the risk of ischemic stroke, both during hospitalization and in follow-up.

Early postoperative AF is commonly considered benign and is believed to have little impact on short- and long-term mortality. Nevertheless, more recent studies have shown that AF after cardiac surgery is associated with an increased rate of postoperative complications, prolonged hospitalization, and increased short-term mortality. For instance, a recently published study from Baylor University Medical Center showed that new-onset AF post-CABG increased mortality. In this study, long-term mortality in patients with new-onset AF was 29% higher than in patients with exactly the same preoperative risk profile who did not develop postoperative AF (**Figure 4.2**). These findings underscore the need for effective prevention.

FIGURE 4.2 — Kaplan-Meier Curves Depicting the Effect of New-Onset Postoperative AF on Survival in Patients Who Underwent CABG at Baylor University Medical Center Between January 1997 and December 2006

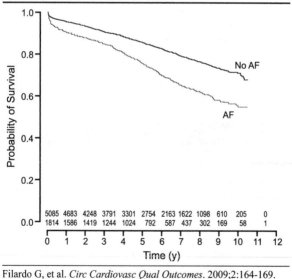

Filardo G, et al. *Circ Cardiovasc Qual Outcomes*. 2009;2:164-169.

Risk Assessment With Ancillary Studies

- Electrocardiographic findings associated with the development of AF include:
  - Frequent premature atrial beats
  - Prolongation of the PR interval
  - Prolongation of intra-atrial and interatrial conduction time
  - Maximum P-wave duration (P maximum) of 110 ms
  - Difference between the maximum and the minimum P-wave duration (P dispersion) of 40 ms
  - LVH
  - Abnormally short or long QT intervals
- Laboratory data associated with the development of AF
  - Elevated level of ANP (>60 pg/mL)
  - Elevated preoperative BNP plasma level
  - Elevated inflammatory markers, such as CRP
  - Low TSH
- Echocardiographic risk factors
  - Increased left atrial size or volume
  - Left atrial reservoir function
  - Increased LV mass
  - Restrictive transmitral Doppler flow pattern
  - Prolonged atrial conduction time as measured by tissue Doppler imaging

Risk Score Assessment for AF

The development of effective preventive strategies for the epidemic of AF requires validation of combined risk factors and a formulation of a risk algorithm that can be used in primary care settings. Recently, the Framingham investigators made the first attempt to establish such a risk-score algorithm. They followed a large cohort of men and women (4764 participants) for 10 years to develop a risk score derived from clinical history, examination, and ECG (**Figure 4.3**). Inclusion of echocardiographic measurements did not significantly improve this risk assessment. The risk score has good

FIGURE 4.3 — Risk Scores for Factors Associated With 10-Year Risk of AF and Predicted 10-Year Risk of AF Assigned to the Risk Score

	Score	
Age (y)	**Women**	**Men**
45-49	-3	1
50-54	-2	2
55-59	0	3
60-64	1	4
65-69	3	5
70-74	4	6
75-79	6	7
80-84	7	7
≥85	8	8
Body Mass Index (kg/m^2)		
<30	0	
≥30	1	
Systolic Blood Pressure (mmHg)		
<160	0	
≥160	1	
Treatment for Hypertension		
No	0	
Yes	1	
PR Interval (ms)		
<160	0	
160-199	1	
≥200	2	
Age at Which Significant Cardiac Murmur Developed (y)		
45-54	5	
55-64	4	
65-74	2	
75-84	1	
≥85	0	
Age of HF (y)		
45-54	10	
55-64	6	
65-74	2	
≥75-84	0	

Risk Score	≤0	1	2	3	4	5	6	7	8	9	≥10
Predicted (%)	≤1	2	2	3	4	6	8	12	16	22	>30

Adapted from Schnabel RB, et al. *Lancet*. 2009;373:739-745.

4

predictive value, although not as easily implemented as the Congestive heart failure, Hypertension, Age >75, Diabetic, and history of Stroke (CHADS2) score to assess embolic risk. Furthermore, this risk score was developed with a middle-aged, elderly, Caucasian group and therefore should not be extrapolated to other ethnic groups or young individuals. Finally, this algorithm requires comprehensive validation before being widely applied in clinical practice.

Key Clinical Points

- The most important etiologies for the development of AF include structural heart disease, such as hypertensive disease, HF, coronary disease with a history of MI, and valvular heart disease.
- Associated noncardiac conditions, such as obesity, hypothyroidism, acute stroke, postoperative state, infections, and alcohol abuse, as well as a changing autonomic nervous system, may lead to AF, even in the absence of underlying heart disease.
- Genetic susceptibility may explain some cases of AF, but there is a complex interplay between heredity and extrinsic factors in most patients.
- Methods to quantify an individual's risk of developing AF are in development but require refinement and validation.

SUGGESTED READING

Arnsdorf M, Ganz L. Causes of atrial fibrillation. In: Basow DS, ed. *UpToDate*. Waltham, MA: UpToDate; 2010.

Bielecka-Dabrowa A, Mikhailidis DP, Rysz J, Banach M. The mechanisms of atrial fibrillation in hyperthyroidism. *Thyroid Res*. 2009;2(1):4.

Filardo G, Hamilton C, Hebeler RF Jr, Hamman B, Grayburn P. New-onset postoperative atrial fibrillation after isolated coronary artery bypass graft surgery and long-term survival. *Circ Cardiovasc Qual Outcomes*. 2009;2:164-169.

Fuster V, Rydén LE, Cannom DS, et al; American College of Cardiology/American Heart Association Task Force on Practice Guidelines; European Society of Cardiology Committee for Practice Guidelines; European Heart Rhythm Association; Heart Rhythm Society. ACC/AHA/ESC 2006 Guidelines for the Management of Patients with Atrial Fibrillation: a report of the American College of Cardiology/American Heart Association Task Force on Practice Guidelines and the European Society of Cardiology Committee for Practice Guidelines (Writing Committee to Revise the 2001 Guidelines for the Management of Patients With Atrial Fibrillation): developed in collaboration with the European Heart Rhythm Association and the Heart Rhythm Society [erratum appears in *Circulation*. 2007;116(6):e138]. *Circulation*. 2006;114(7):e257-e354.

Gudbjartsson DF, Arnar DO, Helgadottir A, et al. Variants conferring risk of atrial fibrillation on chromosome 4q25. *Nature*. 2007;448(7151):353-357.

Gudbjartsson DF, Holm H, Gretarsdottir S, et al. A sequence variant in ZFHX3 on 16q22 associates with atrial fibrillation and ischemic stroke. *Nat Genet*. 2009;41(8):876-878.

Lubitz SA, Yi BA, Ellinor PT. Genetics of atrial fibrillation. *Cardiol Clin*. 2009;27(1):25-33, vii.

Mont L, Elosua R, Brugada J. Endurance sport practice as a risk factor for atrial fibrillation and atrial flutter. *Europace*. 2009;11(1):11-17.

Podrid P. Etiology and pathogenesis of atrial fibrillation. In: Kowey PR, Naccarelli GV, eds. *Atrial Fibrillation*. New York, NY: Marcel Dekker; 2005:27-60.

Rathore SS, Berger AK, Weinfurt KP, et al. Acute myocardial infarction complicated by atrial fibrillation in the elderly: prevalence and outcomes. *Circulation*. 2000;101(9):969-974.

Schmitt J, Duray G, Gersh BJ, Hohnloser SH. Atrial fibrillation in acute myocardial infarction: a systematic review of the incidence, clinical features and prognostic implications. *Eur Heart J*. 2009;30(9):1038-1045.

4

Schnabel RB, Sullivan LM, Levy D, et al. Development of a risk score for atrial fibrillation (Framingham Heart Study): a community-based cohort study. *Lancet*. 2009;373(9665):739-745.

Schoonderwoerd BA, Smit MD, Pen L, Van Gelder IC. New risk factors for atrial fibrillation: causes of 'not-so-lone atrial fibrillation'. *Europace*. 2008;10(6):668-673.

Tsai CT, Lai LP, Hwang JJ, Lin JL, Chiang FT. Molecular genetics of atrial fibrillation. *J Am Coll Cardiol*. 2008;52(4):241-250.

Watanabe H, Tanabe N, Watanabe T, et al. Metabolic syndrome and risk of development of atrial fibrillation: the Niigata preventive medicine study. *Circulation*. 2008;117(10):1255-1260.

5

Clinical Manifestations

The clinical presentation of new-onset AF varies greatly. Some patients with AF are asymptomatic and are diagnosed when they are seeking unrelated medical attention. Others have only minor palpitations, which do not affect their daily activities. However, most patients with new-onset AF present with significant palpitations, often associated with dyspnea, chest discomfort, fatigue, decreased physical activity, or lightheadedness. Patients may also complain of polyuria due to ANP release. Palpitations in AF are most often described as a rapid, irregular "fluttering in the chest," with or without chest discomfort. A careful history and physical examination are critical in the evaluation of AF patients with chest discomfort, as they may reveal clues to the underlying causes of AF. The differential diagnosis of chest pain associated with AF is presented in **Table 5.1**.

Some patients may have serious complications of AF at the time of initial evaluation. In patients with structural heart disease and/or LV dysfunction, AF may lead to hypotension and/or acute decompensated heart failure (ADHF). This may be additionally true with underlying hypertensive heart disease with diastolic dysfunction, HCM, or aortic stenosis (AS), in which the ventricular rate associated with loss of atrial contribution does not allow for sufficient ventricular filling. Long-lasting AF with rapid ventricular response can also cause tachycardia-mediated cardiomyopathy (especially in patients who are unaware of tachyarrhythmia) and HF.

A new thromboembolic cerebrovascular accident (CVA) may be the initial presentation of AF. Likewise, syncope is rare, but may occur upon termination of AF before sinus rhythm resumes in patients with sinus node dysfunction. This may be the result of an "offset pause," ie, a period of asystole after the termination of an arrhythmia before sinus rhythm resumes. Syncope may also complicate AF with rapid ventricular response in patients

TABLE 5.1 — Differential Diagnosis of Chest Discomfort in Patients With AF

Associated Condition	Description	Distinguishing Features
None	• Abrupt onset of rapid, irregular "fluttering in the chest" (palpitations) • Sometimes described by the patient as a chest discomfort • Often associated with shortness of breath, fatigue, weakness, lightheadedness • Syncope may occur, especially with history of structural heart disease or WPW syndrome (pre-excitation)	• Irregularly irregular heart rate • Peripheral "pulse deficit"
CAD	• Substernal discomfort (may extend to the left or right chest) • Character—pressure, tightness, heaviness, burning • Discomfort often radiates to (or is only located in) neck, jaw, shoulders, arms, or epigastrium	• Angina discomfort precipitated by AF with uncontrolled ventricular response, relieved by slowing the heart rate and/or nitroglycerin (angina) • Acute MI—sudden onset, similar description as angina but usually lasting >30 minutes, associated with shortness of breath, diaphoresis, nausea, or vomiting, unrelieved by nitroglycerin and/or rate control

Pericarditis	• Sharp or stabbing pain • Substernal or left precordial • Constant but may wax and wane • Radiates to trapezius ridge	• Often relieved by changing body position (ie, sitting up and leaning forward) • Pericardial friction rub
Pneumonia/pleuritis	• Sharp or stabbing pain, usually brief • Unilateral, localized • Worse with deep breath or cough	• Associated with dyspnea and cough • Fever and crackles may be present on physical examination
PE	• Acute onset, pain is pleuritic and often on the side of the embolus	• Classically associated with tachypnea, tachycardia, and dyspnea in a patient with a normal or near-normal chest x-ray (atelectasis) • Irregularly irregular rhythm with signs of right HF or shock
Anxiety	• Variable location of pain • Character: tightness or aching, often lasting for prolonged period of time, unrelated to exertion or movement • Associated with dyspnea and fear of losing control or dying	• Emotional factors may induce symptoms • Symptoms of panic attacks, anxiety disorder, somatization, anxiety, or depression often revealed by history

5

with HCM or AS or in WPW syndrome (pre-excitation) secondary to rapid conduction through accessory pathway. In extreme cases, cardiac arrest may occur with WPW syndrome when the rapid ventricular response over the accessory pathway converts into ventricular fibrillation. Although uncommon, AF with a rapid ventricular response may precipitate myocardial ischemia or MI in patients with underlying CAD.

Newly diagnosed AF may either be self-limited or may require medical intervention for termination. After termination of the first detected episode, AF can be classified as paroxysmal, persistent, or permanent (see *Chapter 1*). Multiple patterns may occur in patients in the natural course of the disease or in response to treatment.

A poor correlation exists between clinical manifestations and the presence of AF. Although up to 90% of patients will have recurrent episodes of AF, most episodes are asymptomatic. Furthermore, 40% of patients report symptoms attributable to AF in the absence of a documented recurrence.

The majority of patients, especially older or sedentary individuals with effective rate control, have few symptoms, but some individuals are aware of the irregular rhythm even in the absence of tachycardia. Fatigue is often present and may be the only clinical manifestation of AF. Finally, in the absence of palpitations, decreased physical capacity or dyspnea with exertion may be evidence for poor rate control with exertion.

Key Clinical Points

- The clinical presentation of new-onset AF varies greatly. Some patients are asymptomatic. Others have minor palpitations. Most patients present with significant palpitations often associated with dyspnea, chest discomfort, fatigue, decreased physical capacity, lightheadedness, and/or polyuria.
- Some patients may have serious complications of AF at the time of presentation, particularly in the presence of structural heart disease. Such patients

may present with HF due to tachycardia-mediated cardiomyopathy, CVA due to a new thromboembolic event, or syncope with "offset pause."

- There is a poor correlation between clinical manifestation and recurrent AF. Up to 90% of patients with recurrent episodes of AF are asymptomatic. Furthermore, 40% of patients have symptoms attributable to AF in the absence of a documented recurrence.
- Fatigue, decreased physical capacity, or dyspnea on exertion may be the manifestation of poor heart-rate control with exertion.

5

SUGGESTED READING

Fuster V, Rydén LE, Cannom DS, et al; American College of Cardiology/American Heart Association Task Force on Practice Guidelines; European Society of Cardiology Committee for Practice Guidelines; European Heart Rhythm Association; Heart Rhythm Society. ACC/AHA/ESC 2006 Guidelines for the Management of Patients with Atrial Fibrillation: a report of the American College of Cardiology/American Heart Association Task Force on Practice Guidelines and the European Society of Cardiology Committee for Practice Guidelines (Writing Committee to Revise the 2001 Guidelines for the Management of Patients With Atrial Fibrillation): developed in collaboration with the European Heart Rhythm Association and the Heart Rhythm Society [erratum appears in *Circulation*. 2007;116(6):e138]. *Circulation*. 2006;114(7):e257-e354.

Lee TH. Chest discomfort. In: Fauci A, Braunwald E, Kasper DL, et al, eds. *Harrison's Principles of Internal Medicine*. 17th ed. New York, NY: McGraw-Hill Companies, Inc; 2008:87-90.

Prystowsky EN, Waldo A. Atrial fibrillation, atrial flutter, and atrial tachycardia. In: Fuster V, O'Rourke R, Walsh R, Poole-Wilson P, eds. *Hurst's The Heart*. 12th ed. New York, NY: McGraw-Hill Companies, Inc; 2008:953-982.

6

Evaluation of the Patient With Atrial Fibrillation

Evaluation of the Patient With New-Onset AF

Although the basis of the diagnosis of AF rests on the analysis of an ECG recording, a complete clinical history and physical examination are instrumental in the evaluation of a patient with suspected or proven AF. This approach may characterize the pattern of the arrhythmia, reveal a possible underlying cause or trigger, and lead to a logical and focused workup. Additional studies that may complete the workup and guide effective therapy include:

- Limited blood studies (eg, to rule out hyperthyroidism)
- Transthoracic echocardiography (TTE) or transesophageal echocardiography (TEE)
- Chest imaging
- Holter or event monitoring
- Stress testing
- Electrophysiology study (EPS) (rarely).

A list of basic and diagnostic tests recommended in evaluating patients with AF by ACC/AHA/ESC Guidelines is presented in **Table 6.1**.

■ History

In a patient with newly diagnosed AF, clinicians should attempt to define:

- Time of discovery
- Frequency and duration of episodes (eg, clinical pattern—paroxysmal vs persistent)
- Precipitating factors
- Associated symptoms
- Attempts of termination of AF and response to drug therapy (if applicable).

TABLE 6.1 — Clinical Evaluation of Patients With AF

Minimum Evaluation

- History and physical examination, to define:
  - Presence and nature of symptoms associated with AF
  - Clinical type of AF (eg, first episode, paroxysmal, persistent, or permanent)
  - Onset of the first symptomatic attack or date of discovery of AF
  - Frequency, duration, precipitating factors, and modes of termination of AF
  - Response to any pharmacologic agents that have been administered
  - Presence of any underlying heart disease or other reversible conditions (eg, hyperthyroidism or alcohol consumption)
- ECG, to identify:
  - Rhythm (verify AF)
  - LV hypertrophy
  - P-wave duration and morphology or fibrillatory waves
  - Pre-excitation
  - Bundle-branch block
  - Prior MI
  - Other atrial arrhythmias
  - To measure and follow the R-R, QRS, and QT intervals in conjunction with antiarrhythmic drug therapy
- Transthoracic echocardiogram, to identify:
  - Valvular heart disease
  - LA and RA size
  - LV size and function
  - Peak RV pressure (pulmonary HTN)
  - LV hypertrophy
  - LA thrombus (low sensitivity)
  - Pericardial disease
- Blood tests of thyroid, renal, and hepatic function:
  - For a first episode of AF, especially when the ventricular rate is difficult to control

Additional Testing (one or several tests may be necessary)

- Six-minute walk test:
  - If the adequacy of rate control is in question
- Exercise testing:
  - If the adequacy of rate control is in question (permanent AF)
  - To reproduce exercise-induced AF
  - To exclude ischemia before treatment of selected patients with a Class IC AAD

Continued

TABLE 6.1 — *Continued*

Additional Testing (one or several tests may be necessary)
(continued)
- Holter monitoring or event recording:
  - If diagnosis of the type of arrhythmia is in question
  - As a means of evaluating rate control
- TEE:
  - To identify LA thrombus (in the LA appendage)
  - To guide cardioversion
- Electrophysiologic study:
  - To clarify the mechanism of wide–QRS-complex tachycardia
  - To identify a predisposing arrhythmia, such as atrial flutter or paroxysmal SVT
  - To seek sites for curative ablation or AV conduction block/modification
- Chest radiograph, to evaluate:
  - Lung parenchyma, when clinical findings suggest an abnormality
  - Pulmonary vasculature, when clinical findings suggest an abnormality

ACC/AHA/ESC 2006 Guidelines for the Management of Patients With Atrial Fibrillation. *J Am Coll Cardiol.* 2006;48:854-906.

The Canadian Cardiovascular Society Severity in Atrial Fibrillation (CCS-SAF) and European Heart Rhythm Association (EHRA) scoring systems of AF-related symptoms may be used to access a patient's symptomatic status (**Table 6.2**).

In addition to these evaluations, the history should focus on the presence of underlying heart disease (eg, hypertension, HF, etc), medical conditions associated with AF (eg, obesity, OSA), or potentially reversible causes of AF (eg, hyperthyroidism).

Family history is also important, due to an increased evidence of genetic predisposition.

Social history should include any information concerning endurance exercise (especially in young adults with AF), alcohol use, sleep deprivation, emotional stress, and use of stimulants. Most commonly, AF triggers are related to increased sympathetic tone. Vagally mediated AF may occur during sleep or after a large meal. As such,

TABLE 6.2 — EHRA Score: Classification of AF-Related Symptoms

EHRA Class	Explanation of Symptoms
I	None
II	Mild: normal daily activity not affected
III	Severe: normal daily activity affected
IV	Disabling: normal daily activity discontinued

Modified from the Task Force for the Management of Atrial Fibrillation of the European Society of Cardiology (ESC). *Eur Heart J.* 2010;31:2369-2429.

a detailed history of sleep and meal habits should also be obtained.

Finally, a careful medication history should be sought, including over-the-counter medications (eg, nasal decongestants), sympathomimetic agents (eg, theophylline), drugs increasing vagal tone (eg, digoxin), or recent history of withdrawal of β-blockers.

■ **Physical Examination**

Heart rate, BP, and signs of systemic hypoperfusion are key elements in the initial examination of the patient with a symptomatic episode of AF. Heart rate and pulse are typically very irregular and rapid in patients with AF. Since stroke volumes vary because of different periods of diastolic filling, not all ventricular contractions lead to a palpable peripheral pulse. The difference between the heart rate and the pulse rate is called the "pulse deficit" and is a typical feature of AF. The heart rate may be slow and regular if a patient has complete heart block and/or a permanent ventricular pacemaker.

Other clues to the presence of AF during a physical examination include irregular jugular venous pulsations, variation in the intensity of the first heart sound (S1), and loss of a fourth heart sound (S4) in hypertensive patients.

Physical examination is also useful in detecting underlying CV abnormalities that could serve as a substrate for arrhythmias, such as HF (eg, elevated jugular venous pressure, third heart sound, laterally displaced apical impulse), hypertrophic cardiomyopathy (eg, harsh systolic ejection murmur along the left sternal border that increases with Valsalva maneuver), valvular heart disease (eg, murmur of mitral regurgitation), or hypertension.

■ Electrocardiogram

The 12-lead ECG is key to verifying the presence of AF (the electrocardiographic criteria for the diagnosis of AF are presented in *Chapter 1*). However, an ECG can also identify underlying structural causes of AF (eg, LVH, prior MI) and electrophysiologic abnormalities associated with AF (other atrial arrhythmias or pre-excitation). Additionally, R-R, QRS, and QTc intervals should be analyzed for baseline measurements, especially if therapy with antiarrhythmic drugs (AADs) is planned as they may prolong these intervals.

■ Echocardiogram

All patients with AF should have a TTE as part of their initial evaluation. This study should always include assessment of left atrial size/volume, ventricular size and function, valvular abnormalities, pulmonary artery pressures, and pericardium. These data may be helpful in determining the etiology of AF, the risk of stroke and recurrence of AF, and the choice of treatment strategy. TTE is the single best study for detecting underlying structural heart disease as a cause of AF (eg, LVH, ischemic cardiomyopathy, valvular heart disease, pericardial disease). In the absence of LV dysfunction, an elevated right ventricular pressure may suggest underlying lung pathology (eg, acute PE, OSA) as a trigger. Measurement of LA size (LA size >6 cm in diameter on the parasternal long axis view) is predictive of failure of the maintenance of NSR after cardioversion. The LA should also be screened for the presence of thrombus, although it is rarely seen on TTE because most thrombi are located in the left atrial appendage, and this structure is not easily visualized on TTE.

TTE may also help in guiding the therapy for AF. TTE defines patients at increased risk for a hemodynamic compromise with AF, eg, hypertropic cardiomyopathy, hypertensive disease, mitral or aortic stenosis, severely decreased systolic function, or Doppler evidence of diastolic dysfunction. Such patients may require more aggressive antiarrhythmic strategy. The presence of LVH, as well as LV systolic or diastolic dysfunction on TTE helps in choosing appropriate antiarrhythmic and antithrombotic therapy. For example, decreased LV systolic function independently predicts an increased risk of stroke and thus necessitates the use of antithrombotic therapy.

Although TTE can provide anatomic imaging of the LA, it is not sensitive to detect left atrial thrombus. TEE provides superior imaging of the left atrial appendage and proves especially helpful in the detection of clots. Its invasive nature precludes its use unless the results will lead to alterations in therapy. For the detection of left atrial thrombus prior to early cardioversion, TEE is used most frequently in inpatients with AF lasting >48 hours or in high-risk patients with AF of any duration. In patients with paroxysmal, persistent, or permanent AF, TEE is used to identify increased risk of thromboembolic complications, including left atrial appendage thrombus or spontaneous echocardiogram contrast, reduced left atrial appendage flow velocity of ≤20 cm/s, and the presence of a complex aortic plaque. In the Stroke Prevention in Atrial Fibrillation (SPAF) trial, the rate of stroke was increased more than three times with dense spontaneous echo contrast in the LA, three times with left atrial appendage thrombus or reduced left atrial appendage peak flow velocity, and four times with complex aortic plaque.

A complete discussion on assessment of thromboembolism risk is presented in *Chapter 12*.

■ Blood Tests

Focused blood work is an essential part of the initial evaluation of all patients with AF. Since silent hypothyroidism is common (especially in the elderly), obtaining a TSH level is routine in all patients with new-onset AF, even in the absence of clinical features. A complete blood count is useful in screening for anemia or an ongoing infectious process as a trigger for tachyar-rhythmia. Baseline platelet count, prothrombin time, and partial thromboplastin times should be assessed prior to the initiation of systemic anticoagulation. Baseline renal and liver function tests, as well as serum electrolytes, are measured prior to the initiation of antiarrhythmic therapy.

■ Chest Imaging

A baseline chest x-ray is commonly used to screen for underlying lung disease as well as for the presence of HF in patients with AF. Chest computed tomography (CT) may be indicated as the initial imaging modality if acute PE (associated with new-onset AF) is suspected or as a further workup of abnormal chest x-ray findings.

The previously mentioned baseline studies are often sufficient in the evaluation of patients with new-onset AF. However, additional studies may be necessary for diagnosing and guiding safe and effective therapy in selected patients.

■ Ambulatory Arrhythmia Monitoring

Long-term arrhythmia recording may be indicated in patients with new-onset AF who are rate controlled, asymptomatic, and hemodynamically stable at rest. Such patients do not require hospitalization. The monitor may assess rate control. The recording elucidates the pulse rate range with various activities throughout a 24-hour period. Ambulatory ECG recordings and device-based monitor-ing are indicated in the initial evaluation of patients with suspected but unproven AF, in assessing the burden of newly diagnosed paroxysmal AF, and as a part of the workup for cryptogenic stroke. Further discussion on the role of AF monitoring will be presented in the follow-up evaluation section of this chapter.

■ Exercise Stress Testing

Stress testing is indicated if new-onset AF was pre-cipitated by exercise or if electrocardiographic ischemic changes accompany AF. An ischemic evaluation should also be considered prior to starting antiarrhythmic therapy with Class IC agents (two of which were shown in the

Cardiac Arrhythmia Suppression Trial [CAST] to have proarrhythmic effect in post-MI patients). If a rate-control strategy is chosen, stress testing may be performed in order to evaluate the efficacy of rate-control therapy with exercise, particularly in patients taking digoxin as the sole AV nodal blocking agent since accelerated ventricular rates with low levels of exercise are not uncommon.

■ Electrophysiology Study

An EPS does not play a role in the routine evaluation of patients with new-onset AF. However, it may be required in certain settings. For example, in patients with a diagnosis of AF and a history of syncope, the presence of δ wave on the an ECG (suggesting pre-excitation) should be followed by EPS and often ablation of the bypass tract. An EPS is also indicated in the case of wide QRS complex tachycardia when the ECG is inconclusive in differentiating between AF (with bundle branch block) and ventricular tachycardia.

AF Evaluation on Follow-Up Encounters

All components of the initial assessment may also apply to the follow-up care of patients with AF; however, some aspects of the subsequent evaluation and monitoring of the disease are worth particular attention.

The symptoms of AF do not correlate with either its frequency or duration. Also, the absence of symptoms does not equate to the absence of the arrhythmia. Therefore, outpatient monitoring may be needed. If poor rate control of AF is detected on the follow-up visit (especially in the setting of underlying heart disease), the patient should be questioned about symptoms of HF. In the elderly population, a group at high risk for thromboembolism, a neurologic evaluation must be considered to rule out deficits secondary to subclinical stroke. Patients with inadequate anticoagulation are more susceptible to such thromboembolic events.

Heart rhythm and rate, as well as previously unseen abnormalities on the ECG, should be determined at each office visit. Careful assessment of heart rate, QRS, and

QTc intervals is necessary to monitor efficacy and safety of AADs.

TTE is an important component of the evaluation of all patients experiencing their first episode of AF. However, repeat TTE for paroxysmal or persistent AF on follow-up visits is not indicated unless the clinical presentation has changed. TEE, but not repeat TTE, may be indicated if cardioversion for recurrent or persistent AF is planned. This would be needed if the patient has not been therapeutically anticoagulated for several weeks prior to the cardioversion.

Depending on the AAD used, renal or liver function tests as well as serum electrolytes need to be routinely monitored to ensure drug efficacy and safety. Measurements of TSH and free T_4 should be considered in initially stable AF patients who then present with uncontrolled ventricular response or in patients who fail to stay in NSR early after successful cardioversion. In the absence of LV dysfunction, an elevated BNP is associated with an increased risk of thromboembolism and more frequent paroxysms of AF.

An EPS plays a key role in patients who require invasive therapy for AF. An EPS is an essential tool for localizing target sites of ablation in the left and right atria. EPS may also be required in certain cases of AF with a complicated clinical course. EPS may be helpful when AF is associated with supraventricular reentrant tachycardias, such as atrial flutter. EPS, followed by ablation procedure for reentrant tachycardia, may eliminate or decrease the burden of AF. In patients with AF and uncontrolled ventricular rate despite maximal medical therapy, EPS is performed as part of AV nodal ablation and permanent pacemaker implantation.

The use of devices for extended ambulatory monitoring has gained wide acceptance. They may be used as an initial diagnostic tool or to assess the efficacy of therapy.

Clinical scenarios that may require ambulatory monitoring include:

- Establishing the etiology of AF if the basic workup is unrevealing, eg, associated atrial arrhythmias or vagally mediated AF during sleep
- Ruling out asymptomatic episodes of AF

- Investigating the correlation between the patient's symptoms and episodes of AF
- Assessing efficacy of rate-control therapy in persistent or permanent AF
- Establishing the safety of stopping anticoagulation.

This choice of monitoring strategy depends on the duration, frequency, and severity of symptoms, as well as on the risk of serious AF complication. The most common strategies for AF monitoring are shown in **Table 6.3**.

Key Clinical Points

- History, physical examination, and ECG analysis are the cornerstones of the initial evaluation and long-term management of patients with AF.
- On initial evaluation, history and physical examination should focus on detecting underlying heart disease, medical conditions associated with AF, and potentially reversible causes of AF.
- TTE and focused blood work, including TSH level, are indicated in all patients with new-onset AF.
- In patients on rhythm-control therapy with AADs, blood work assessment of electrolytes, renal function, and/or hepatic function (depending on drug metabolism) should be routinely obtained.
- TEE should be considered if cardioversion is planned for paroxysmal or recurrent persistent AF of >48 hours in duration or for patients who are not adequately anticoagulated.
- Ambulatory ECG monitoring and exercise stress testing may be useful in follow-up evaluation of patients with AF, regardless of whether rhythm- or rate-control strategy is chosen.

TABLE 6.3 — Recording Options in AF

Telemetry Type	Indication(s)	Limitation(s)
In-hospital telemetry	• Critically ill patients • Hemodynamic instability • Assessment of antiarrhythmic therapy • Assessment of adequacy of rate control	• Inconvenience of hospitalization
Ambulatory ECG (Holter monitor)		• Limited sensitivity due to short duration
Event recorders	• Symptomatic patients • Intermittent symptoms (not daily)	• Asymptomatic patients • Patients unable to trigger device to record
Mobile cardiac outpatient telemetry monitoring	• Symptomatic and asymptomatic recording transmitted • Improved sensitivity compared with many other options • Longer recording time—better assessment of AF burden • Assessment of antiarrhythmic therapy	• Cost
Implanted loop recorders	• Long-term monitoring • Often higher clinical risk patients	• Invasive
Interrogation of memory function of PPMs or defibrillators	• Detect asymptomatic and symptomatic episodes • Assess AF burden • Establish effectiveness of medical therapy	• Not applicable for majority of patients

6

SUGGESTED READING

Auer J, Scheibner P, Mische T, Langsteger W, Eber O, Eber B. Subclinical hyperthyroidism as a risk factor for atrial fibrillation. *Am Heart J.* 2001;142(5):838-842.

Fuster V, Rydén LE, Cannom DS, et al; American College of Cardiology/American Heart Association Task Force on Practice Guidelines; European Society of Cardiology Committee for Practice Guidelines; European Heart Rhythm Association; Heart Rhythm Society. ACC/AHA/ESC 2006 Guidelines for the Management of Patients with Atrial Fibrillation: a report of the American College of Cardiology/American Heart Association Task Force on Practice Guidelines and the European Society of Cardiology Committee for Practice Guidelines (Writing Committee to Revise the 2001 Guidelines for the Management of Patients With Atrial Fibrillation): developed in collaboration with the European Heart Rhythm Association and the Heart Rhythm Society [erratum appears in *Circulation.* 2007;116(6):e138]. *Circulation.* 2006;114(7):e257-e354.

Israel CW, Grönefeld G, Ehrlich JR, Li YG, Hohnloser SH. Long-term risk of recurrent atrial fibrillation as documented by an implantable monitoring device: implications for optimal patient care. *J Am Coll Cardiol.* 2004;43(1):47-52.

Rothman SA, Laughlin JC, Seltzer J, et al. The diagnosis of cardiac arrhythmias: a prospective multi-center randomized study comparing mobile cardiac outpatient telemetry versus standard loop event monitoring. *J Cardiovasc Electrophysiol.* 2007;18(3):241-247.

Manning W. Role of echocardiography in atrial fibrillation. In: Basow, DS, ed. *UpToDate.* Waltham, MA: UpToDate; 2010.

Page RL, Wilkinson WE, Clair WK, McCarthy EA, Pritchett EL. Asymptomatic arrhythmias in patients with symptomatic paroxysmal atrial fibrillation and paroxysmal supraventricular tachycardia. *Circulation.* 1994;89(1):224-227.

7

Nonpharmacologic and Pharmacologic Prevention

Introduction

The growing epidemic of AF has led to multiple investigations and clinical trials in search of effective approaches to prevent this arrhythmia and its complications. However, as the pathogenesis of AF is not fully understood and is complex (with multiple pathways leading to progression of the condition), relatively few data exist on effective preventive strategies.

This lack of strategies to prevent AF led the National Heart, Lung, and Blood Institute to form an expert panel to identify goals and directions for prevention. The recently published recommendations by this expert panel stress the complexity of AF pathogenesis and identify multiple targets for AF prevention (**Figure 7.1**).

Based on this model, prevention of AF may be targeted on multiple levels of its development and progression. These include lifestyle and therapeutic modifications of preventable risk factors, arrhythmia substrates, and triggers. Once AF develops, preventive strategies should be directed to stop progression to persistent or permanent AF.

Nonpharmacologic Prevention of AF

Structural heart diseases, such as hypertensive heart disease, LV dysfunction with HF, valvular heart disease, and coronary disease with MI, are associated with an increased risk of AF. Also, CV risk factors, such as hypertension, obesity, metabolic syndrome, cigarette smoking, and environmental stress, are well-established risk factors. As such, nonpharmacologic lifestyle modifications (eg, weight loss, moderate physical exercise, low-salt diet, cessation of smoking) should decrease the incidence of AF.

FIGURE 7.1 — Opportunities for AF Prevention

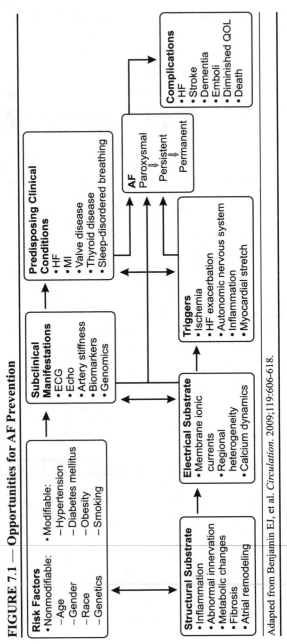

Risk Factors
- Nonmodifiable:
  - Age
  - Gender
  - Race
  - Genetics
- Modifiable:
  - Hypertension
  - Diabetes mellitus
  - Obesity
  - Smoking

Subclinical Manifestations
- ECG
- Echo
- Artery stiffness
- Biomarkers
- Genomics

Predisposing Clinical Conditions
- HF
- MI
- Valve disease
- Thyroid disease
- Sleep-disordered breathing

AF
Paroxysmal
Persistent
Permanent

Complications
- HF
- Stroke
- Dementia
- Emboli
- Diminished QOL
- Death

Structural Substrate
- Inflammation
- Abnormal innervation
- Metabolic changes
- Fibrosis
- Atrial remodeling

Electrical Substrate
- Membrane ionic currents
- Regional heterogeneity
- Calcium dynamics

Triggers
- Ischemia
- HF exacerbation
- Autonomic nervous system
- Inflammation
- Myocardial stretch

Adapted from Benjamin EJ, et al. *Circulation.* 2009;119:606-618.

However, there are few data proving benefit of lifestyle modifications on an individual's risk of developing AF.

Excessive endurance training has been implicated to increase the risk of AF in younger athletes and middle-aged adults. However, the pathogenesis of AF is most likely different in the older adults, in whom CV risk factors and structural heart disease play a major role in risk of AF. Since regular, moderate physical activity reduces the risk of major CV conditions (eg, hypertension, CHF, MI), regular physical activity might be expected to reduce the incidence of AF. This concept was proven in a recently published report from a prospective analysis of 5446 adults ≥65 years of age followed for 12 years in the CHS. Habitual, long-term, light-to-moderate level physical activity was associated with a lower incidence of AF. Furthermore, greater leisure-time activity and walking lowered the risk as time and intensity increased (**Table 7.1**).

AF is more commonly found in patients with established CV conditions than in those with only classic CV risk factors.

Epidemiologic data from Europe and North America show that despite most classic CV risk factors being better controlled, the prevalence of AF is increasing. Furthermore, African Americans and Hispanics have a lower incidence of AF despite the greater prevalence of CV risk factors.

In the future, the key to nonpharmacologic prevention of AF may lie in the genetic identification of susceptible phenotypes (traits predisposing to disease) and aggressive lifestyle and pharmacologic modifications in subjects at risk.

Pharmacologic Prevention of AF

Atrial injury and inflammation in susceptible subjects lead to structural and electrophysiologic changes called atrial remodeling. This process is crucial not only in the development, but also in the maintenance, of AF as tachyarrhythmia itself perpetuates atrial remodeling (AF begets AF). Changes in extracellular matrix

TABLE 7.1 — Risk of New-Onset AF in 5446 Older Adults[a] According to Walking Habits in the Cardiovascular Health Study

			Adjusted for…	
	Events (N)	Person-Years	Age and Gender	Multiple Variables[b]
Walking Distance, Blocks/Week (n[c])				
0-4 (n = 1145)	272	8867	1.0 (reference)	1.0 (reference)
5-11 (n = 855)	218	9188	0.78 (0.65-0.93)	0.78 (0.65-0.94)
12-23 (n = 981)	212	9452	0.71 (0.59-0.86)	0.76 (0.63-0.91)
24-59 (n = 1205)	191	9789	0.62 (0.51-0.75)	0.67 (0.55-0.81)
≥60 (n = 1260)	168	9984	0.51 (0.42-0.63)	0.56 (0.45-0.69)
P for trend	—	—	<0.001	<0.001
Walking Pace (n[c])				
<2 mph (n = 1656)	527	16,805	1.0 (reference)	1.0 (reference)
2-3 mph (n = 2314)	427	22,494	0.62 (0.55-0.71)	0.68 (0.59-0.77)
>3 mph (n = 1476)	107	7982	0.51 (0.41-0.63)	0.59 (0.48-0.74)
P for trend	—	—	<0.001	<0.001

[a] Adults ≥65 years of age.

[b] Adjusted for age (years), gender (male/female), race (white/nonwhite), enrollment site (four sites), education (<high school, high school, >high school), smoking status (never, former, current), pack-years of smoking (four categories), CHD (yes/no), chronic pulmonary disease (yes/no), diabetes mellitus (yes/no), alcohol use (six categories), and β-blocker use (yes/no).

[b] Number of individuals in each category at baseline.

Mozaffarian D, et al. *Circulation.* 2008;118:800-807.

composition followed by fibrosis are key sequelae of structural remodeling in the atria. Different signaling pathways are involved in the development and progression of fibrosis such as the renin-angiotensin-aldosterone system (RAAS), transforming growth factor-β (TGF-β), and platelet-derived growth factor (PDGF). Structural changes in the atria (ie, fibrosis and atrial dilatation) can facilitate changes in the electrical system, such as creating ectopic triggers and promoting reentry circuits. Additionally, changes in the autonomic nervous system and accumulation of reactive oxygen species (secondary to inflammation) can contribute to structural and electrophysiologic changes in the atria and promote AF.

Based on these pathophysiologic principles, it is reasonable to assume that AF could be prevented by altering the structural and electrical remodeling of the atria. Strategies can be used to achieve regression of both atrial inflammation and fibrosis, as well as to protect from initial atrial insult (eg, LVH leading to atrial dilatation).

Certain nonantiarrhythmic agents with established efficacy in modulating the above pathways have been investigated in primary and secondary prevention of AF. Possible mechanisms of atrial remodeling predisposing to AF and pharmacologic strategies to inhibit these pathways are presented in **Figure 7.2**.

A summary of the possible mechanisms of action of different pharmacologic agents used in AF prevention is presented in **Table 7.2**.

■ Renin-Angiotensin-Aldosterone System Blockade

Inhibition of RAAS with angiotensin-converting enzyme (ACE) inhibitors, angiotensin receptor blockers (ARBs), and aldosterone antagonists are mainstays of antiremodeling therapy in various CV disorders. Increasing evidence supports the role of the RAAS in the pathogenesis of AF and the possible beneficial effects of RAAS inhibitors in AF prevention. ACE inhibitors and ARBs have been shown to cause regression of LVH, decreased left atrial pressure, and decreased atrial wall stress. RAAS-modulating agents inhibit atrial fibrosis and decrease arrhythmogenicity of atrial tissue. RAAS inhibition blocks inflammation and thrombosis in the LA.

FIGURE 7.2 — Different Mechanisms of Atrial Remodeling Predisposing to AF and Compounds That Can Inhibit These Pathways

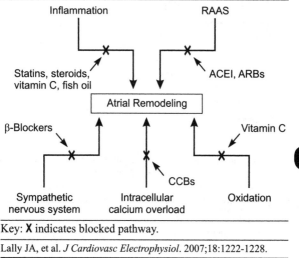

Key: **X** indicates blocked pathway.

Lally JA, et al. *J Cardiovasc Electrophysiol.* 2007;18:1222-1228.

The efficacy of ACE inhibitors and ARBs has been studied in the primary and secondary prevention of AF. Results vary depending on the population studied, but despite some individual trial results, it is safe to conclude that no greater benefit has been demonstrated with either class of agent.

Postanalyses of major CV randomized trials have suggested that ACE inhibitors and ARBs may reduce the incidence of new-onset AF in patients with HF, LV systolic dysfunction, and LVH.

A retrospective analysis of Trandolapril Cardiac Evaluation (TRACE) demonstrated that trandolapril reduced the incidence of AF in patients with LV dysfunction (ejection fraction [EF] <36%) after acute MI. In this study, 1577 patients had sinus rhythm at the time of randomization and were assigned to either trandolapril or placebo. During the 2- to 4-year follow-up period, 5.3% in the placebo group developed AF compared with 2.8% in the trandolapril group (*P*<0.05). In the retrospective analysis of SOLVD on the effectiveness of enalapril in

TABLE 7.2 — Mode of Action of Current Pharmacologic Therapies in AF Prevention

Statins
- Anti-inflammatory effect
- Antioxidant effect
- Improvement of endothelial function
- Reduction of neurohormonal activation:
  - Decreased angiotensin type I receptor signaling
  - Decreased cardiomyocytes response to β-adrenergic stimulation
- Stabilization of cardiac membrane

Glucocorticoids
- Anti-inflammatory effect:
  - Atrial tissue
  - Pericardium in postoperative patients
- Attenuation of tachycardia-induced atrial remodeling
- Decreased nausea/vomiting in postoperative patients (improved absorption of oral medications, ie, β-blockers)

ACE/ARB
- Antiremodeling effect:
  - Decreased LVH
  - Decreased LA pressure
  - Decreased atrial stretch
  - Inhibition of atrial fibrosis
- Anti-inflammatory effect
- Decreased arrhythmogenecity of atrial tissue

Aldosterone Antagonists
- Reduction of atrial fibrosis
- Reduction of vascular collagen turnover
- Increased intracellular potassium and magnesium
- Direct effect on cardiac action potential

LV dysfunction (EF <35%), 374 patients in sinus rhythm at the beginning of the study were randomized to either enalapril or placebo. After a mean follow-up of 2.9 years, 5.4% of patients in the enalapril group vs 24% in the placebo group developed AF (P<0.0001).

Similar findings have been noted in ARB trials. The incidence of new-onset AF in patients with HF was a prespecified secondary end point in the Candesartan in Heart Failure: Assessment of Reduction in Mortality and Morbidity (CHARM) trial. Analysis of this trial included a total of 6379 patients without AF on the baseline ECG who were randomized to candesartan or placebo. Patients in this trial had symptomatic CHF (NYHA class II-IV) and systolic or diastolic dysfunction. After a median follow-up of 38 months, 6% of patients on candesartan developed new-onset AF vs 6.7% of the placebo group ($P=0.048$).

A retrospective analysis of the Valsartan Heart Failure Trial (Val-HeFT) examined the benefit of valsartan for prevention of AF during a mean follow-up of 23 months. In this study, 4395 patients with chronic symptomatic HF (NYHA class II-IV) and LV dysfunction (EF <40%) were randomized to either valsartan or placebo, added to standard HF therapy (including ACE inhibitors and β-blockers). In the valsartan group, 5.1% of patients developed AF compared with 7.95% in the placebo group (relative risk reduction [RRR] of 37%).

Losartan Intervention For End Point Reduction in Hypertension (LIFE) trial examined the benefit of an ARB compared with a β-blocker in patients with hypertension and LVH. In this trial, 8851 patients in sinus rhythm were randomized to losartan or atenolol and followed for a mean of 4.8 years. Although there was no BP difference between therapy groups, new-onset AF occurred in 3.5% patients treated with losartan vs 5.3% in the atenolol group ($P<0.001$). The reduction in this arrhythmia appeared to have been a direct drug effect independent of lowering BP.

Although recent analysis of the Valsartan Antihypertensive Long-term Use Evaluation (VALUE) trial suggested a possible benefit of valsartan over amlodipine in reducing risk of new-onset AF, other trials in hypertensive patients without LVH, such as the Captopril Prevention Project (CAPP) and the Swedish Trial in Old Patients with Hypertension-2 (STOP-2), showed no reduction in new-onset AF associated with the use of ACE inhibitors compared with other antihypertensive agents.

A meta-analysis of 11 randomized controlled trials confirmed the benefit of ACE inhibitors and ARBs in preventing AF. The 11 trials and 56,308 patients included in this meta-analysis enrolled patients with different CV comorbidities such as HF, hypertension, post-MI, and patients after cardioversion for AF. All trials that enrolled patients with HF showed a significant reduction in AF with ACE inhibitor and ARB therapy, with a 44% RRR in the onset of AF. Additionally, the ACE inhibitor and ARB lowered the rate of AF in patients after MI but only if concomitant LV dysfunction was present. ACE inhibitors and ARBs were also effective in AF prevention in hypertensive patients if LVH was present. The benefit of ACE inhibitors and ARBs in secondary prevention of AF (postcardioversion patients) was also noted.

The results of two large prospective, randomized, double-blind studies, Telmisartan Randomized Assessment Study in ACE Intolerant Subjects With Cardiovascular Disease (TRANSCEND) and Ongoing Telmisartan Alone and in Combination with Ramipril Global Endpoint Trial (ONTARGET), were recently published. In these trials, the role of an ARB (telmisartan) and/or an ACE inhibitor (ramipril) were studied as a secondary end point for the occurrence of new-onset AF in patients at high risk for CV disease (eg, CAD, peripheral vascular disease [PVD], CVA, diabetes mellitus with end-organ damage). In ONTARGET, patients were randomized to the ACE inhibitor ramipril ($n = 8576$), the ARB telmisartan ($n = 8542$), or both ($n = 8502$). After median follow-up of 56 months, new-onset AF occurred in 6.9% of patients receiving ramipril, in 6.7% patients in the telmisartan group, and in 6.5% receiving combination therapy. In TRANSCEND, 5926 patients at high risk for CV events and intolerant to ACE inhibitors, were randomized to telmisartan ($n = 2954$) or placebo ($n = 2972$). After a median follow-up of 56 months, the rate of new-onset AF was 6.4% in the telmisartan group vs 6.3% in placebo.

The results of ONTARGET and TRANSCEND failed to show a benefit of RAAS blockade in the prevention of new-onset AF. These results are concordant with the analysis of some other trials which supported use of ACE inhibitors and ARBs for prevention of AF only in patients with HF, LV systolic dysfunction, or hypertension with LVH. Patients with HF were excluded from ONTARGET/TRANSCEND and only 12.7% to 13.5% of patients had LVH in these trials.

ACE inhibitors and ARBs were also studied in secondary prevention of AF. ACE inhibitors and ARBs used postcardioversion as an add-on therapy to amiodarone were found to decrease the risk of AF recurrence. However, a recently published, large, prospective, randomized GISSI-AF trial failed to show benefit of valsartan in preventing recurrent AF postcardioversion. In this trial, 1442 patients on established antiarrhythmic therapy were randomized to either valsartan ($n=722$) or placebo ($n=720$). After 1 year, the incidence of recurrent AF was almost identical in the two groups (valsartan 51.4% and placebo 52.1%).

The possible benefit of aldosterone-antagonist agents in AF prevention has a very strong pathophysiologic basis. Aldosterone antagonists have been shown to reduce collagen turnover/atrial fibrosis and to have an antiarrhythmic effect. However, clinical data on the role of aldosterone antagonists for AF prevention come from case reports and small observational studies. Large prospective, randomized trials are needed to support the concept of AF prevention with aldosterone antagonists.

■ **HMG-CoA Reductase Inhibitors (Statins)**

Several potential mechanisms support the benefit of statin use in AF prevention. On a molecular level, the development of AF is associated with proinflammatory state, impairment of endothelial function, oxidative stress, and neurohormonal activation. In addition to their lipid-lowering and anti-ischemic effects, statins exert anti-inflammatory properties, improve endothelial function, increase nitric oxide bioavailability, reduce release of reactive oxygen, reduce neurohormonal activation, decrease angiotensin type I receptor signaling, and blunt cardiomyocytes response to β-adrenergic stimulation. Finally, statins may exert an antiarrhythmic effect by altering serum levels of polyunsaturated fatty acids, thus stabilizing cardiac membranes.

Such strong preclinical evidence for the potential benefit of statins led to multiple studies to assess their role in AF. Unfortunately, most of these studies had significant limitations; some were retrospective, some were not randomized, and the few completed prospective trials were small in size. Furthermore, these studies observed the effect of statins in patients with diverse forms of AF (eg, paroxysmal AF, AF with underlying ischemic heart disease or HF, AF after electrical cardioversion, or postoperative AF). As such, the results of these studies were conflicting, ie, where some showed beneficial effect of statins on risk of AF (especially in patients with postoperative AF), others did not. Therefore, the beneficial role of statins in AF prevention is substantiated by only a few prospective, randomized trials.

The Atorvastatin for Reduction of Myocardial Dysrhythmia After Cardiac Surgery (ARMYDA3) trial was the first prospective, randomized, double-blind, placebo-controlled trial on statin pretreatment for the reduction of postoperative AF incidents. In ARMYDA3, 200 patients without a prior history of AF and scheduled to undergo CABG were randomized to 7 days of atorvastatin 40 mg/day or placebo. After 30 days, the primary end point of postoperative AF occurred in 35% of the atorvastatin group compared with 57% of the placebo group (P=0.003).

On the other hand, a recently published, randomized, double-blind, placebo-controlled trial evaluating effect of statins on AF recurrence after successful cardioversion failed to show a benefit of statins in maintaining sinus rhythm. This study included 234 patients with persistent AF and a clinical indication for cardioversion. The study evaluated the effect of atorvastatin in keeping patients in sinus rhythm 30 days after cardioversion. Patients were randomized to treatment with atorvastatin 80 mg daily (n=118) or placebo (n=116) in a prospective, double-blind fashion. Treatment was initiated 14 days before cardioversion and was continued 30 days after cardioversion. An intention-to-treat analysis showed that 57 patients (51%) in the atorvastatin group and 47 patients (42%) in the placebo group were in sinus rhythm 30 days after cardioversion (OR 1.44, 95% CI 0.85–2.44, P=0.18). As such, atorvastatin was not statistically superior to placebo in maintaining sinus rhythm 30 days after cardioversion in patients with persistent AF.

Table 7.3 presents characteristics of prospective statin trials of postcardioversion AF in comparison with postoperative AF.

Because of the pleiotropic effects of statins and their variable effect in different subsets of patients with AF, a potential different mechanism of action needs to be considered. A dose-dependent effect of statins on the incidence of AF was evaluated in a recent retrospective analysis of Pravastatin or Atorvastatin Evaluation and Infection (PROVE IT)–Thrombolysis in Myocardial Infarction (TIMI) PROVE IT–TIMI 22 and phase Z of the Aggrastat to Zocor (A to Z) Trial. This analysis showed that intensive (high-dose) statin therapy did not reduce the short-term incidence of AF among patients with acute coronary syndrome (ACS) when compared with standard dose. In the PROVE IT-TIMI 22 trial, 4162 patients who enrolled within 10 days of hospitalization for an ACS were assigned to atorvastatin 80 mg daily or pravastatin 40 mg daily and follow for 2 years. In phase Z of the A to Z Trial, 4497 patients were randomized to therapy with simvastatin 40 mg daily for 30 days followed by 80 mg daily or placebo for 4 months, followed by simvastatin 20 mg daily. Median time of follow-up was 2 years. Both studies failed to show AF prevention by a high-dose statin. In PROVE IT–TIMI 22, 2.9% vs 3.3% and in the A to Z Trial, 1.6% vs 1.0% patients in the high vs standard statin therapy experienced the onset of AF over 2 years.

Although statins have been shown to decrease CRP levels, not all studies support an anti-inflammatory mode of action. For example, in the ARMYDA3 study, elevated postoperative CRP levels were associated with a higher risk of AF. However, there was no statistical relationship between statin use and plasma CRP levels, suggesting that statins may protect from AF independent of CRP levels. Statins are known to modify neurohormonal activation by decreasing angiotensin I receptor signaling and blunting the effect of β-adrenergic stimulation of cardiomyocytes. Combined treatment with statins and β-blockers appears to be more effective in preventing AF than statins alone.

7

TABLE 7.3 — Association of Statin Therapy and Incidence of AF

Study	Data	Randomized/PBO-Controlled	Population	Patients (N)	Design	Drug	End Point	Results
Siu et al[1]	O	No/No	Lone persistent AF + cardioversion	62	Statin vs no statin	S, A	Incidence of AF postcardioversion	Statin therapy reduced AF incidence; RR 0.31 (0.103-0.905)
Tveit et al[2]	P	Yes/No	Persistent AF + cardioversion	112	Pravastatin 40 mg/d vs no therapy 3 wk before to 6 wk after cardioversion	P	Incidence of AF postcardioversion	Pravastatin not superior to no statin therapy
Ozaydin et al[3]	P	Yes/No	Persistent AF + cardioversion	48	Atorvastatin 10 mg/d, 48 h before to 3 mo after vs no therapy	A	Incidence of AF postcardioversion	Atorvastatin therapy reduced AF incidence; RR 0.23 (0.064-0.82)
Patti et al[4]	P	Yes/Yes	Patients undergoing elective cardiac surgery	2000	Atorvastatin 40 mg/d vs placebo started 7 days before surgery	A	Postoperative incidence of AF	Atorvastatin therapy reduced AF incidence; OR 0.39 (0.18-0.85)
Almroth et al[5]	P	Yes/Yes	Persistent AF + cardioversion	234	Atorvastatin 80 mg/d vs placebo	A	Incidence of AF day 30 postcardioversion	Atorvastatin therapy not statistically superior to placebo; OR 1.37 (0.82-2.3)

Key: A, atorvastatin; AF, atrial fibrillation; O, observational; OR, odds ratio; P, prospective; RR, relative risk; S, simvastatin.

[1] Siu CW, et al. *Am J Cardiol.* 2003;92:1343-1345.
[2] Tveit A, et al. *Am J Cardiol.* 2004;93:780-782.
[3] Ozaydin M, et al. *Am J Cardiol.* 2006;97:1490-1493.
[4] Patti G, et al. *Circulation.* 2006;114:1455-1461.
[5] Almroth H, et al. *Eur Heart J.* 2009;30:827-833.

7

Patients who were taking β-blockers randomized to atorvastatin in ARMYDA3 study had impressive (90%) risk reduction in the rate of postoperative AF. Retrospective analysis of the Cocktail Attenuation of Rotational Ablation Flow Effects (CARAF) I and II studies showed that the recurrence of AF after successful cardioversion was reduced by 74% in patients taking statins and β-blockers. Statin or β-blocker therapy alone was not associated with significant changes in AF recurrence.

Larger, prospective and randomized trials are clearly needed to examine effectiveness of statins in preventing AF in different subsets of patients. Other unanswered questions include statin dosing and possible benefit of combination therapy with other agents in the prevention of AF.

■ Glucocorticosteroids

Conflicting data exist on the role of inflammation in the development of AF. It is unclear if inflammation plays a direct causal role in the development and progression of AF or whether it is merely a marker for other conditions associated with AF. Different strategies have been developed to limit recurrences of AF with reduction of the inflammatory state as assessed by decreased CRP level. Corticosteroids are well-known, potent, anti-inflammatory agents, and the beneficial effects of steroids have been studied in diverse subsets of patients with AF.

In a trial of methylprednisolone to prevent recurrent AF, 104 patients with a first episode of symptomatic and persistent AF were randomized to either a 5-month regimen of methylprednisolone (16 mg methylprednisolone for 4 weeks tapered to 4 mg for 4 months) or placebo. CRP levels in these patients were elevated at baseline with a median value of 1.14 mg/dL. After a median follow-up of 2 years, five patients (9.6%) in the methylprednisolone group developed recurrent AF compared with 26 patients (50%) in the placebo group ($P<0.001$). Also, permanent AF was lower in the methylprednisolone group (2%) than in placebo group (29%). The methylprednisolone group was noted to have lowered CRP levels by 80% within the first month of therapy, and this decrease persisted throughout the study. Thus, in this small study, oral steroids appeared to be helpful in both the prevention of recurrent AF and the progression of persistent to permanent AF.

An exaggerated inflammatory response is thought to be an etiologic factor for many post–cardiac surgery complications. The role of corticosteroid prophylaxis has been studied extensively. Until recently, the studies were small and not randomized or prospective. A prospective, double-blind, randomized, multicenter trial from Finland showed that intravenous (IV) hydrocortisone reduced the incidence of AF after cardiac surgery (eg, CABG, aortic valve replacement, or combined CABG and aortic valve replacement). Two hundred forty-one consecutive patients (without prior history of AF) were randomized to 100 mg of IV hydrocortisone (first dose in the evening of the operative day, followed by 100 mg every 8 hours for 3 days) or placebo. All patients in the study were also receiving oral metoprolol. The incidence of postoperative AF in the first 48 hours was 30% in the hydrocortisone group and 48% in the placebo group (adjusted HR, 0.54; 95% CI, 0.35-0.83; $P=0.004$; NNT, 5.6). As such, the RR of postoperative AF in the hydrocortisone group was decreased by 37%. Steroid therapy was not associated with any significant side effects. A meta-analysis of this trial and two previous randomized, controlled trials confirmed the beneficial effect of corticosteroid treatment (**Figure 7.3**).

In contrast, a recent prospective, randomized, double-blind study from the Cleveland Clinic failed to show a beneficial effect of dexamethasone on the development of postoperative AF after combined CABG and valve surgery. However, the importance of these results were limited by the small study size ($n=78$).

Different corticosteroid preparations, eg, methyl-prednisolone, dexamethasone, and hydrocortisone, and different doses of steroids were used in AF-prevention trials. Also, the duration of steroid therapy has varied. Not all studies examined the safety of steroid use. Some of these questions were addressed in the recent meta-analysis of randomized controlled trials on the use of corticosteroids in adult cardiac surgery. Three thousand

FIGURE 7.3 — Meta-analysis of Randomized, Controlled Trials of Corticosteroid Therapy for the Prevention of AF After Cardiac Surgery

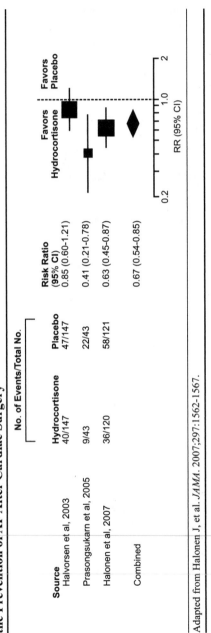

	No. of Events/Total No.		
Source	**Hydrocortisone**	**Placebo**	**Risk Ratio (95% CI)**
Halvorsen et al, 2003	40/147	47/147	0.85 (0.60-1.21)
Prasongsukarn et al, 2005	9/43	22/43	0.41 (0.21-0.78)
Halonen et al, 2007	36/120	58/121	0.63 (0.45-0.87)
Combined			0.67 (0.54-0.85)

Adapted from Halonen J, et al. *JAMA.* 2007;297:1562-1567.

three hundred twenty-three patients from 50 randomized, controlled trials were included. Low-dose corticosteroid was defined as a total dose of <1000 mg hydrocortisone or its equivalent, medium dose as 1000 to 10,000 mg, and high dose as >10,000 mg hydrocortisone (or equivalent). Compared with placebo, corticosteroid therapy decreased the risk of AF (25.1% vs 35.1%, P<0.01), and length of both ICU and hospital stay. Low-dose corticosteroid was as effective as high-dose corticosteroid in reducing the risk of AF. Short courses of steroids (<24 to 72 hours) did not increase the risk of perioperative infections; however, steroid-induced hyperglycemia requiring insulin infusion was common.

In summary, a corticosteroid represents a potent, well-tolerated, and inexpensive anti-inflammatory drug that appears to be safe and effective in low doses for AF prevention. However, these preliminary data require confirmation by larger, randomized trials, which should provide protocols for steroid use in AF prophylaxis. Most importantly, the safety of using large doses of corticosteroids needs to be weighed against the benefit of sinus rhythm preservation, in particular in the self-limited syndrome of postoperative AF.

■ Antioxidants

Elevated atrial oxidative stress may cause contractile dysfunction of the atria, leading to initiation and perpetuation of AF. Atrial tachycardia was found to be associated with decreased tissue levels of vitamin C, enhanced oxidative stress, and a shortened atrial effective refractory period. Reactive oxygen species also have a procoagulant effect, thus increasing the risk of left atrial thrombus.

Several studies have examined the role of antioxidants in AF prevention. Small studies of vitamin C supplementation in AF prophylaxis suggest possible benefit in post-CABG and post-cardioversion patients. However, larger prospective and randomized trials are needed to draw any firm conclusions. Supplementation of vitamin E 600 IU in 38,933 healthy women enrolled in the Women's Health Study and followed for an average of 10.2 years did not reduce the risk of developing AF. A recent, prospective, randomized, double-blind, placebo-controlled study of 115 patients undergoing cardiac surgery showed that another antioxidant agent, N-acetylcysteine (NAC) decreased the incidence of postoperative AF. Patients were randomized to the NAC group ($n=58$) or placebo ($n=57$) and followed for up to 10 days. Three patients (5.2%) in the NAC group and 12 patients (21%) in the placebo group developed AF in the follow-up period (OR 0.20; 95% CI 0.05 to 0.77; $P=0.019$).

■ **Fish Oil**

n-3 Polyunsaturated fatty acids (PUFA), the active component in fish oils, are used to treat lipid disorders, primarily hypertriglyceridemia. They have anti-inflammatory effects and have been shown to reduce ventricular arrhythmias. In addition, preclinical studies clearly indicate that they have an effect on atrial and ventricular electrical properties.

However, studies of the effectiveness of n-3 fatty acids for the prevention of AF have had mixed results. In a prospective, population-based cohort study in 4815 adults >65 years of age, consumption of broiled and baked fish correlated with elevated plasma levels of long-chain n-3 fatty acids. During 12 years of follow-up, intake of fish one to four times a week lowered the incidence of AF by 28% ($P=0.005$), while intake of five or greater times a week lowered the incidence by 31% ($P=0.008$). In a prospective, randomized, controlled trial, pretreatment with PUFAs also decreased the risk of AF after CABG surgery. In this study, 160 patients were randomized to receive 2 g/day of fish oil or placebo starting 5 days before CABG and continued throughout their hospital stay. Postoperative AF developed in 33% of the placebo group vs 15.2% of the fish oil group ($P=0.013$).

However, analyses of the large cohorts from the Danish Diet, Cancer and Health Study ($n=47,949$ patients), the Rotterdam Study ($n=5184$), and the Women's Health Initiative Study ($n=46,704$) showed no association between fish oil ingestion and incidence of AF.

A prospective, randomized, double-blind, placebo-controlled trial enrolled >600 patients with symptomatic AF. For entry, the patients were required to have no substantial structural heart disease and be in NSR at baseline.

Patients were randomized to fish oil pills at 8 g/day for 7 days, then 4 g/day for 23 weeks vs placebo. The primary end point was symptomatic recurrence of AF in up to 6 months of follow-up. There was no significant difference between the two groups, ie, 48% in the placebo group and 52% in the fish oil group ($P=0.26$).

Role of Device-Based Therapy in Prevention of AF

The physiologic sequence of activation of the atria and ventricles is altered with RV pacing. Atrial activation follows RV pacing (AV dyssynchrony) and the right ventricle contracts before the intraventricular septum, followed by the LV lateral wall as in left bundle branch block (ventricular dyssynchrony). AV and ventricular dyssynchrony are thought to be responsible for the increased incidence of AF noted with RV pacing. The benefit of the physiologic mode of pacing (dual chamber or atrial) on the development of AF has been showed in a several clinical trials. Both the Canadian Trial of Physiologic Pacing (CTOPP) and Mode Selection Trial (MOST) showed a lower incidence of AF in patients associated with physiologic pacing vs ventricular pacing. The Search AV Extension and Managed Ventricular Pacing for Promoting Atrio-Ventricular Conduction (SAVEPace) trial showed that use of dual-chamber pacemakers with minimal ventricular pacing is associated with a lower likelihood of developing AF. Also, meta-analysis of several major trials showed that compared with ventricular pacing, atrial-based pacing reduces the incidence of AF and may modestly reduce stroke. However, the magnitude of AF reduction, although statistically significant, was not clinically important and pacing did not reduce CV death or improve overall survival.

Based on outcomes of the above trials, the following recommendations were made in the ACC/AHA/HRS device guidelines:

- Patients with a history of AF who require a permanent pacemaker for bradycardia should have an implanted dual-chamber or atrial pacing device.

- After dual-chamber pacemaker implantation in patients with intact AV conduction, the pacemaker should be programmed to minimize the amount of ventricular pacing.
- Permanent pacing is not indicated to prevent AF in the absence of another indication for pacemaker placement.

In a patient at risk for AF who requires a pacemaker for bradycardia indications, physiologic pacing (as opposed to RV pacing) may be the modality of choice since it is associated with a reduced incidence of AF. Stand-alone pacing for AF treatment is not advocated.

The role of device-based therapy in the cardioversion of AF will be discussed further in *Chapter 10*.

Key Clinical Points

- Light-to-moderate physical activity (eg, walking), is associated with a lower incidence of AF in older adults.
- RAAS blockade with ACE inhibitors or ARBs may prevent the development of AF, especially in patients with LV systolic dysfunction, HF, or hypertension associated with concentric LVH.
- Currently, there are insufficient data to recommend the use of statins in primary prevention of AF or secondary prevention after successful cardioversion.
- Growing evidence supports a possible beneficial effect of statins in primary prevention of AF in post–cardiac surgery patients.
- Steroids appear to be effective for AF prevention, especially in post–cardiac surgery patients, but their safety needs to be better elucidated.
- Large, prospective, randomized, placebo-controlled trials that target specific groups of patients with AF are needed to establish the benefit of pharmacologic prevention of AF.

- In patients with permanent pacemakers, physiologic pacing (atrial or dual chamber) is beneficial in the prevention of AF but is not advocated as stand-alone therapy.

SUGGESTED READING

Adam O, Neuberger HR, Böhm M, Laufs U. Prevention of atrial fibrillation with 3-hydroxy-3-methylglutaryl coenzyme A reductase inhibitors. *Circulation.* 2008;118(12):1285-1293.

Almroth H, Höglund N, Boman K, et al. Atorvastatin and persistent atrial fibrillation following cardioversion: a randomized placebo-controlled multicentre study. *Eur Heart J.* 2009;30(7):827-833.

Benjamin EJ, Chen PS, Bild DE, et al. Prevention of atrial fibrillation: report from a National Heart, Lung, and Blood Institute workshop. *Circulation.* 2009;119(4):606-618.

Cheng J, Arnsdorf M. The role of pacemakers in the prevention of atrial fibrillation. In: Basow, DS, ed. *UpToDate.* Waltham, MA: UpToDate; 2010.

Connolly SJ, Kerr CR, Gent M, et al. Effects of physiologic pacing versus ventricular pacing on the risk of stroke and death due to cardiovascular causes. Canadian Trial of Physiologic Pacing Investigators. *N Engl J Med.* 2000;342(19):1385-1391.

Dernellis J, Panaretou M. Relationship between C-reactive protein concentrations during glucocorticoid therapy and recurrent atrial fibrillation. *Eur Heart J.* 2004;25(13):1100-1107.

Ducharme A, Swedberg K, Pfeffer MA, et al; CHARM Investigators. Prevention of atrial fibrillation in patients with symptomatic chronic heart failure by candesartan in the Candesartan in Heart failure: Assessment of Reduction in Mortality and morbidity (CHARM) program. *Am Heart J.* 2006;152(1):86-92.

Fuster V, Rydén LE, Cannom DS, et al; American College of Cardiology/American Heart Association Task Force on Practice Guidelines; European Society of Cardiology Committee for Practice Guidelines; European Heart Rhythm Association; Heart Rhythm Society. ACC/AHA/ESC 2006 Guidelines for the Management of Patients with Atrial Fibrillation: a report of the American College of Cardiology/American Heart Association Task Force on Practice Guidelines and the European Society of Cardiology Committee for Practice Guidelines (Writing Committee to Revise the 2001 Guidelines for the Management of Patients With Atrial Fibrillation): developed in collaboration with the European Heart Rhythm Association and the Heart Rhythm Society [erratum appears in *Circulation.* 2007;116(6):e138]. *Circulation.* 2006;114(7):e257-e354.

7

Gao X, Peng L, Adhikari CM, Lin J, Zuo Z. Spironolactone reduced arrhythmia and maintained magnesium homeostasis in patients with congestive heart failure. *J Card Fail.* 2007;13(3):170-177.

GISSI-AF Investigators, Disertori M, Latini R, Barlera S, et al. Valsartan for prevention of recurrent atrial fibrillation [erratum appears in *N Engl J Med.* 2009;360(22):2379]. *N Engl J Med.* 2009;360(16):1606-1617.

Guglin M, Garcia M, Yarnoz MJ, Curtis AB. Non-antiarrhythmic medications for atrial fibrillation: from bench to clinical practice. *J Interv Card Electrophysiol.* 2008;22(2):119-128.

Halonen J, Halonen P, Järvinen O, et al. Corticosteroids for the prevention of atrial fibrillation after cardiac surgery: a randomized controlled trial. *JAMA.* 2007;297(14):1562-1567.

Hansson L, Lindholm LH, Ekbom T, et al. Randomised trial of old and new antihypertensive drugs in elderly patients: cardiovascular mortality and morbidity the Swedish Trial in Old Patients with Hypertension-2 study. *Lancet.* 1999;354(9192):1751-1756.

Hansson L, Lindholm LH, Niskanen L, et al. Effect of angiotensin-converting-enzyme inhibition compared with conventional therapy on cardiovascular morbidity and mortality in hypertension: the Captopril Prevention Project (CAPPP) randomised trial. *Lancet.* 1999;353(9153):611-616.

Healey JS, Baranchuk A, Crystal E, et al. Prevention of atrial fibrillation with angiotensin-converting enzyme inhibitors and angiotensin receptor blockers: a meta-analysis. *J Am Coll Cardiol.* 2005;45(11):1832-1839.

Ho KM, Tan JA. Benefits and risks of corticosteroid prophylaxis in adult cardiac surgery: a dose-response meta-analysis. *Circulation.* 2009;119(14):1853-1866.

Iravanian S, Dudley SC Jr. The renin-angiotensin-aldosterone system (RAAS) and cardiac arrhythmias. *Heart Rhythm.* 2008;5(6 suppl):S12-S17.

Kaireviciute D, Aidietis A, Lip GY. Atrial fibrillation following cardiac surgery: clinical features and preventative strategies. *Eur Heart J.* 2009;30(4):410-425.

Kalahasty G, Ellenbogen K. The role of pacemakers in the management of patients with atrial fibrillation. *Cardiol Clin.* 2009;27(1):137-150.

Kowey PR, Reiffel JA, Ellenbogen KA, Naccarelli GV, Pratt CM. Efficacy and safety of prescription omega-3 fatty acids for the prevention of recurrent symptomatic atrial fibrillation: a randomized controlled trial. *JAMA.* 2010;304(21):2363-2372.

Lally JA, Gnall EM, Seltzer J, Kowey PR. Non-antiarrhythmic drugs in atrial fibrillation: a review of non-antiarrhythmic agents in prevention of atrial fibrillation. *J Cardiovasc Electrophysiol.* 2007;18(11):1222-1228.

Lamas GA, Lee KL, Sweeney MO, et al; Mode Selection Trial in Sinus-Node Dysfunction. Ventricular pacing or dual-chamber pacing for sinus-node dysfunction. *N Engl J Med*. 2002;346(24):1854-1862.

Maggioni AP, Latini R, Carson PE; Val-HeFT Investigators. Valsartan reduces the incidence of atrial fibrillation in patients with heart failure: results from the Valsartan Heart Failure Trial (Val-HeFT). *Am Heart J*. 2005;149(3):548-557.

McLean DS, Ravid S, Blazing M, Gersh B, Shui A, Cannon CP. Effect of statin dose on incidence of atrial fibrillation: data from the Pravastatin or Atorvastatin Evaluation and Infection Therapy-Thrombolysis in Myocardial Infarction 22 (PROVE IT-TIMI 22) and Aggrastat to Zocor (A to Z) trials. *Am Heart J*. 2008;155(2):298-302.

Mohammed KS, Kowey PR, Musco S. Adjuvant therapy for atrial fibrillation. *Future Cardiol*. 2010;6(1):67-81.

Mozaffarian D, Furberg CD, Psaty BM, Siscovick D. Physical activity and incidence of atrial fibrillation in older adults: the cardiovascular health study. *Circulation*. 2008;118(8):800-807.

Patti G, Chello M, Candura D, et al. Randomized trial of atorvastatin for reduction of postoperative atrial fibrillation in patients undergoing cardiac surgery: results of the ARMYDA-3 (Atorvastatin for Reduction of MYocardial Dysrhythmia After cardiac surgery) study. *Circulation*. 2006;114(14):1455-1461.

Pedersen OD, Bagger H, Kober L, Torp-Pedersen C. Trandolapril reduces the incidence of atrial fibrillation after acute myocardial infarction in patients with left ventricular dysfunction. *Circulation*. 1999;100(4):376-380.

Schmieder RE, Kjeldsen SE, Julius S, McInnes GT, Zanchetti A, Hua TA; VALUE Trial Group. Reduced incidence of new-onset atrial fibrillation with angiotensin II receptor blockade: the VALUE trial. *J Hypertens*. 2008;26(3):403-411.

Sweeney MO, Bank AJ, Nsah E, et al; Search AV Extension and Managed Ventricular Pacing for Promoting Atrioventricular Conduction (SAVE PACe) Trial. Minimizing ventricular pacing to reduce atrial fibrillation in sinus-node disease. *N Engl J Med*. 2007;357(10):1000-1008.

Telmisartan Randomised Assessment Study in ACE Intolerant Subjects With Cardiovascular Disease (TRANSCEND) Investigators; Yusuf S, Teo K, Anderson C, et al. Effects of the angiotensin-receptor blocker telmisartan on cardiovascular events in high-risk patients intolerant to angiotensin-converting enzyme inhibitors: a randomised controlled trial [erratum appears in *Lancet*. 2008;372(9647):1384]. *Lancet*. 2008;372(9644):1174-1183.

Vermes E, Tardif JC, Bourassa MG, et al. Enalapril decreases the incidence of atrial fibrillation in patients with left ventricular dysfunction:

7

insight from the Studies Of Left Ventricular Dysfunction (SOLVD) trials. *Circulation*. 2003;107(23):2926-2931.

Vidt DG. Telmisartan, ramipril, or both in patients at high risk for vascular events. *Curr Hypertens Rep*. 2008;10(5):343-344.

Wachtell K, Lehto M, Gerdts E, et al. Angiotensin II receptor blockade reduces new-onset atrial fibrillation and subsequent stroke compared to atenolol: the Losartan Intervention For End Point Reduction in Hypertension (LIFE) study. *J Am Coll Cardiol*. 2005;45(5):712-719.

8
Goals of Therapy

A broad overview of therapeutic goals in AF and the approaches to achieve these goals are presented in this chapter (**Figure 8.1**). Specific aspects of AF therapy are discussed in detail in subsequent chapters.

In the acute setting, the main goal of AF therapy is assuring the patient's hemodynamic stability via control of ventricular rate or restoration of NSR. Every patient with AF also needs immediate stroke-risk assessment and effective strategy to avoid thromboembolic complications. If AF is symptomatic, control of patient's symptoms is another goal in acute AF management. The negative impact of the arrhythmia on the underlying heart disease needs to be minimized.

Once initial goals are achieved, long-term aims in AF therapy are set. The presence of AF is associated with increased mortality. As such, improving patient's survival is a primary long-term goal of AF therapy. This may be achieved with limiting AF sequelae, such as stroke and tachycardia-induced cardiomyopathy, although studies to prove mortality benefit have not been forthcoming.

Due to the myriad of possible symptoms associated with AF, relief of symptoms, maintenance of exercise tolerance, and improvement in QoL are key goals in the management of patients with AF. Reductions in hospitalization, limiting side effects of therapy, and cost-effectiveness are also important.

Large, randomized clinical trials are the primary source for an evidence-based approach to AF therapy. The major clinical trial results are applicable only to the patient population group enrolled in these trials and may not apply to every patient with AF. As such, each patient needs an individualized strategy to achieve long-term goals. This individualized approach should focus on the choice between rate vs rhythm control with pharmacologic or nonpharmacologic therapy and the need for chronic anticoagulation.

FIGURE 8.1 — Individualized Strategy to Achieve Primary and Long-Term Goals in AF Therapy

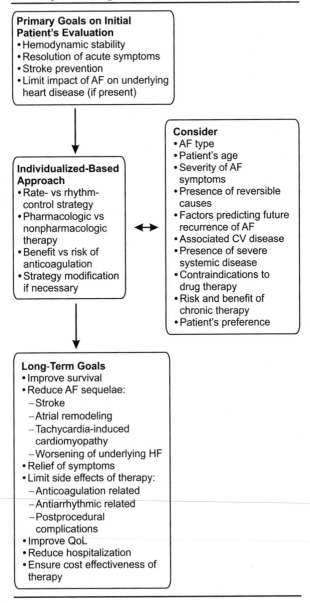

Primary Goals on Initial Patient's Evaluation
- Hemodynamic stability
- Resolution of acute symptoms
- Stroke prevention
- Limit impact of AF on underlying heart disease (if present)

Individualized-Based Approach
- Rate- vs rhythm-control strategy
- Pharmacologic vs nonpharmacologic therapy
- Benefit vs risk of anticoagulation
- Strategy modification if necessary

Consider
- AF type
- Patient's age
- Severity of AF symptoms
- Presence of reversible causes
- Factors predicting future recurrence of AF
- Associated CV disease
- Presence of severe systemic disease
- Contraindications to drug therapy
- Risk and benefit of chronic therapy
- Patient's preference

Long-Term Goals
- Improve survival
- Reduce AF sequelae:
  - Stroke
  - Atrial remodeling
  - Tachycardia-induced cardiomyopathy
  - Worsening of underlying HF
- Relief of symptoms
- Limit side effects of therapy:
  - Anticoagulation related
  - Antiarrhythmic related
  - Postprocedural complications
- Improve QoL
- Reduce hospitalization
- Ensure cost effectiveness of therapy

Therapeutic approaches to AF are presented in **Figure 8**.2.

Several factors may influence the long-term AF management of a particular patient. These include:

- AF subtype (eg, paroxysmal, persistent, permanent)
- Patient's age
- Severity of AF symptoms
- Presence of reversible causes of AF
- Factors predicting future recurrence of AF, history of underlying heart disease or severe systemic disease, as well as contradictions to drug therapy (especially to antiarrhythmics) and patient's preference.

FIGURE 8.2 — Therapeutic Approaches to AF

Preventive Therapy

Nonpharmacologic (risk-factor modification, eg, light physical activity in the elderly)

Pharmacologic (ACEI/ARB, aldosterone inhibitors, statins, fish oil, steroids)

Rhythm and Rate Management

Rhythm control
- Acute:
  - Electrical cardioversion
  - Pharmacologic cardioversion
- Chronic:
  - Pharmacologic (chronic AADs therapy, 'pill in the pocket')
  - Nonpharmacologic (radiofrequency ablation, atrial defibrillators, surgical techniques)
  - Combination of ablation with AADs therapy

Rate control
- Pharmacologic (eg, β-blockers, nondihydropyridine CCBs, digoxin)
- Nonpharmacologic (AV nodal ablation with PPM implantation)

Hybrid therapy
- AADs with rate-control properties (eg, sotalol, amiodarone, dronedarone)
- Combination of AADs with rate-control agents
- Combination of ablation with rate-control agents

Stroke Prevention

Antithrombotic therapy ——→ Acute (UFH, LMWH)
                          ——→ Chronic (warfarin, dabigatran, ?other newer anticoagulants)

Antiplatelet therapy ——→ ASA or ASA + clopidogrel:
                         • Low-stroke-risk patients
                         • Contraindications for oral anticoagulation

Device therapy ——→ Embolic prevention (eg, Watchman device)

8

SUGGESTED READING

Camm J, Reiffel JA. Defining endpoints in clinical trials on atrial fibrillation. *Eur Heart J Suppl.* 2008;10(suppl H):H55-H78.

Fuster V, Rydén LE, Cannom DS, et al; American College of Cardiology/American Heart Association Task Force on Practice Guidelines; European Society of Cardiology Committee for Practice Guidelines; European Heart Rhythm Association; Heart Rhythm Society. ACC/AHA/ESC 2006 Guidelines for the Management of Patients with Atrial Fibrillation: a report of the American College of Cardiology/American Heart Association Task Force on Practice Guidelines and the European Society of Cardiology Committee for Practice Guidelines (Writing Committee to Revise the 2001 Guidelines for the Management of Patients With Atrial Fibrillation): developed in collaboration with the European Heart Rhythm Association and the Heart Rhythm Society [erratum appears in *Circulation.* 2007;116(6):e138]. *Circulation.* 2006;114(7):e257-e354.

Padanilam BJ, Prystowsky EN. Atrial fibrillation: goals of therapy and management strategies to achieve the goals. *Med Clin North Am.* 2008;92(1):217-235.

Rothman SA, Laughlin JC, Seltzer J, et al. The diagnosis of cardiac arrhythmias: a prospective multi-center randomized study comparing mobile cardiac outpatient telemetry versus standard loop event monitoring. *J Cardiovasc Electrophysiol.* 2007;18(3):241-247.

9

Therapy: Rate vs Rhythm Control

Background

At the time of the initial evaluation of a patient with AF, a critical issue must be addressed: whether to restore and attempt to maintain NSR or to control ventricular rate but allow AF to persist. These are the two major approaches to therapy of this rhythm disturbance. In the rate-control strategy, therapy is aimed to control any rapid ventricular rate associated with AF without an attempt to restore and maintain sinus rhythm. In the rhythm-control strategy, cardioversion to NSR and maintenance of sinus rhythm is the goal. Pharmacologic, nonpharmacologic, and hybrid therapies may be used in both strategies (**Figure 8.2**). Based on the AF course and the patient's response to therapy, the initial strategy may need to be changed when the first choice of treatment is ineffective or is associated with significant side effects.

Reestablishing NSR appears to be a logical goal of therapy, and for years, pharmacotherapy in AF was focused on the development of effective drugs to achieve this goal. However, restoration of NSR with AADs did not protect from AF sequelae such as stroke. It also became apparent that although maintenance of sinus rhythm is used as a goal of AAD therapy, there are no foolproof methods to ensure absence of AF in clinical practice. Additionally, results of clinical trials of AADs (eg, CAST), showed ineffectiveness and toxicity of AADs in a post-MI premature ventricular contraction (PVC)–suppression trial. Furthermore, some epidemiologic studies suggested that the mortality and morbidity in patients with AF may be at least partially related to the underlying cause of AF but not to the arrhythmia itself. As such, the benefit of AAD therapy in AF was placed in question. In contrast, the well-established efficacy and safety of rate-control agents, combined with remarkable effectiveness of oral anticoagulation for stroke prevention, made a rate-control strategy a logical option in many AF patients.

These observations and unanswered questions led to five randomized clinical trials of the relative value of rate vs rhythm control in patients with AF. These classic trials include:

- PIAF
- AFFIRM
- RACE
- STAF
- HOT CAFE.

An overview of these randomized trials on rhythm- vs rate-control strategy is presented in **Table 9.1**.

Other trials which focused on rate vs rhythm strategy in specific AF populations will be discussed separately.

Outcomes of Rhythm- vs Heart Rate-Control Strategy in Major AF Trials

Patients enrolled in the five major trials on rhythm vs rate control had similar characteristics: older age (average age ~68 years), presenting mostly with recurrent persistent AF, symptomatic (but ~50% of patients in AFFIRM were symptomatic less often than once per month), and the majority with underlying CV disease (but only a few with advanced HF). As such, the results of these trials should be attributable only to this patient population. Outcomes of these trials were similar. Since the AFFIRM trial was much larger than the other four trials, the results of AFFIRM will be presented as a representative example.

The AFFIRM trial was a multicenter, randomized, controlled trial of 4060 patients with AF assigned to rhythm- ($n = 2033$) vs rate- ($n = 2027$) control therapy. Patients enrolled in this trial had persistent (majority) or paroxysmal AF. Mean age was 69.7 years, with 71% of patients having a history of hypertension and 38% with CAD. The most common AADs used for rhythm control were amiodarone and sotalol. Rate control was achieved with digoxin, β-blockers, or CCBs. Target heart rate for the patients in the rate-control arm included: resting ≤80 BPM, with a 6-minute walk ≤110 BPM, 24-hour Holter average ≤100 BPM, and no heart rate >110% of the age-predicted maximum. Five percent of patients in the rate-control arm required AV nodal ablation and pacemaker implantation. Only 1% of patients in the rhythm-control arm were treated with radiofrequency ablation of AF or a surgical ablation procedure. In the rhythm-control arm, 17% of patients at 1 year and 38% at 5 years crossed over to the rate-control arm, mostly due to failure to maintain NSR or drug intolerance. In the rate-control arm, the crossover to rhythm control was 8% at 1 year and 15% at 5 years, mostly due to failure to control AF symptoms or HF. Over 85% of patients in the rate-control group were receiving warfarin compared with approximately 70% in the rhythm-control arm. Discontinuation of warfarin was permitted in the rhythm-control arm after NSR had been maintained for 1 month.

■ Total Mortality

There was no statistically significant difference in all-cause mortality in the AFFIRM trial between the two strategies. A strong trend toward a higher death rate in the rhythm-control group was observed. Overall mortality in the AFFIRM trial at 5 years was 23.8% for rhythm control vs 21.3% for rate control (HR 1.15, 95 % CI, 0.99 to 1.34, $P = 0.08$). Meta-analysis of the five trials had a similar trend, suggesting a hazard of antiarrhythmic therapy and favoring the use of a rate-control approach (HR 1.12, 95% CI = 0.98–1.29; $P = 0.087$).

Two subgroups in the AFFIRM trial had a significantly lower mortality with rate control than with rhythm control: patients without a history of HF (adjusted HR 0.69) and patients >65 years of age (HR 0.76). Interestingly, the excess deaths in the rhythm-control arm were due to non-CV deaths, primarily pulmonary disease and cancer.

The deleterious effect associated with use of AADs was further proven in a substudy of the AFFIRM trial. In this analysis, AADs therapy was associated with 49% increased mortality, which offset the benefits of conver-

TABLE 9.1 — Overview of Published Randomized Trials of Rhythm Control vs Heart-Rate Control in the Management of AF

	PIAF	AFFIRM	RACE	STAF	HOT CAFE
Subjects (N)	252	4060	522	200	205
Follow-up duration (y)	1	3.5	2.3	1.7	1
Patient characteristics	60 years old; 92% male; 50% HTN and 23% CAD; 16% no heart disease; few CHF	70 years old; 61% male; 71% HTN and 38% CAD; 13% no heart disease; 9% CHF	68 years old; 63% male; 49% HTN and 27% CAD; 21% no heart disease; half CHF	65 years old; 64% male; 63% HTN and 44% CAD; 11% no heart disease; 46% CHF	61 years old; 65% male; 64% HTN and 44% CAD; 21% no heart disease; ~half CHF
AF characteristics	Persistent 7 days to 1 year	Persistent (≥69%) and paroxysmal	Persistent; median 32 days; recurrent after ECV	Persistent >4 wk	Persistent 7 days to 2 years
Rhythm control	Amiodarone; ECV	Amiodarone; sotalol; propafenone; other class 1; ECV; few nonpharmacologic	Sotalol, flecainide/propafenone, amiodarone; ECV (prescribed sequence)	Amiodarone; propafenone; flecainide; ECV	ECV followed by propafenone, sotalol, or disopyramide; repeat ECV, new drug, or amiodarone for recurrence
Rate control therapies used	Diltiazem; β-blockers; digitalis; AV junction RF ablation	β-Blockers; diltiazem; verapamil; digitalis; AV junction RV ablation	β-Blockers; diltiazem; verapamil; digitalis; AV junction RV ablation	β-Blockers; diltiazem; verapamil; digitalis; AV junction RF ablation	β-Blockers; diltiazem; verapamil; digitalis; AV junction RF ablation
Anticoagulant use	Continued for duration of study	Discontinuation for SR permitted by guidelines	Discontinuation for SR permitted by guidelines	Discontinuation for SR permitted by guidelines	Discontinuation for SR permitted at physician discretion
Primary end points	Proportion symptomatically improved	Death	Composite of clinical events	Composite of clinical events	Composite of death and death and clinical events

Other end points	QoL; functional capacity; hospitalization; adverse drug effects; bleeding	Composite of clinical events; QoL; functional capacity; hospitalization; cost	Individual components of the composite; QoL; bleeding; cost	Individual components of the composite; QoL; echo measurements; worsening HF; bleeding	Measures of rate and rhythm control; discontinuation of therapy; hemorrhage; hospitalization; new or worsening CHF; exercise tolerance; echo measurements
Summary of results	No difference in primary end point and QoL; rhythm = slightly better functional capacity; rate = fewer hospitalizations and adverse drug effects	No difference in primary end point (trend favors rate) and QoL; rates = fewer hospitalizations and adverse drug effects; rhythm = slightly better functional capacity	Rate not inferior on primary end point; no difference in QoL; rate = fewer hospitalizations and adverse drug effects	No difference in primary end point and all secondary end points; rate = fewer hospitalizations	No difference in primary end point; rate = fewer hospitalizations; rhythm = better exercise tolerance and slight increase in fractional shortening; all 3 strokes in rhythm

New York Heart Association Class ≥II.

Adapted from Wyse DG, *J Cardiovasc Electrophysiol.* 2003;14:S35-S39; Hersi A, et al. *Curr Prob Cardiol.* 2005;30:175-234; Wyse DG. *Int J Cardiol.* 2006;110:301-312.

sion and maintenance of NSR (associated with a 53% reduction in mortality).

■ CV Mortality

There was no difference between the rhythm- and rate-control arms of the AFFIRM study in the incidence of cardiac death, death from arrhythmia, or death due to ischemic or hemorrhagic stroke. Although an increased death rate from proarrhythmic complications of AADs might have been expected in the rhythm-control arm, there was no excess in mortality from cardiac arrhythmia (**Figure 9.1**).

FIGURE 9.1 — Cumulative Mortality From Any Cause in the Rhythm-Control Group and the Rate-Control Group in the AFFIRM Trial

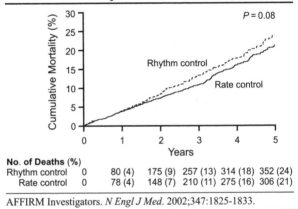

No. of Deaths (%)						
Rhythm control	0	80 (4)	175 (9)	257 (13)	314 (18)	352 (24)
Rate control	0	78 (4)	148 (7)	210 (11)	275 (16)	306 (21)

AFFIRM Investigators. *N Engl J Med.* 2002;347:1825-1833.

■ Thromboembolic Complications

The AFFIRM trial showed a trend toward a higher risk of ischemic stroke with rhythm control than with rate control (7.1% vs 5.5%), but the difference did not reach statistical significance. Most strokes occurred after discontinuation of anticoagulation or with a subtherapeutic international normalized ratio (INR) (<2.0). Subanalysis of this study showed that use of warfarin was associated with a large reduction in stroke risk (HR=0.33, 95% confidence limits=0.14, 0.77, $P = 0.01$), and it was suggested that a higher incidence of stroke in the rhythm-control arm was secondary to underuse of warfarin in patients who were presumably in NSR on antiarrhythmic treatment (**Figure 9.2**).

Since the majority of AF patients in the AFFIRM and RACE trials had more than one risk factor for stroke, these data suggest that anticoagulation therapy should not be discontinued after successful restoration of sinus rhythm in patients at risk for stroke. Because of the absence of reliable methods to continuously monitor maintenance of NSR on antiarrhythmic treatment, long-

FIGURE 9.2 — Hazard Ratios for Death in Prespecified Subgroups in the AFFIRM Trial

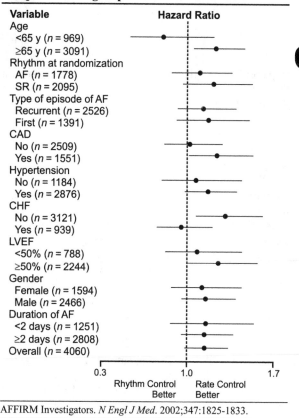

AFFIRM Investigators. *N Engl J Med.* 2002;347:1825-1833.

term anticoagulation should be continued based on the stroke risk, regardless of the chosen rhythm strategy.

■ Impact on Heart Failure

The presence of AF is known to have a negative hemodynamic effect in patients with HF. However, there was no significant difference in either the development or deterioration of HF in the rhythm- and rate-control arms of AFFIRM, RACE, STAF, and HOT CAFÉ trials. Further subgroup analyses in AFFIRM trial suggested there may be a benefit of rhythm-control strategy in patients with a previous history of HF. Additionally, in a substudy of the DIAMOND trial of patients with EF <35%, maintenance of NSR with dofetilide or placebo was associated with a significant reduction in mortality (RR 0.44).

These results led to the first dedicated trial testing the hypothesis that rhythm control is better than rate control in patients with HF and paroxysmal AF (AF-CHF). In this large, prospective randomized trial in patients with AF and HF, outcomes were similar with rhythm- and rate-control strategy. Results of the AF-CHF trial will be discussed later.

■ Symptoms and Quality of Life

Both symptomatic improvement and change in QoL are important therapeutic goals. Unfortunately, objective data are sparse. Patients with similar clinical scenarios of AF may have completely different severity of symptoms and QoL. Additionally, the majority of AF patients have asymptomatic episodes of arrhythmia, and many of those who maintain NSR still report poor QoL. Side effects of therapies for rhythm or rate control and chronic anticoagulation, along with frequent blood testing, may significantly impact QoL.

Although there was no difference in QoL reported in the two study arms of AFFIRM, RACE, PIAF, and STAF, further subanalysis of RACE, the Canadian Trial of Atrial Fibrillation (CTAF), and Sotalol Amiodarone Atrial Fibrillation Efficacy Trial (SAFE-T) showed that restoration and maintenance of NSR was associated with improved QoL. Relief of symptoms and improved QoL in AF have also been reported with a rhythm-control strategy achieved with radiofrequency ablation and surgical procedures.

■ **Exercise Tolerance**

Rhythm-control appears to be superior to rate-control strategy for exercise capacity in patients with AF. In the PIAF and HOT CAFE studies, rhythm control resulted in better exercise tolerance. Also, in a substudy of the AFFIRM trial, rhythm control was associated with a mildly better performance in a 6-minute–walk test.

In a substudy of SAFE-T, exercise tolerance in the SR group was significantly better than that in the AF group at 8 weeks and at 1 year. Patients most likely to improve with treatment were younger, nonobese, and with the greatest pretest incapacity. However, significant differences in exercise capacity between SR and AF arms were not seen in the asymptomatic patients at 8 weeks and 1 year (**Figure 9.3**).

FIGURE 9.3 — SR vs AF Comparisons on Mean Increase in Maximal Exercise Duration From Baseline to 8 Weeks and From Baseline to 1 Year

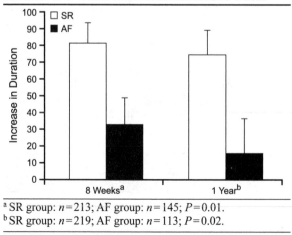

[a] SR group: $n=213$; AF group: $n=145$; $P=0.01$.
[b] SR group: $n=219$; AF group: $n=113$; $P=0.02$.

Singh SN, et al. *J Am Coll Cardiol*. 2006;48:721-730.

■ Hospitalization

During a mean 3.5 years of follow-up in AFFIRM, the number of patients requiring hospitalization was significantly higher with the rhythm- than with the rate-control arm (80% vs 73%). Admission for cardioversion was found to be the main driver.

■ Cost-Effectiveness

There is a significant economic advantage of rate control over rhythm control, mostly due to more frequent hospitalizations with the rhythm-control approach. During a mean follow-up of 3.5 years in the AFFIRM trial, the rate-control strategy was associated with $2,200 to $5,500 savings per person.

In summary, these five randomized trials suggest that in older patients with persistent AF and mild symptoms, rate control with chronic anticoagulation may be a reasonable therapeutic alternative. They also showed that in the absence of reliable methods to monitor maintenance of NSR after cardioversion, anticoagulation should be continued in all patients.

The use of AADs is associated with increased mortality. This will need reevaluation with the development of new AADs. However, these trials have proven that NSR is desirable with regard to symptomatic improvement and QoL, and a strategy to maintain sinus rhythm without the adverse effects of antiarrhythmic medications may have a benefit over rate control.

The results of the above studies should not be extrapolated to other populations, especially younger and severely symptomatic patients with AF who may benefit from antiarrhythmic therapy with newer, less-toxic AADs or ablation/surgical procedures.

Trials of Rhythm vs Rate Control in Specific AF Populations

Results of randomized, controlled trials, including AFFIRM, RACE, PIAF, STAF, and HOT CAFE, are applicable to the majority of patients with AF (ie, elderly with recurrent, persistent AF). There are several other trials that pertain to other important AF populations. The results of these studies provide help in the choice of AF therapy in particular clinical settings.

■ Patients With Symptomatic, Paroxysmal AF

The Paroxysmal Atrial Fibrillation-2 (PAF-2) trial focused on highly symptomatic patients with paroxysmal AF in whom antiarrhythmic therapy had failed, following which they then underwent atrioventricular ablation and pacemaker implantation. Since permanent AF frequently develops in patients treated with this strategy, a total of 137 patients were randomized to either further antiarrhythmic therapy to maintain sinus rhythm or no subsequent AAD use after AV nodal ablation and pacemaker implantation.

Development of permanent AF was a primary end point, while QoL, worsening of CHF, rate of hospitalizations, and echocardiographic measurements were secondary end points. The drugs included were amiodarone, propafenone, flecainide, or sotalol.

After a mean follow-up of 16 months, compared with the rate-control arm, fewer patients randomized to AADs progressed to permanent AF (OR 0.43, 95% CI 0.18-0.95). The difference in the two arms was much less significant at 24 months than at 12 months, suggesting that the benefit of AADs in preventing the development of permanent AF decreases with time.

Quality of life and echocardiographic measurements (eg, left atrial diameter, LV end diastolic diameter, LV ejection fraction) were similar between the two study groups. Additionally, fewer patients in the rate-control group developed HF or required hospitalization. Based on the above outcomes, investigators concluded that antiarrhythmic therapy reduces the risk of developing permanent AF (at least during a relatively short period of follow-up). However, the benefit of this strategy is unclear and maintenance of NSR with AADs in patients after AV nodal ablation and pacemaker implantation is not warranted.

The Japanese Rhythm Management Trial for Atrial Fibrillation (J-RHYTHM) studied the rhythm vs rate strategies in patients with paroxysmal AF. This study had some unique characteristics since it was conducted exclusively in Japan (where there may be a higher frequency of vagally mediated AF), and in relatively younger patients (mean ~65 years of age) with normal LV systolic function. Over 40% of patients had a history of hypertension but very few had a history of CHF. Additionally, Class I AADs were used in this trial, some of which are not available in the United States (eg, pilsicainide, cibenzoline, aprindine). Only 0.5% of patients in the rhythm-control–strategy group were treated initially with amiodarone. β-Blockers were predominantly used in the rate-control arm (51.5%). Approximately 60% of patients in both arms were anticoagulated with warfarin.

In this prospective, randomized control study, a total of 823 patients with paroxysmal AF were randomized to rhythm- or rate-control therapy and followed for a mean of 578 days. There was no difference in overall mortality or CV morbidity between the groups; however, physiologic/psychological disability (which was also a primary end point) was significantly lower in the rhythm-control group (11% vs 16%) and, in several cases, required crossover. The investigators concluded that rhythm-control strategy was preferred over rate control. Interestingly, in the AFFIRM and AF-CHF trials that focused on different populations, crossover was higher in the rhythm-control arm. This difference underscores the importance of individualizing therapy based on the type of AF, its pathophysiology, comorbidities, and patient expectations.

■ Patients With AF and Heart Failure

The loss of AV synchrony, as well as rapid and/or irregular heart rate, are deleterious in patients with AF and HF. Intuitively, restoration and maintenance of NSR should be an important therapeutic goal in patients with HF. However, substudies of randomized control trials comparing rhythm vs rate control have demonstrated similar outcomes in HF patients.

The AF-CHF trial was the first large, multicenter, prospective, randomized trial comparing rhythm vs rate control in HF patients with AF. In this trial, 1376 patients with HF symptoms, ejection fraction ≤35%, and AF were assigned to a rhythm control (*n*=682) or rate control ($n=694$). The mean age of patients enrolled in this study was 67 years. AF was persistent in 69% and paroxysmal in 31% of patients. The most common AAD used in the rhythm-control arm was amiodarone and rate-control therapies included mostly β-blockers and digitalis. Approximately 90% of patients in both groups were treated with oral anticoagulation.

After a mean follow-up of 37 months, death from CV causes (primary outcome) was not statistically different—26.7% vs 25.2%, with an annual death rate of approximately 8% in both groups. There was also no significant difference in all-cause mortality, stroke, or worsening HF (secondary outcomes). Hospitalization for AF (mostly for electrical cardioversion) was higher in the rhythm-control group. Crossover rates were also higher with initial assignment to the rhythm rather than to the rate-control strategy (21% vs 10%), respectively.

These results suggest that either the benefit of NSR in HF is attenuated by ineffective and toxic agents used to achieve this goal or that there is no benefit in restoration of NSR once AF develops. The correct conclusion will be determined with the use of newer approaches to restore and maintain NSR in HF patients with AF.

■ Young Patients With AF and Valvular Heart Disease

The Control of Rate versus Rhythm in Rheumatic Atrial Fibrillation Trial (CRRAFT) studied patients with AF due to rheumatic valve disease. Patients in this trial were young (mean age, 39 years), all had AF due to RHD and normal LV systolic function, and the majority had a previous history of valvular surgery. A total of 144 patients enrolled in this trial were randomized to electrical cardioversion alone or electrical cardioversion with amiodarone (rhythm control) vs diltiazem (rate control). The investigators constructed a group of those treated with electrical cardioversion and amiodarone, and compared them with rate-control alone (diltiazem). At 1 year, QoL and exercise capacity were superior in the rhythm-control group. As amiodarone toxicity with long-term therapy would likely occur, a relatively short follow-up was a major limitation of the study.

Although rhythm control appears to be a desirable goal in AF therapy, the results of large clinical trials suggest that a rate-control strategy is satisfactory for many patients. This may reflect the limitations of current rhythm-control therapies rather than lack of benefit in restoration of NSR. Factors to be considered in choosing between rhythm- and rate-control strategy are presented in *Chapter 8* (**Figure 8.1**).

After the results of AFFIRM study were published, the American Academy of Family Physicians and the American College of Physicians 2003 Clinical Practice Guidelines stated that most patients with first-detected AF should be treated with a rate-control strategy and chronic anticoagulation. Most cardiologists would attempt to reestablish NSR with a first episode of AF in the majority of patients with a relatively low risk of recurrence (eg, AF due to reversible causes, normal LA size, no valvular or hypertensive heart disease, or absence of LV dysfunction or CHF). This approach was supported by the 2006 ACC/AHA/ESC Guidelines, which stressed the risk of missing an opportunity to prevent permanent AF with a general preference for an early rhythm-control approach in the majority of patients.

The discrepancy between general practitioners and cardiologists in the approach to rate vs rhythm strategy was recently illustrated in a retrospective analysis of 155,731 hospitalizations from 464 hospitals. Rhythm-control strategy was chosen in 48%. Care by family or internal medicine physicians (vs cardiologists) and patient age >65 years favored rate-control therapy (OR 0.33, 95% CI, 0.31-0.36).

We believe that there is no first-line therapy for AF. The choice of strategy should be individualized and based on the clinical scenario. Frequently, the initially chosen strategy may need to be changed. Patient characteristics favoring rhythm- vs rate-control strategy are presented in **Table 9.2**.

TABLE 9.2 — Patient Characteristics Favoring Rhythm- vs Rate-Control Strategy

Rhythm Control	Rate Control
Younger	Older (especially >70 years old)
Symptomatic	Asymptomatic or mildly symptomatic
Physically active	Limited physical activity
Complaint	Refuses hospitalizations
First detected or recurrent lone AF	Long-standing AF with high risk of failing cardioversion
AF due to known precipitants	Underlying severe systemic disease associated with increased risk of AAD toxicity
Uncontrolled heart rate with rate-control strategy	Intolerance or contradiction to AAD therapy

Anticoagulation for both groups based on stroke risk and *not* based on choice of rhythm- vs rate-control strategy.

9

Key Clinical Points

- A rate-control strategy is favored in elderly and mildly symptomatic patients without a contraindication to chronic anticoagulation.
- A rhythm-control strategy is favored in younger, symptomatic patients with first-detected or lone AF.
- There is most likely a benefit of maintenance of NSR, but it may be counterbalanced by the toxicity of commonly used AADs. Newer pharmacologic agents with a better safety profile or invasive approaches for rhythm control may shift the focus of AF therapy to rhythm control in the future.
- Patients with AF should always be anticoagulated based on stroke risk independent of choice of rhythm- vs rate-control strategy.

SUGGESTED READING

Allen Lapointe NM, Sun JL, Kaplan S, d'Almada P, Al-Khatib SM. Rhythm versus rate control in the contemporary management of atrial fibrillation in-hospital. *Am J Cardiol.* 2008;101(8):1134-1141.

Anter E, Callans DJ, Wyse DG. Pharmacological and electrical conversion of atrial fibrillation to sinus rhythm is worth the effort. *Circulation.* 2009;120(14):1436-1443.

Atwood JE, Myers JN, Tang XC, Reda DJ, Singh SN, Singh BN. Exercise capacity in atrial fibrillation: a substudy of the Sotalol-Amiodarone Atrial Fibrillation Efficacy Trial (SAFE-T). *Am Heart J.* 2007;153(4):566-572.

Brignole M, Menozzi C, Gasparini M, et al; PAF 2 Study Investigators. An evaluation of the strategy of maintenance of sinus rhythm by antiarrhythmic drug therapy after ablation and pacing therapy in patients with paroxysmal atrial fibrillation. *Eur Heart J.* 2002;23(11):892-900.

Carlsson J, Miketic S, Windeler J, et al; STAF Investigators. Randomized trial of rate-control versus rhythm-control in persistent atrial fibrillation: the Strategies of Treatment of Atrial Fibrillation (STAF) study. *J Am Coll Cardiol.* 2003;41(10):1690-1696.

Chung MK, Shemanski L, Sherman DG, et al; AFFIRM Investigators. Functional status in rate- versus rhythm-control strategies for atrial fibrillation: results of the Atrial Fibrillation Follow-Up Investigation of Rhythm Management (AFFIRM) Functional Status Substudy. *J Am Coll Cardiol.* 2005;46(10):1891-1899.

Dorian P, Mangat I. Quality of life variables in the selection of rate versus rhythm control in patients with atrial fibrillation: observations from the Canadian Trial of Atrial Fibrillation. *Card Electrophysiol Rev.* 2003;7(3):276-279.

Hagens VE, Ranchor AV, Van Sonderen E, et al; RACE Study Group. Effect of rate or rhythm control on quality of life in persistent atrial fibrillation. Results from the Rate Control Versus Electrical Cardioversion (RACE) Study. *J Am Coll Cardiol.* 2004;43(2):241-247.

Hohnloser SH, Kuck KH, Lilienthal J. Rhythm or rate control in atrial fibrillation--Pharmacological Intervention in Atrial Fibrillation (PIAF): a randomised trial. *Lancet.* 2000;356(9244):1789-1794.

Ogawa S, Yamashita T, Yamazaki T, et al; J-RHYTHM Investigators. Optimal treatment strategy for patients with paroxysmal atrial fibrillation: J-RHYTHM Study. *Circ J.* 2009;73(2):242-248.

Opolski G, Torbicki A, Kosior DA, et al; Investigators of the Polish How to Treat Chronic Atrial Fibrillation Study. Rate control vs rhythm control in patients with nonvalvular persistent atrial fibrillation: the results of the Polish How to Treat Chronic Atrial Fibrillation (HOT CAFE) Study. *Chest.* 2004;126(2):476-486.

Pedersen OD, Bagger H, Keller N, Marchant B, Køber L, Torp-Pedersen C. Efficacy of dofetilide in the treatment of atrial fibrillation-flutter in patients with reduced left ventricular function: a Danish investigation of arrhythmia and mortality on dofetilide (diamond) substudy. *Circulation.* 2001;104(3):292-296.

Podrid P, Manning W. Rhythm control versus rate control in atrial fibrillation. In: Basow DS, ed. *UpToDate.* Waltham, MA: UpToDate; 2010.

Reiffel JA. A contemporary look at classic trials in atrial fibrillation: what do they really show and how might they apply to future therapies? *Am J Cardiol.* 2008;102(6A):3H-11H.

Roy D, Talajic M, Nattel S, et al; Atrial Fibrillation and Congestive Heart Failure Investigators. Rhythm control versus rate control for atrial fibrillation and heart failure. *N Engl J Med.* 2008;358(25):2667-2677.

Singh SN, Tang XC, Singh BN, et al; SAFE-T Investigators. Quality of life and exercise performance in patients in sinus rhythm versus persistent atrial fibrillation: a Veterans Affairs Cooperative Studies Program Substudy. *J Am Coll Cardiol.* 2006;48(4):721-730.

Van Gelder IC, Hagens VE, Bosker HA, et al; Rate Control versus Electrical Cardioversion for Persistent Atrial Fibrillation Study Group. A comparison of rate control and rhythm control in patients with recurrent persistent atrial fibrillation. *N Engl J Med.* 2002;347(23):1834-1840.

Wyse DG, Anter E, Callans DJ. Cardioversion of atrial fibrillation for maintenance of sinus rhythm: a road to nowhere. *Circulation.* 2009;120(14):1444-1452.

Wyse DG, Waldo AL, DiMarco JP, et al; Atrial Fibrillation Follow-up Investigation of Rhythm Management (AFFIRM) Investigators. A comparison of rate control and rhythm control in patients with atrial fibrillation. *N Engl J Med.* 2002;347(23):1825-1833.

Wyse DG. Pharmacologic approaches to rhythm versus rate control in atrial fibrillation–where are we now? *Int J Cardiol.* 2006;110(3):301-312.

Wyse DG. Rate control versus maintenance of sinus rhythm. In: Kowey PR, Naccarelli GV, eds. *Atrial Fibrillation.* New York, NY: Marcel Dekker; 2005:109.

9

10

Therapy: Restoration and Maintenance of Normal Sinus Rhythm

Restoration of NSR is emergently required when a patient with AF is hemodynamically unstable (eg, hypotensive, in decompensated HF, or symptomatic from CAD). A rhythm-control strategy is also often chosen as a long-term strategy for patients with AF, especially in the following situations:

- Severely symptomatic
- Young age
- First episode of AF
- When AF is due to reversible causes.

A complete discussion on rhythm vs rate approach in AF is presented in *Chapter 9*.

Restoration of NSR may be achieved with electrical shock or with the use of an AAD. Electrical cardioversion is safe, highly efficacious (>90% success rate with biphasic shock), and is generally preferred over pharmacologic cardioversion. A transthoracic electrical cardioversion is almost exclusively performed, although certain patients may benefit from internal electrical cardioversion or implantation of devices with atrial defibrillation properties. Once sinus rhythm is restored, with either electrical or pharmacologic cardioversion, AADs are frequently used for maintenance of NSR (see *Chapter 11*).

Restoration and maintenance of NSR may also be attempted with invasive procedures in an attempt to permanently cure AF. Approximately 90% of patients with AF achieve restoration and long-term maintenance of NSR with a surgical procedure when performed by an experienced operator. Catheter ablation of AF is successful in approximately 75% of cases. This procedure is less invasive and associated with fewer complications.

Regardless of the modality chosen to restore NSR, a longer duration of AF, enlargement of the atria, and more advanced age are all associated with procedural failure. Furthermore, whether cardioversion is performed emergently or as a part of a long-term strategy, anticoagulation to prevent thromboembolic complications should always be addressed. Treatment modalities used for restoration of NSR are presented below. Thromboembolic risk and stroke prevention with cardioversion of AF are discussed in detail in *Chapter 13*.

Electrical Cardioversion

■ Overview

Electrical cardioversion performed under appropriate conditions is well tolerated, rapid, and more effective than pharmacologic cardioversion (success rate with biphasic electrical cardioversion is approximately 90%). Electrical cardioversion is the modality of choice for restoration of NSR in hemodynamically unstable patient or as an elective procedure in patients with AF.

Direct-current (DC) cardioversion is used for cardioversion of AF. It implies that delivery of an electrical shock is synchronized with the intrinsic QRS complex, which prevents shock-induced arrhythmia following electrical stimulation during the vulnerable period of the cardiac cycle. Although the term "electrical cardioversion" almost always refers to a transthoracic procedure, electrical shock may be delivered with internal cardioversion or via atrial defibrillator. Although DC cardioversion is safe and well tolerated, attention to detail is required to prevent procedural failure and possible complications (**Table 10.1**).

■ Indications for DC Cardioversion of AF

The 2006 ACC/AHA/ESC Guidelines for the management of AF concluded that immediate electrical cardioversion for AF is recommended when:

- AF with rapid ventricular rate (and associated with ongoing myocardial ischemia, symptomatic hypotension, angina, or HF) does not respond to pharmacologic therapy.

TABLE 10.1 — DC Cardioversion Checklist Prior to the Procedure

- Presence of AF confirmed prior to cardioversion
- Informed consent signed
- Patient fasting (preferably >8 hours)
- Reliable IV access available
- Relevant history reviewed and physical exam obtained
- Known duration of AF (consider AADs load prior to cardioversion if AF >3 months)
- Known anticoagulation strategy
- Laboratory data reviewed:
  - Hypokalemia and hypomagnesemia present? If so, postpone procedure until corrected
  - Therapeutic level of PTT and/or INR?
- Medications list reviewed:
  - Patient receiving any AADs?
  - Patient on digoxin? If so, check ECG for signs of digoxin toxicity; cancel the procedure if present
- Sedation plan and anesthesia backup available
- Continuous vital sign monitoring available (conscious sedation protocol)
- Continuous electrocardiographic monitoring available
- Shock delivery in "synchronized" mode

- AF with underlying pre-excitation is associated with very rapid tachycardia or hemodynamic instability.

The 2006 ACC/AHA/ESC Guidelines recommend elective cardioversion in the absence of hemodynamic instability when symptoms of AF are unacceptable to the patient.

Additionally, according to the guidelines, DC cardioversion may be useful to restore sinus rhythm as part of a long-term rhythm-control strategy for patients with AF. Infrequently, repeated cardioversions for the management of symptomatic or recurrent AF may also be considered based on patient's preference.

■ Practical and Technical Aspects of Electrical Cardioversion
Anesthesia

DC cardioversion should be performed in a place with full advanced cardiac life-support (ACLS) capability. Electrical shock is associated with significant pain; as such, elective DC cardioversion should generally be performed under moderate sedation. Rapid-onset and short-acting agents (eg, midazolam, fentanyl, propofol) are preferred to allow rapid recovery after cardioversion. In some cases, especially in patients with severe lung disease, general anesthesia with endotracheal intubation may be required. In patients with severely decreased LV systolic function, etomidate is preferred over propofol. BP and pulse oximetry should be monitored in the peri-procedural period.

Anticoagulation

A detailed discussion on anticoagulation strategies with cardioversion for AF is presented in *Chapter 13*. Only key aspects are presented below.

The need for anticoagulation with cardioversion of AF must be considered prior the procedure. Patients with AF undergoing DC cardioversion are at an especially high risk for stroke because electrical shock may cause embolization of preexisting thrombus. Additionally, atrial mechanical function is significantly impaired (stunning) for up to 4 weeks following cardioversion to sinus rhythm. The duration of atrial stunning appears to be directly related to the duration of AF prior to cardioversion.

It is generally accepted that if AF has been present for <48 hours, cardioversion may be performed without anticoagulation prior to the procedure. However, this concept is not based on data from large, randomized trials.

For AF lasting >48 hours (or for an uncertain duration), the risk of a thromboembolic event post-cardioversion may be as high as 5% in the absence of anticoagulation. This elevated risk of stroke is observed in the first month postcardioversion, although the vast majority of strokes occur within the first 10 days. As such, two basic anticoagulation strategies for cardioversion in patients with AF >48 hours are used.

In the first strategy, a patient is anticoagulated with warfarin with a therapeutic INR (ie, 2 to 3) for 3 to 4 weeks before the procedure. Warfarin is then continued for at least 4 weeks postprocedure. In the second approach, TEE is performed. In the absence of thrombus, heparin is started before cardioversion. Postcardioversion, oral anticoagulation with warfarin is initiated. Heparin (or LMWH) is stopped 48 hours after therapeutic INR is achieved with oral anticoagulation. Warfarin is then continued for at least 4 weeks postprocedure. Further anticoagulation after 4 weeks is based on the patient's stroke risk. Case reports have described embolic strokes in patients who underwent electrical cardioversion without periprocedure anticoagulation despite preprocedure TEE showing no thrombus.

In the hemodynamically unstable patient, the restoration of sinus rhythm outweighs the risk of stroke, and cardioversion should be performed emergently. Anticoagulation with heparin should be started before cardioversion. Postprocedure heparin and warfarin should be continued as per appropriate recommendations as previously discussed.

Appropriate Pads/Paddles Use

A paddle size of 8 to 12 cm is recommended for AF cardioversion.

Electrodes for DC cardioversion may be placed in two positions (**Figure 10.1**):

- Anterolateral (anterior electrode—right parasternal second and third intercostal space, lateral—midaxillary line below the fourth intercostal space) (**Figure 10.1**, *left figure*)
- Anteroposterior (anterior electrode—right parasternal second and third intercostal space, posterior electrode—just below the left scapula) (**Figure 10.1**, *middle and right figures*).

Some claim that the success rate is higher and less energy is necessary with the anteroposterior electrode position. However, available data do not clearly support this position. If DC cardioversion with one configuration is ineffective, the procedure may be repeated with another position.

FIGURE 10.1 — Electrode Positions: Anterolateral and Anteroposterior

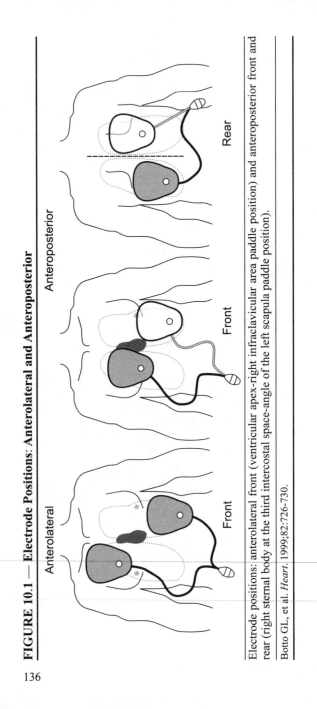

Electrode positions: anterolateral front (ventricular apex-right infraclavicular area paddle position) and anteroposterior front and rear (right sternal body at the third intercostal space-angle of the left scapula paddle position).

Botto GL, et al. *Heart.* 1999;82:726-730.

Shock Synchronization

The delivery of an electric shock during the ventricle vulnerable period, upstroke of the T wave, can lead to ventricular fibrillation (VF). As such, shock delivery is synchronized with the QRS complex. The shock is delivered on the sensed intrinsic R wave. At this time, the ventricle is depolarized and least susceptible to the induction of VT. The presence of accurate synchronization should be verified since large T or P waves, R' in RsR' complex of right bundle branch block, and artifacts may lead to inappropriate synchronization.

Shock Waveforms

Traditionally, transthoracic electrical cardioversion and defibrillation was performed with a monophasic shock wave, characterized by a single discharge with an initial high voltage peak, followed by an exponential decay to zero. Biphasic shock waves have an initial positive peak current (lower than monophasic) followed by a second phase with negative polarity (**Figure 10.2**).

Biphasic defibrillators have been shown to be more effective than monophasic in cardioverting patients with AF. Cardioversion with biphasic waveforms requires fewer shocks and, due to lower energy, results in less dermal injury.

Energy Delivered

An initial energy of 200 joules (J) (monophasic shock) or 150-200 J (biphasic shock) is usually recommended for successful cardioversion of AF. However, in cases of AF of >48 hours' duration or patients weighing >85 kg (187 lb), an initial energy of 360 J (monophasic shock) and 200 J (biphasic shock) is frequently used.

Some practitioners advocate using high energy for every cardioversion of AF (360 J biphasic). This increases the probability of successful restoration of NSR with the first shock and shortens sedation time. Thermal injury to the skin is a potential concern with high-energy shocks (monophasic more than biphasic), however, the theoretical concern of myocardial injury caused by high-energy shocks does not appear to have clinical significance.

FIGURE 10.2 — Defibrillation Waveforms

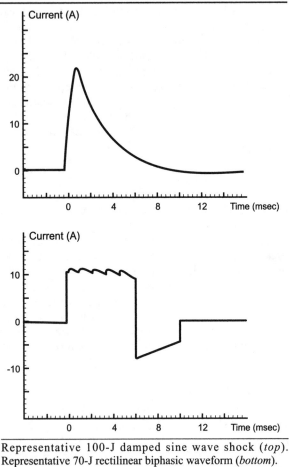

Representative 100-J damped sine wave shock (*top*).
Representative 70-J rectilinear biphasic waveform (*bottom*).

Mittal S, et al. *Circulation*. 2000;101:1282-1287.

A lower initial shock energy may be used for cardioversion of atrial flutter (100 J biphasic). Monophasic and biphasic defibrillation appear to be equally effective in restoration of NSR in patients with atrial flutter.

Special Populations

Patients With an Implanted Device

External cardioversion in patients with implanted devices (PPMs and implantable cardioverters and defibrillators [ICDs]) may lead to distortion in the electrical circuit (programmed data) and electrode–myocardial interference (endocardial injury). However, cardioversion can be safely performed with appropriate precautions.

Paddles should be placed in the AP position as far as possible from the implanted device. As a rule, creating maximal electrical current parallel to PPM/ICD leads (one paddle over the device and the other at the apex) should always be avoided. The device should be also interrogated pre- and postcardioversion and reprogrammed postprocedure if necessary. In patients with AF and an ICD, cardioversion may be performed with shock delivered by the device. However, this will decrease the battery life of the ICD. In patients with atrial flutter and ICD, antitachycardia pacing through the device may be tried before sedation and delivery of an internal shock.

Patients With Acute MI

DC cardioversion of AF in hemodynamically unstable patients with acute MI is safe and does not result in significant additional myocardial injury.

Patients Post–Cardiac Surgery

Electrical cardioversion can be effective in patients with postoperative AF who are hemodynamically unstable. However, the efficacy of cardioversion may be decreased in poststernotomy patients for up to 1 month postsurgery. If epicardial wires or transvenous electrodes are still in place postoperatively, internal cardioversion should be considered.

Patients With Hyperthyroidism

AF should be initially treated with rate-control strategy since the majority of patients will convert spontaneously to NSR when thyroid hormones normalize with antithyroid therapy. Cardioversion should be considered after approximately 4 months of a euthyroid state. After restoration of NSR, the vast majority of euthyroid patients remain in NSR without antiarrhythmics.

Pregnancy

DC cardioversion may be sometimes necessary in pregnancy, especially in patients with underlying structural heart disease (eg, mitral stenosis) who are hemodynamically unstable. Electrical cardioversion appears to be safe for the fetus as long as the paddles are kept as far as possible from the uterus.

■ Possible Complications of DC Cardioversion

Complications related to sedation, arrhythmias, and stroke are the most common concerns with DC cardioversion.

Electrical cardioversion is frequently complicated by benign arrhythmias (PVCs, premature atrial contractions [PACs], bradycardia, or short periods of sinus arrest), which often resolve spontaneously. AF may be associated with sinus node dysfunction, and DC cardioversion in these cases may lead to asystole. As such, in patients with suspected conduction-system disease (eg, very elderly presenting with AF with slow ventricular rates), DC cardioversion should be performed only after insertion of a temporary pacemaker lead.

Electrocardiographic changes commonly follow electrical cardioversion. ST-segment elevation and depression, as well as T-wave inversion, may occur. The significance of electrocardiographic changes postcardioversion is unclear since they are not associated with elevation of enzymatic markers of myocardial injury.

Myocardial necrosis may occur with multiple, high-energy shocks. However, the energy range used for DC cardioversion of AF should not lead to a significant increase in cardiac enzymes levels. As such, a substantial elevation of cardiac troponins (>2 mcg/L) noted after standard DC cardioversion is unlikely from the procedure itself.

Atrial systolic function may be impaired (atrial stunning) for up to several weeks postcardioversion despite restoration and maintenance of NSR. This phenomenon has clinical consequences leading to a higher risk of stroke in the postcardioversion period.

Patients with AF who do not receive proper anticoagulation prior to cardioversion have up to a 7% risk for thromboembolic complications. However, the risk is minimal (<1%) in a fully anticoagulated patient. A discussion of anticoagulation therapy in AF will be presented in *Chapter 14*.

Minor complications of cardioversion, such as chest muscle or skeletal pain and first-degree burns, frequently occur with high-energy shocks.

Finally, complications related to procedural sedation depend on comorbidities and the sedative agent used. Aspiration of stomach contents into the lung is always a concern with sedation. The injury risk is lessened if the patient is kept fasting for 8 hours prior to the elective cardioversion.

■ Outcomes of Electrical Cardioversion and Further Management

DC cardioversion may lead to successful restoration of NSR, restoration of sinus rhythm followed by immediate reinitiation of AF, or cardioversion failure (when shock does not interrupt arrhythmia even for a single sinus beat).

Restoration of NSR

The success rate of electrical cardioversion of AF with monophasic shocks is reported to be 75% to 93% and is higher with biphasic shocks (>90%). The duration of AF is the most important prognostic factor of cardioversion success. AF duration of >1 year is associated with a lower probability of cardioversion success. New-onset AF, normal left atrial size, younger patient, and low transthoracic impedance are prognostic of successful cardioversion.

Recurrence of AF is high after successful cardioversion if therapy with AADs is not initiated postprocedure. More than 50% of patients will have recurrent AF in the month postcardioversion, and the majority of these within the first 5 days. This early reinduction of AF postcardioversion is related to an increased vulnerability of the atrial tissue due to a delay in resolution of atrial remodeling for up to 1 week after restoration of NSR. After two successful cardioversions, followed by recurrent AF in a short period of time, repeat cardioversion is not generally recommended.

AF recurrence postcardioversion has been classified depending on the time of recurrence (**Figure 10.3**). Immediate recurrence of AF (IRAF) occurs in the first few minutes postcardioversion. Early or subacute recurrence of AF (ERAF), in <2 weeks, and late recurrence, from 2 weeks to 1 year postcardioversion.

FIGURE 10.3 — Hypothetical Illustration of Cardioversion Failure

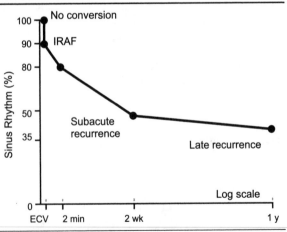

Three types of recurrences after electrical cardioversion of persistent AF are shown.

Van Gelder IC, et al. *Am J Cardiol.* 1999;84:147R-151R.

Immediate Recurrence of AF

The incidence of IRAF postcardioversion is reported as 5% to 25%.

The diagnosis of IRAF has important prognostic value since patients with IRAF (eventually cardioverted to sinus rhythm) may have similar long-term freedom from AF as those with immediate cardioversion to NSR. As such, careful ECG monitoring during cardioversion is crucial. Patients with even one sinus beat postcardioversion (IRAF) may eventually achieve significantly better rhythm control than patients who fail cardioversion completely.

Given the high probability of freedom from AF after successful cardioversion, aggressive strategies using pretreatment with AADs were developed to increase the chance of maintenance of NSR in patients with a history of IRAF.

Current ACC/AHA/ESC Guidelines recommend pretreatment with AADs prior to a second cardioversion attempt in patients with IRAF or ERAF. Choice of AADs recommended to enhance success of cardioversion and prevent recurrence of AF include amiodarone, flecainide, ibutilide, propafenone, or sotalol (Class IIa, level of evidence B).

Lists of AADs known to be effective in facilitation of electrical cardioversion in patients with IRAF are presented in **Table 10.2** and **Table 10.3**.

TABLE 10.2 — AADs Studied for Acute Loading in Patients With IRAF Prior to Repeat Cardioversion

AAD	Route	Dosing[a]
Ibutilide	IV	1 mg over 10 min
Amiodarone	IV	300 mg over 10 min
Sotalol[b]	IV	1.5 mg/kg over 30 min
Propafenone[b]	IV	1.5 mg/kg over 10 min
Verapamil[c]	IV	10 mg over 10 min

[a] Dosing as in original studies.
[b] IV formulation not available in the United States.
[c] Efficacy not well established.

TABLE 10.3 — AADs Studied for Outpatient Loading in Patients With IRAF Prior to Repeat Cardioversion

AAD	Route	Dosing[a]
Amiodarone	PO	600 mg/d for 4 wk prior to and 200 mg/d for 4 wk postcardioversion; or 400 mg/d for 1 mo prior to and 200 mg/d for 2 mo postcardioversion
Propafenone	PO	750 mg/d for 2 days prior to cardioversion
Propafenone + verapamil[b]	PO	900 mg propafenone and 240 mg verapamil for 3 days prior to and 3 mo postcardioversion
Quinidine	PO	1.2 g 1 day prior to cardioversion

[a] Dosing as in original studies.

[b] In this study, combination of propafenone and verapamil until 3 months postcardioversion was found to be more effective than either propafenone alone or adding verapamil for 3 days postcardioversion.

The diagnosis of IRAF made immediately after electrical cardioversion may prompt IV loading of ibutilide or amiodarone prior to repeat shocks (efficacy of IV verapamil is controversial). An alternative approach includes outpatient loading with AADs (eg, amiodarone, propafenone ± CCB) prior to repeat DC cardioversion.

Commonly, patients with IRAF are pretreated with an AAD, which is chosen for chronic rhythm control postcardioversion (with the exception of ibutilide).

A more detailed discussion of AADs for cardioversion will be presented later in this chapter (see *Pharmacologic Cardioversion*).

Failed DC Cardioversion

Shock failure is defined as failure to interrupt AF even for one beat.

It is estimated that electrical cardioversion fails to restore sinus activity in approximately 10% of patients with AF. Long-standing AF (>1 year), left atrial enlargement (>4.5 cm—diameter measurement in long-axis parasternal echocardiographic view), advanced patient age, and increased transthoracic impedance are associated with cardioversion failure. A retrospective analysis of patients in whom cardioversion failed suggested that a history of hypertension and obesity is associated with an increased risk of cardioversion failure.

If further attempts to restore NSR are planned, therapeutic options include optimization of electrical cardioversion or facilitation of cardioversion with AADs.

Repeat DC Cardioversion

Effective flow of electrical current through atrial myocardium is necessary for successful electrical cardioversion of AF.

Electrical current flow is directly proportional to shock energy and inversely related to transthoracic impedance. As such, approaches to improve efficacy of electrical cardioversion originate from procedural and technical aspects related to these factors (**Table 10.4**).

10

TABLE 10.4 — Approaches to Increase Likelihood of Successful Electrical Cardioversion

- High-energy shock:
  - 720 J monophasic shock[a]
  - 360 J biphasic shock[a]
- Changing monophasic defibrillator to biphasic
- Changing paddles position and energy vector
- Lowering transthoracic impedance:
  - Optimal pad size
  - Contact medium
  - Firm electrode pressure
  - Chest shaving
  - Shock during expiratory phase
- Pretreatment with AADs prior to electrical cardioversion
- Internal cardioversion

[a] Recommended only in patients with large body habitus or high impedance due to severe lung disease.

Pharmacologic Facilitation of Failed DC Cardioversion

Pretreatment with AADs is recommended after true failure of electrical cardioversion (no single sinus beat postcardioversion). It becomes a true emergency in hemodynamically unstable patients with AF in whom electrical cardioversion failed. IV amiodarone, procainamide, or ibutilide is frequently used (**Table 10.5**).

TABLE 10.5 — Pharmacologic Facilitation of Failed DC Cardioversion in Hemodynamically Unstable Patients

AAD	Route	Dosing
Amiodarone	IV	150 mg bolus over 10 min (may repeat once), followed by 1 mg/min for 6 h and then 0.5 mg/min
Procainamide	IV	Load: 20 mg/min over 30 min or 100-mg boluses every 10 min up to a total of 1.2 g; maintenance 1-4 mg/min
Ibutilide	IV	1 mg over 10 min

Although all of these agents may cause hypotension, amiodarone appears to be the safest in hemodynamically unstable patients. Procainamide decreases contractility, has a vasodilatory effect, and prolongs QTc. Ibutilide cannot be used in patients with low EF and is associated with increased risk of torsade de pointes (TdP). As such, use of ibutilide should be carefully considered in acutely ill patients.

Current ACC/AHA/ESC Guidelines recommend pretreatment with amiodarone, flecainide, ibutilide, propafenone, or sotalol to enhance success of cardioversion and prevent recurrence of AF in hemodynamically stable patients (**Table 10.6**). However, strong evidence for effective facilitation of restoration of NSR after failed cardioversion exists only for use of amiodarone and ibutilide.

Ibutilide may be preferred in patients with normal systolic function who are not candidates for chronic

TABLE 10.6 — AADs Studied for Pharmacologic Facilitation After Failed DC Cardioversion in Hemodynamically Stable Patients

AAD	Route	Dosing[a]
Amiodarone	PO	600 mg/d for 4 wk prior to and 200 mg/d for 4 wk postconversion; *or* 10-15 mg/kg/d for up to total of 6-g load prior to cardioversion, followed by 200 mg/d for 12 mo
Ibutilide	IV	1 mg over 10 min

[a] Dosing as in original studies.

therapy with amiodarone. Due to increased risk of TdP associated with ibutilide, the patient should be monitored for at least 6 hours after drug infusion. This may be an issue for the patient in the emergency department who desires cardioversion and prompt discharge.

Outpatient pretreatment with amiodarone is preferred in patients with a history of LV dysfunction or in those patients who are to be maintained on long-term amiodarone (**Table 10.6**).

■ **Internal Cardioversion**

Internal cardioversion uses a transvenous electrode system to deliver shocks in proximity of the atrial myocardium. This technique involves placement of intracardiac catheters under fluoroscopic guidance. Internal cardioversion is more effective than traditional monophasic shocks, requires less energy than external cardioversion, and may be performed only under anesthesia.

■ **Atrial Defibrillators**

The high efficacy of internal cardioversion for AF and technical advances related to development of implantable ventricular defibrillators led to development of the atrial defibrillator. Cardioversion with an atrial defibrillator seemed to be an attractive therapeutic strategy not only for treating highly symptomatic patients with frequent episodes of AF, but also for possible prevention of AF. Recurrent episodes of AF led to the development of electrical remodeling and perpetuation of the arrhythmia. However, frequent AF recurrences led to multiple shocks and poor tolerability of the therapy. Additionally, the theoretical concern of shock-induced ventricular arrhythmias was an issue. Furthermore, in contrast to the ICD, which has a significant impact on CV mortality, implantable atrial defibrillators (IADs) have not shown this benefit. Manufacturing of stand-alone atrial defibrillators has been discontinued.

Another therapeutic option utilizing atrial defibrillators is a combined dual-chamber atrial and ventricular defibrillator. These devices allow "tiered therapy" for AF. This begins with reducing the risk of AF recurrence due to the presence of backup-pacing capabilities, which allows the use of AADs without the risk of bradyarrhythmia (especially in the elderly). Therapy for atrial tachyarrhythmia recurrence starts with painless antitachycardia pacing followed by extremely rapid 50 Hz burst pacing. If these therapies are unsuccessful, shock therapy is delivered. In the future, hybrid approaches (combination of electrical atrial defibrillation and new antiarrhythmic therapies) and further advancements in multichamber-device technology may expand the role of this modality in AF therapy.

Pharmacologic Cardioversion

■ Introduction

Although the success rates of pharmacologic vs electrical cardioversion have not been compared directly in prospective randomized studies, the pharmacologic approach is regarded as simpler but less efficacious and associated with a risk of AAD toxicity.

Pharmacologic cardioversion appears to be effective in 35% to 75% of patients, depending on the drug used, the duration of AF, and the population studied. However, spontaneous cardioversion occurs in up to 50% of patients within 24 to 48 hours of an AF episode. The rate of spontaneous cardioversion may be even higher if a rapid heart rate is controlled with rate-control agents.

Therefore, in patients without structural heart disease and with short-duration AF, the use of AADs for cardioversion is not associated with significantly increased success rates when compared with placebo. It is rather accepted that pharmacologic cardioversion accelerates conversion to sinus rhythm in recent-onset AF, but the benefit over placebo is small after 24 to 48 hours. The pathophysiologic reason for this observation is related to electrical remodeling in the atria (AF-induced changes in electrical current and/or channel expression that perpetuate AF). Once remodeling takes place, changes in ionic currents and channels reduce the effectiveness of some AADs. As such, pharmacologic cardioversion is less effective after 7 days of AF.

■ Indications

Electrical cardioversion is the modality of choice for cardioversion in acute settings and as an elective procedure since it is relatively safe and highly effective. Restoration of NSR with catheter ablation and surgical techniques offer the potential of a decreased burden of arrhythmia. As such, indications for pharmacologic cardioversion are limited and include:

- Highly symptomatic patients who have little or no structural heart disease and present with short-duration AF (first episode or recurrent). Pharmacologic cardioversion may be conveniently performed in an outpatient setting using the pill-in-the-pocket approach.
- Patients who fail electrical cardioversion or have IRAF
- Patients who are poor candidates for anesthesia yet require cardioversion for AF
- Patients with a strong preference to undergo pharmacologic and not electrical cardioversion.

■ Safety of Pharmacologic Cardioversion
Anticoagulation

The principles of comprehensive stroke prevention with anticoagulation therapy apply to all strategies of cardioversion whether performed electrically, pharmacologically, or with ablative techniques. General rules were previously outlined (see *Electrical Cardioversion,* this chapter), and a detailed discussion is presented in *Chapter 13.* Some AADs with the ability to restore NSR (eg, amiodarone) may be used in patients with AF for other reasons than cardioversion (eg, for rate control in patients with HF). However, as conversion to sinus rhythm may occur, anticoagulation principles should be applied.

Outpatient use of oral Class IC AADs (eg, propafenone, flecainide) with the pill-in-the-pocket approach also requires an assessment of stroke risk and anticoagulation strategy.

Toxicity of AADs

All AADs used for pharmacologic cardioversion may have proarrhythmic effects (induce new or worsen preexisting arrhythmias). Previous MI and advanced patient age have been associated with increased risk. Class IC drugs may convert AF to atrial flutter in up to 5% of patients. Decreased atrial rates in atrial flutter may result in more rapid AV nodal conduction to the ventricles, sometimes in a 1:1 ratio, and lead to life-threatening ventricular rhythms. As such, β-blockers or CCBs are sometimes given to slow ventricular conduction prior to attempted cardioversion with these agents. Class IC drugs may cause broad, complex, incessant ventricular arrhythmias that may be hard to distinguish from AF with aberration caused by slow conduction.

Class III agents used for cardioversion (eg, ibutilide or dofetilide) can cause polymorphic VT (TdP). Almost all AADs used for cardioversion can cause bradycardia, especially in elderly patients with underlying conduction-system disease. Class I agents have negative inotropic effects and should not be used for cardioversion in patients with significant LV dysfunction.

Inpatient vs Outpatient Settings

The risk of adverse cardiac side effects, such as proarrhythmia and bradyarrhythmias *(see above)*, often favor the inpatient setting for the initiation of AAD therapy. Although some of the AADs may be initiated safely in outpatient settings (eg, low-dose amiodarone), the 2006 ACC/AHA/ESC Guidelines support only the use of propafenone and flecainide for pharmacologic cardioversion in outpatient settings (this list may expand with the approval of newer agents).

The rationale for this strategy came from a study of 268 patients without significant structural heart disease who underwent cardioversion for recent-onset AF with a single dose of either flecainide or propafenone. Patients in whom a pharmacologic cardioversion failed or who had significant side effects were excluded from the study. Two hundred ten patients who were successfully cardioverted under observation without major side effects, then received a prescription for the effective AAD at the time of discharge and were asked to take the drug 5 minutes after the onset of palpitations. Patients weighing >70 kg were prescribed 300 mg flecainide or 600 mg propafenone, while those weighing <70 kg were prescribed 200 mg flecainide or 450 mg propafenone.

At a mean follow-up of 15 months, self-administered oral therapy of either propafenone or flecainide was successful in 94% of outpatient episodes. The mean time to resolution of symptoms was approximately 2 hours. The number of emergency room visits and hospital admissions decreased significantly after the initiation of this management strategy. Only 7% of patients developed some noncardiac side effects of therapy (eg, nausea, vertigo), and there was only one report of a serious cardiac adverse effect (atrial flutter with 1:1).

This study showed the efficacy and safety of the pill-in-the-pocket strategy to treat symptomatic, recent-onset AF in patients without significant structural heart disease. Class IC agents have rapid onset of action and are safe and effective in a select population of patients with AF. Therefore, the pill-in-the-pocket approach may be useful in terminating short episodes of AF in patients who are highly symptomatic. This strategy may be considered only in patients who have previous history of Class IC drug use without complications, no underlying structural heart disease, and a normal baseline ECG.

■ Choice of AADs for Pharmacologic Cardioversion

The evidence of the effectiveness of AADs for cardioversion of AF is limited by small trial size, inconsistency in inclusion criteria, varying durations for outcome assessments, and different delivery and route doses. Furthermore, outcomes from large, randomized trials may be difficult to generalize due to each trial's specific entry criteria.

Based on the evidence from available trials as well as progress in understanding electrical remodeling, the 2006 ACC/AHA/ESC Guidelines made important changes in recommendations for pharmacologic cardioversion of AF. Dofetilide, flecainide, ibutilide, propafenone, and amiodarone are the recommended agents based on the duration of AF (**Table 10.7**).

TABLE 10.7 — Recommended AADs for Pharmacologic Cardioversion Based on Duration of AF

	<7 Days	>7 Days
Class I	Dofetilide	Dofetilide
	Flecainide	
	Ibutilide	
	Propafenone	
Class IIA	Amiodarone	Amiodarone
		Ibutilide

Administration of the Class IA AADs (eg, disopyramide, procainamide, and quinidine) for AF cardioversion is not generally recommended (Class IIb) due to unproven success rate and toxicity risk. Use of digoxin and sotalol for AF cardioversion is discouraged (Class III).

There are some exceptions to the above classification. Procainamide, which is not regarded as a preferred agent by the guidelines (Class IIb), may be useful for cardioversion of hemodynamically unstable patients with AF. It is frequently given in 100-mg boluses (up to a total dose of 1.2 g over 60 minutes) or 10-mg/kg bolus followed by IV infusion at 1 to 4 mg/minute. Hypotension and prolongation of the QTc are the major side effects.

Several general factors should be considered in a stepwise fashion before choosing among the recommended AADs (**Table 10.8**). Frequently, the same AAD is chosen for cardioversion and for maintenance of NSR postcardioversion. Due to the potentially toxic effect of AADs, the side effect profile and patient safety must always be considered. Specific characteristics of recommended AADs are presented in **Tables 10.8** through **10.12**.

TABLE 10.8 — Factors to Consider in the Choice of AAD for Pharmacologic Cardioversion

- Duration of AF
- AAD route of administration
- AAD conversion time and rate
- Presence of underlying heart disease
- Outcome of previous pharmacologic cardioversions
- Other medications (especially AAD) used by the patient
- Plan of AAD therapy postcardioversion

10

■ New AADs for Pharmacologic Cardioversion
Atrial Selective Agents for AF

Many new AADs are currently under development (eg, amiodarone congeners, β-blockers with Class I and III properties) and may play a role in the future in restoration and maintenance of NSR in patients with AF. AADs with highly specific affinity to ion channels involved in repolarization in the atria but not the ventricles ("atrial selective" agents) are recognized as possibly ideal agents for pharmacologic cardioversion of AF.

The electrophysiologic properties, ionic channels, and membrane proteins of atria differ from those of the ventricles (**Figure 10.4**). Electrical currents, such as ultrarapid delayed-rectifier (IKur) and acetylcholine-regulated current (IKACh), are important components of atrial, but not ventricular, electrophysiology. Also, some of the channel proteins (eg, Kv1.5) are expressed only in the atria.

Progress in understanding differences in atrial and ventricle electrophysiology led to critical review of the use of available AADs in AF.

TABLE 10.9 — Ibutilide for Pharmacologic Cardioversion of AF

- Class III AAD—prolongs QT interval and mildly slows sinus rate
- Prolongs repolarization and increases atrial and ventricular refractoriness and refractoriness of:
  - AV node
  - His-Purkinje system
  - Accessory pathways
- Available only in IV form with an elimination half-life of 2 to 12 hours (mean 6 hours)
- Exhibits reverse-use dependence (less effective with high rates)
- More effective for cardioversion of atrial flutter (80%) than of short-duration AF (up to 50%)
- Limited efficacy for AF >3 weeks' duration
- Effective in termination of immediate recurrence of AF post-electrical cardioversion and AF postcardiac surgery
- Recommended dose:
  - For patients <60 kg: 0.01 mg/kg over 10 minutes
  - For patients >60 kg: 1 mg IV over 10 minutes (dose may be repeated after 10 minutes if the arrhythmia persists)
- May cause transient hypotension and bradycardia postinfusion
- Mean AF termination time approximately 30 minutes (useful when rapid cardioversion required)
- Requires monitoring for at least 4 h; prolongation of QT after infusion—comes back to baseline usually in 2 to 4 hours
- Up to 8% risk of TdP limits its use (2% requires electrical termination); highest risk of TdP within 1 hour postinfusion
- Risk of TdP with ibutilide is increased in women, HF patients, higher dose of drug, slow ventricular rate, and low levels of K and Mg
- Magnesium sulfate (4 g IV) can increase the chance of cardioversion and lower the risk of TdP
- Contraindicated in patients with:
  - Prolonged QT
  - Severe structural heart disease
  - HF
  - Sinus node dysfunction
- Should not be administered to patients already taking drugs that prolong the QT interval because of increased risk of TdP

TABLE 10.10 — Dofetilide for Pharmacologic Cardioversion

- Class III drug—prolongs QT without changing PR or QRS interval
- Available only in oral form in the United States[a]
- Bioavailability exceeds 90% with an elimination half-life of 8 to 9 hours
- Long onset of action; requires 24 to 36 hours to produce cardioversion
- AAD of choice for pharmacologic cardioversion of AF duration >1 week
- Cardioversion rate of 30% for patients with AF duration >2 weeks reported in pivotal study (SAFIRE-D)
- In the absence of significant heart disease, cardioversion rate may be much higher (recently reported as 85% with 500 mcg bid and 44% with 250 mcg bid)
- Can be safely used in post-MI and HF patients
- Exhibits reverse-use dependence (less effective with high rates)
- Contraindicated in patients with:
  - Renal failure (CrCl <20 cc/min)
  - Prolonged QTc
  - Profound bradycardia
- Up to 4% risk of TdP (highest in first 3 days of therapy)
- Requires monitoring in the hospital for first 3 days of therapy and predose adjustment based on renal function and postdose QTc
- Replacement for hypokalemia and hypomagnesemia required prior to use
- Metabolized by CYP 3A4 and has numerous drug interactions (inhibitors of CYP 3A4, such as verapamil, will increase dofetilide level)

[a] IV dofetilide has been shown to be more effective than IV amiodarone for cardioversion of AF and can effectively terminate AF in patients with WPW syndrome.

TABLE 10.11 — Propafenone and Flecainide for Cardioversion of AF

- Class IC agents—prolong PR and QRS interval
- Slow conduction in atrial, AV node, His-Purkinje system, ventricle and accessory pathways; propafenone also has β-blocker activity
- Available only in oral form in the United States
- Half-life: 20 hours for flecainide and 6 hours for propafenone (up to 12 hours in 10%—"slow metabolizers")
- Success rate in termination of recent-onset AF is 70% to 80% within 8 hours (cardioversion usually within 3 to 4 hours with oral drug)
- Favored for pill-in-the-pocket strategy (rapid action, no organ toxicity, and limited risk of proarrhythmia)
- Recommended single oral dose for cardioversion of AF:
  - Immediate-release propafenone (450 mg in patients weighing <70 kg, 600 mg if ≥70 kg)
  - Flecainide (200 mg in patients weighing <70 kg, 300 mg if ≥70 kg)
- For breakthrough AF on maintenance therapy with propafenone or flecainide: extra dose 6 hours after the last scheduled dose (not to exceed 900-mg/day immediate-release propafenone or 400 mg/day flecainide)
- Class IC agents are contraindicated in patients with:
  - Structural heart disease (particularly post-MI)
  - Sinus node dysfunction
  - Conduction disease
- Class IC agents are not effective in immediate recurrence of AF after electrical cardioversion
- Use a rate-control agent concomitantly with Class IC drugs, as used alone these drugs may cause:
  - Hypotension (rare)
  - Bradycardia
  - induction of atrial flutter with a rapid ventricular rate
- Propafenone may increase level of:
  - Metoprolol
  - Digoxin
  - Warfarin
- Propafenone and carvedilol have the same hepatic metabolism involving the CYP2D6 pathway; oral loading with propafenone (pill-in-the-pocket strategy) in a patient on carvedilol may cause high plasma levels of propafenone and potential adverse effects

TABLE 10.12 — Amiodarone for Cardioversion of AF

- Class III agent, but also has class I, II and IV activity—causes sinus bradycardia, increased PR and QRS duration, and QT prolongation (but very rarely TdP)
- Success rate for AF cardioversion depends on total dose, route of administration, and whether single bolus was followed by further therapy
- IV formulation is useful in hemodynamically unstable patients for simultaneous rate control and possible cardioversion (300-mg bolus IV usually slows the rate, 1-2 g/24 hours required for cardioversion)
- Oral amiodarone has a relatively long time to onset of action (>24 to 48 hours)
- Cardioversion rate with recent-onset AF <48 hours is approximately 60%
- Higher conversion rates reported with very high doses of the drug: 30 mg/kg PO (cardioverted 50% of patients at 8 hours and >85% at 24 hours) or IV infusion of 125 mg/hour until conversion or a maximum of 3 g (success rate >90%); intolerance rate is high with these doses
- In patients with recent-onset AF, the use of amiodarone is associated with delayed cardioversion (it is inferior to Class IC drugs at 8 hours, but has similar efficacy at 24 hours)
- Amiodarone is not superior to other AADs for cardioversion of recent-onset AF but is relatively safe in patients with structural heart disease and HF
- Cardioversion rate in persistent AF is reported between 25% and 50% at 4 weeks and appears to be higher if single bolus is continued by further oral therapy for 4 weeks
- Oral amiodarone and sotalol appear equally effective in converting persistent AF to sinus rhythm (SAFE-T study)
- In patients with persistent AF (duration >3 weeks), success rate with amiodarone and propafenone were similar (reported as 40% at 4 weeks); cardioversion with propafenone occurred between 1 and 14 days vs 7 and 28 days with amiodarone
- Adverse effects of amiodarone associated with cardioversion include bradycardia, hypotension, and nausea/constipation, or phlebitis
- Amiodarone increases warfarin level (bleeding), digoxin level (digoxin toxicity), and simvastatin level (myopathy and rhabdomyolysis); it has additive proarrhythmic effects when used with drugs that prolong the QT interval

10

FIGURE 10.4 — Regional Difference in Ionic Current Contribution to Action Potential (AP): Differences in Key Ion Currents Between Atrial and Ventricular APs

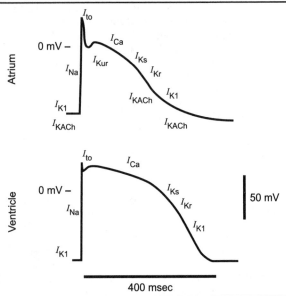

Atrial APs have smaller AP amplitude and less negative resting membrane potential. Currents identified above the line illustrating the APs are present in both regions; atrially expressed ionic currents are illustrated below the AP schematic.

Ehrlich JR, et al. *J Am Coll Cardiol.* 2008;51:787-792.

The use of traditional AADs for cardioversion of AF has several limitations. Most of the AADs prolong repolarization in both atria and ventricles, and were in fact initially developed for treatment of ventricular arrhythmias. Therefore, ventricular proarrhythmia is common, eg, occurrence of TdP in patients with QT prolongation. AF induces electrical remodeling (electrophysiologic changes in current/channel expression in the atria, which lead to maintenance of AF). These changes include decreased contribution of IKr current to atrial repolarization, which reduces the efficacy of Class III drugs. IKr is a target of most Class III drugs, such as ibutilide, dofetilide, and sotalol.

Therefore, the development of AADs that can exert their action only in the atrium and preserve (or increase) their efficacy during AF-induced electrophysiologic remodeling is an attractive target of AF therapy. Because of negligible effect on ventricular repolarization, these agents should be relatively free of ventricular proarrhythmic effects.

Although known as atria "selective," all of these agents target more than one type of ion channel, and at high doses, will most likely have electrophysiologic effects on ventricular tissue.

Vernakalant

The best studied atrial selective agent is vernakalant, which acts on IKur (delayed-rectifier potassium current), Ito (transient outward potassium current), INa (inward sodium current), and IKACh (acetylcholine-regulated potassium current) ion channels. It slows conduction velocity within the atrium and prolongs atrial recovery. Vernakalant is a rate- and voltage-dependent agent, with increased blocking activity in depolarized tissue and at higher heart rates.

Relative atrial selectivity (with low risk of proarrhythmia and conduction disturbances), short half-life (2 to 3 hours), and lack of significant hemodynamic effects, make this drug desirable for safe and effective pharmacologic cardioversion.

Furthermore, although vernakalant is metabolized by the CYP2D6 system, differential expression of CYP2D6 was not reported to significantly change the pharmacokinetics of this agent. Renal or hepatic impairment, concomitant β-blocker use, history of HF, and patient's age also do not change the pharmacokinetics of this agent. The risk of serious CV adverse effects is low (hypotension, 1.2%; significant bradyarrhythmias, <1%; VF, 0.3%). TdP is extremely rare (only one reported case). Mild side effects, such as dysgeusia, paresthesia, sneezing, nausea and cough, are common. The drug interaction profile of vernakalant is not well established.

The safety and efficacy of IV vernakalant has been studied in several studies. In a phase 2 trial, Controlled Randomized Atrial Fibrillation Trial (CRAFT) enrolled 56 patients with recent-onset AF (duration, 3 to 72 hours). Vernakalant (2 mg/day, followed by 3 mg/day) was significantly better than placebo in the termination of AF (61% vs 5%, respectively; P <0.0005) with a shorter median time to conversion (14 minutes vs 162 minutes, P=0.016).

The safety and efficacy of vernakalant have been investigated in four phase 3 studies. In the randomized, double-blind, placebo-controlled Atrial Arrhythmia Conversion Trial (ACT) I study of 416 patients with AF, successful conversion of recent-onset AF (duration, 3 hours to 7 days) was achieved in 52% of patients receiving vernakalant compared with 4% of patients receiving placebo (P <0.001). The overall success rate of converting AF of any duration (3 hours to 45 days) was 38% in the vernakalant group vs 3% of patients receiving placebo (P<0.001). Vernakalant had a rapid onset of action with a median time to conversion of 11 minutes.

Results of the randomized, double-blind, placebo-controlled ACT III study of 276 patients with AF were similar to those of ACT I (**Figure 10.5**). Conversion of recent-onset AF (duration of 3 hours to 7 days) was achieved in nearly 52% of patients receiving vernakalant vs 4% of patients receiving placebo (P<0.0001); overall conversion rate AF of any duration (3 hours to 45 days) was achieved in 38% vs 3% of patients (P<0.0001). Much lower conversion rates occurred in patients with AF duration of >7 days (8%), and those with flutter (9%).

No TdP was reported. Mild side effects with vernakalant included transient taste disturbances (30%), sneezing (16%), paresthesias (11%), nausea (9%), and hypotension (6.3%—transient and resolved without pharmacologic intervention).

The results of the ACT I and III studies prove the safety and efficacy of vernakalant for the conversion of recent-onset AF. ACT III demonstrates its ineffectiveness for conversion of long-standing AF or atrial flutter.

ACT II evaluated the efficacy of IV vernakalant for cardioversion in 150 patients who had AF within 7 days

FIGURE 10.5 — Success Rates of Vernakalant in the Short-Duration, Long-Duration, and Overall AF Populations

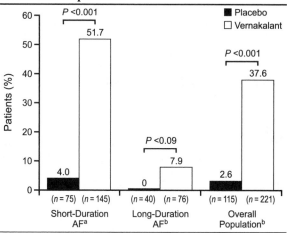

[a] Success rate defined as the percentage of patients who demonstrated conversion to SR within 90 minutes of the first infusion.

[b] Success rate defined as the percentage of patients who demonstrated termination of AF within 90 minutes of the first infusion.

Roy D, et al. *Circulation*. 2008;117:1518-1525.

after CABG or valve replacement surgery. Conversion to SR was observed in approximately 45% of patients receiving active therapy with vernakalant vs 15% of patients receiving placebo ($P=0.0002$). The median time to conversion with vernakalant was 12 minutes.

ACT IV was an open-label study conducted to provide additional safety information regarding vernakalant in patients with recent-onset AF. The 236 patients enrolled had AF for 3 hours to 45 days. Among patients with AF for 3 hours to 7 days, 50.9% converted to NSR after vernakalant infusion. Median time to cardioversion was 14 minutes. The side-effect profile of vernakalant was similar to those presented above.

IV vernakalant has been approved in the European Union and has been submitted to the FDA for approval in the United States. Two additional studies that confirmed previously reported efficacy and safety of vernakalant for cardioversion of short-duration AF and AF after cardiac surgery were recently reported.

Studies of the oral formulation are ongoing. Advantages of vernakalant for long-term rhythm control include its excellent safety profile compared with other AADs, an IV form for rapid cardioversion, and an oral formulation for maintenance of NSR.

The interim results of a phase IIb randomized, double-blind study of 446 patients treated with three doses of oral vernakalant (150, 300, and 500 mg twice daily) were encouraging. No statistical difference was found in maintenance of NSR between two lower doses of vernakalant and placebo. However, patients receiving 500-mg vernakalant po twice a day were more likely to maintain NSR at 3 months than placebo group (52% vs 39%, $P < 0.05$). Maintenance antiarrhythmic therapy with 500-mg vernakalant bid was associated with a time to recurrence of AF >90 days compared with 39 days in the placebo group.

Vernakalant has the potential to become the agent of choice for pharmacologic cardioversion of recent-onset AF, however, ibutilide remains an attractive agent for cardioversion of atrial flutter. Specific characteristics of vernakalant related to cardioversion for AF are presented in **Table 10.13**.

Catheter Ablation

■ Background

Results of large clinical trials suggest that restoration and maintenance of NSR is beneficial. However, it is difficult to achieve this goal with the available AADs. As such, nonpharmacologic approaches to rhythm-control therapy in AF have been sought.

Catheter ablation eliminates or isolates arrhythmogenic tissue in atrial myocardium in order to eliminate the tachyarrhythmia. It uses various energy sources, most often thermal energy (radiofrequency or cryotherapy), as well as laser or ultrasound.

TABLE 10.13 — Vernakalant for Cardioversion of AF

- Relatively atrial-selective agent
- Sodium channel (INa) and potassium channels (IKur, Ito, and IK-Ach) blocker
- IV formulation pending FDA approval; studies on oral form ongoing
- Half-life of 2 hours
- Effective at higher heart rates
- Dosing for cardioversion of AF: 3 mg/kg IV over 10 minutes; if cardioversion fails in 15 minutes, IV bolus may be repeated at 2 mg/kg over 10 minutes
- IV vernakalant effective for recent-onset AF lasting ≥7 days (best efficacy in first 24 hours)
- Success rate of 52% in cardioversion of recent-onset AF (most often within 10 to 15 minutes)
- Success rate of 45% for cardioversion within 90 minutes in postcardiac surgery AF
- Less effective for cardioversion of atrial flutter
- Risk of serious cardiovascular adverse effects is low (severe hypotension, 1.2%; significant bradyarrhythmias, <1%; VF, 0.3%); TdP is extremely rare (0.1%)
- Mild side effects, such as dysgeusia, paresthesia, sneezing, nausea, and cough, are common
- Safety and efficacy of vernakalant not studied in patients with Class IV HF or acute MI

Lessons learned from surgical procedures and advances in invasive cardiology techniques greatly contributed to catheter ablation for AF. Progress in the understanding of AF pathophysiology has been a main reason for rapid development of this technique.

The presence of both trigger and arrhythmia substrate were recognized as necessary for the development of AF, which was discovered to be a syndrome with distinct underlying mechanisms rather than a single entity.

In its paroxysmal form, AF is usually triggered by a rapidly firing focus, most commonly localized in the thoracic veins and posterior wall of the atrium. The autonomic nervous system may play an important role in the initiation of these triggered firings (premature atrial beats). Foci near the PVs are the most common sites initiating premature beats leading to AF. Its electrical activity can then be conducted through sleeves of cardiac myocardium that extend from LA to the PV. Based on these observations, it was postulated that focal triggers can create high frequency reentrant circles (rotors), which then degenerate into fibrillatory conduction. **Figure 10.6** presents the role of focal triggers in the initiation of reentry.

The persistence of fibrillatory waves changes the properties of an ion channel (electrical remodeling) and creates a milieu favoring maintenance of AF. This also leads to structural changes in the atria, such as fibrosis (structural remodeling), thus establishing a substrate.

FIGURE 10.6 — Focal Triggers Leading to Initiation of Reentry

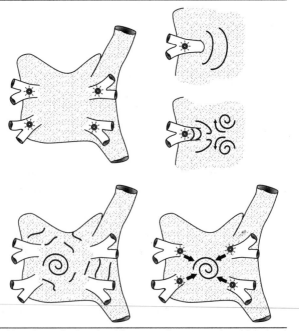

This schematic drawing illustrates the manner in which focal triggers lead to initiation of reentry (rotors). Eventually, atrial remodeling leads to additional focal triggers and perpetuation of reentry.

Calkins H, et al. *Europace*. 2007;9:335-379.

As such, persistent AF may be caused by long-standing, abnormal electrical activity leading to structural atrial remodeling. This structural remodeling of atrial myocardium may also result from underlying heart disease. Regardless of the cause, abnormal atrial substrate is the hallmark of persistent AF. Differences between the underlying pathophysiology of paroxysmal and persistent AF are presented in **Figure 10**.7.

■ Techniques of AF Ablation

These basic advances in the understanding of the pathogenesis of paroxysmal and persistent AF have led to various therapeutic techniques to cure this arrhythmia.

The general goal of ablative therapy in AF is to restore and maintain NSR by removing or isolating triggers that induce AF and thus alter arrhythmia substrate. However, the main focus is different in paroxysmal AF (trigger) vs persistent AF (abnormal substrate). Modulation of autonomic innervation may also play a role in both forms of AF. Effectiveness of different ablative techniques and their combinations are currently being investigated; however, most of them focus on isolation of AF triggers in the PVs. Different ablation procedures are presented in **Figure 10**.8.

Ostial Pulmonary Vein Isolation

Segmental PV isolation is the primary ablation strategy in younger patients with paroxysmal AF without structural heart disease. The goal of this technique is prevention of AF through electrical isolation of triggers in the PVs. It requires sophisticated electroanatomic mapping and significant procedural time. During the procedure, a transvenous catheter is placed into the right atrium and then advanced to the left atrium via transseptal puncture. Catheter position is confirmed and electroanatomic mapping is performed using a circular catheter placed in the ostium of the PV *(see the following* Imaging *discussion)*. Electrical isolation (guided by electroanatomic mapping) is accomplished with ablation of sites of electrical conduction around the ostia of the PVs. Ablation is performed on the atrial site of the PV

10

FIGURE 10.7 — Important Differences Between Paroxysmal and Persistent Forms of AF

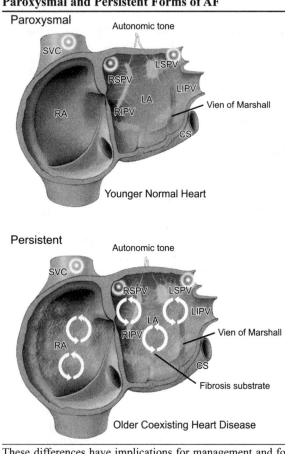

These differences have implications for management and for outcome expectations. Circular arrows represent rotors.

Crandall MA, et al. *Mayo Clin Proc*. 2009;84:643-662.

orifice until electrical disconnection of PV from the LA is evident. Complete isolation of all four pulmonary veins is the generally accepted end point of the procedure. Additional ablation lines are sometimes necessary during this procedure. PV isolation may be performed if the patient is in sinus rhythm or AF. The procedure

FIGURE 10.8 — Catheter Ablation Procedures for Treatment of AF

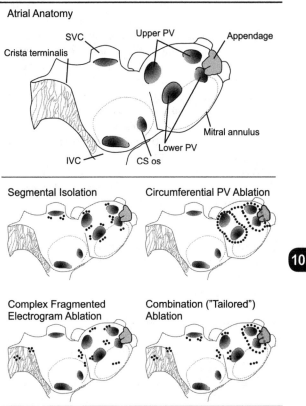

Atrial anatomy is shown at top; black dots denote sites of ablation according to the ablation strategy.

Adapted from Miller J, Zipes D. In: Libby P, et al. *Braunwald's Heart Disease: A Textbook of Cardiovascular Medicine*. 8th ed. Philadelphia, PA: WB Saunders; 2008

may be complicated by PV stenosis (although much less frequently than in the past). Since the size of ablation lesions is now much more limited, other complications are also less common.

Circumferential Left Atrial Ablation

Isolated exclusion of PV triggers initiating AF is much less effective in patients with structural heart disease and persistent AF. For these patients, ablation of the abnormal substrate is beneficial. It is well documented that atrial ostia of PVs can serve as a substrate in maintaining AF, and there is growing evidence suggesting that PVs and atrial ostia of PVs may in fact play a critical role in maintenance of AF. Circumferential PV ablation is more complex and extensive than the PV isolation technique and alternates other mechanisms of AF formation (such as abnormal substrate) besides isolation of triggers in PV. In circumferential left atrial ablation, confluent lesions are created. The ostia of all PVs (usually in two pairs) are separated from atrial tissue and thus create complete conduction block. Additional lines are frequently performed using other anatomic landmarks. This prevents formation of a macroreentry circuit, which can lead to subsequent atrial flutter post–AF ablation. Mapping is usually not necessary since the procedure is based on the anatomical approach. PV stenosis is uncommon after circumferential left atrial ablation, however, a significant extent of ablation may lead to increased rate of other complications *(see below)*.

Other ablative strategies, such as complex fractionated atrial ECG ablation and tailored approach, are also used. Several new technologies are currently under investigation. The ostial ablation with occlusive balloons technique appears to be feasible in eliminating triggers of the arrhythmia. Ablation of autonomic nerves attempts to influence autonomic stimulation in order to decrease propensity of the atria to maintain AF.

■ Periprocedural Management
Imaging

Sophisticated imaging of cardiac anatomy and electrical activity is critical for successful ablation therapy of AF.

Electroanatomic mapping (eg, CARTO, NavX) is nonfluoroscopic, catheter-based technology, which provides real-time, three-dimensional reconstruction of cardiac chamber anatomy and voltage mapping with identification of ablation sites.

CT or MRI performed prior to the procedure provides valuable data on the anatomy of the LA and PVs, which can be incorporated into a three-dimensional mapping system. CT and MRI may be also useful in the diagnosis of postprocedural complications.

Although preprocedure CT and MRI improve catheter navigation during the ablation procedure, real-time cardiac imaging techniques (eg, rotational angiography, 3D TEE, and intracardiac echocardiography with 3D imaging capabilities) are now being tested.

All patients should also have TEE prior to catheter ablation to exclude the presence of an intra-atrial thrombus. Prior to the ablation procedure, patients frequently undergo both CT and TEE. Use of cardiac MRI may detect atrial fibrosis, which is predictive of procedural failure.

Anticoagulation

The risk of thromboembolic events in patients with AF is particularly high during catheter ablation for several reasons. The use of an endovascular catheter may dislodge a preexisting clot and lead to a thromboembolic event. The ablation procedure can also damage the LA endocardium and create a prothrombotic environment. Furthermore, alterations in a chronic anticoagulation regimen and cardioversion to NSR both significantly increase the risk of a thromboembolic event.

As such, patients undergoing catheter ablation require TEE prior to the procedure to exclude the presence of an LA thrombus. Warfarin needs to be withheld prior to the procedure, during which the patient is fully anticoagulated with heparin. Therapy with heparin/LMWH and warfarin is reinitiated postprocedure until the INR level is therapeutic. Warfarin is then continued in all patients for at least 3 months postprocedure. Discontinuation of anticoagulation is not recommended in any patient with a CHADS score ≥2. However, some electrophysiologists would attempt to stop anticoagulation if the patient is free from AF during follow-up monitoring after successful catheter ablation.

■ Complications

Catheter ablation for AF is one of the more complex and sophisticated cardiac invasive procedures and is associated with a 5% risk of major complications (including a 0.05% risk of periprocedural death). Advanced age (>70 years) and female gender were found to be associated with an increased risk of complications. Serious complications are becoming less common with technical advances and progress in imaging techniques. Complications in catheter ablation may be either specific for AF ablation or common for all endovascular interventions. Some serious complications associated with catheter ablation of AF include PV stenosis, atrial-esophageal fistula, and thromboembolic events.

PV stenosis was a common complication of early catheter ablations for AF (up to 10%). Ablation within the PV can lead to injury, followed by narrowing of the vein. Shortness of breath, frequent pulmonary infections and, in severe cases, symptoms related to pulmonary hypertension may occur. The diagnosis is made with CT or MRI. Symptoms may decrease in time, but PV balloon angioplasty may be necessary in severely symptomatic patients. A benefit of stenting is unclear. This complication rate is markedly decreased today since ablation within PVs is avoided. The risk of persistent PV stenosis is reported now at approximately 1.5%. Half of such patients require interventional or surgical treatment.

Atrial-esophageal fistula is a very rare but potentially fatal complication of catheter ablation for AF. It is most often reported after RF ablation involving the LA posterior wall and is caused by direct injury to the esophagus or nerves and vessels supplying the esophagus. Atrio-esophageal fistulae typically become symptomatic 2 to 4 weeks postprocedure and may present as fever, chills, or odynophagia. GI bleeding and neurologic signs due to air emboli prevail. CT and MRI of the chest are the modalities of choice for making a diagnosis. Death can be prevented with urgent surgical intervention.

The thromboembolic event rate is approximately 0.5% to 2.0%. Stroke most commonly occurs in the first 24 hours postprocedure, but the patient has an increased risk of CVA for several weeks postablation. Risk of clinically silent CVA may be substantially higher. In the recent study on 234 consecutive patients with paroxysmal or persistent AF who underwent radiofrequency ablation, pre- and postablation MRI of the brain was performed. A periprocedural symptomatic CVA (TIA) occurred in only one patient (0.4%), however, cerebral MRI 1 day postprocedure was positive for new embolic lesions in 33 patients (14%). Cardioversion to sinus rhythm and intensity of anticoagulation during a procedure correlated with an increased incidence of cerebral embolism. Specifically, periprocedural cardioversion was associated with 2.75 times greater risk of silent cerebral embolism.

Diaphragmatic paralysis is a relatively uncommon complication (0.1% to 0.2%). Clinically, this may vary from asymptomatic to very symptomatic. A chest x-ray that shows an elevated hemidiaphragm is suggestive of this diagnosis. Most often, diaphragmatic paralysis resolves within a year.

Tamponade is rare (1% to 1.5%) but is a leading cause of death. Less-severe complications associated with access site of the catheter intervention are more common and include bleeding, hematoma, AV fistula formation, deep-vein thrombosis, and infection.

A recently published, retrospective case series of patients undergoing catheter ablation for AF from 162 centers worldwide analyzed periprocedural complications and any cause of death. Between 1995 and 2006, there were 32,569 patients who underwent 45,115 procedures. Thirty-two deaths were reported—approximately 1 of 1000 patients (death rate 0.1%). Causes of death are listed in **Table 10.14**. There was no relationship between mortality rate and type of ablation procedure.

■ Follow-Up and Recurrence of AF
Early AF Recurrence

Early recurrence of AF is common. The rate of early recurrence is similar in segmental PV isolation and circumferential ablation of LA. It is estimated that up to 45% of patients may have AF recurrence in the first 3 months postablation. However, AF recurrence is transient in up to one third of these patients. AAD therapy

TABLE 10.14 — Causes of Death in Patients Undergoing Catheter Ablation for AF

Cause of Death	Proportional Cause of Death (%)	Fatality Rate (%)
Cardiac tamponade	25	2.3
Stroke	16	5.1
Atrioesophageal fistula	16	71.4
Massive pneumonia	6	100

Data from Cappato R, et al. *J Am Coll Cardiol.* 2009;53(19):1798-1803.

is commonly used during the first few months after ablation. Outcomes are frequently censored for the first 3 months after ablation. Repeat procedures should not be performed in the first 3 months after ablation (unless symptoms cannot be controlled with pharmacologic therapy). Approximately 15% of patients will be more symptomatic than they were preablation. Early transient postablation AF may be related to an inflammatory response or pericarditis after RF ablation, a proarrhythmic effect of the ablation procedure, or transient autonomic nervous system imbalance.

Atrial flutter and atrial tachycardia account for at least 10% of early tachyarrhythmias. These arrhythmias are caused by reentrant circuit around scar created by radiofrequency ablation. These arrhythmias are commonly resistant to AAD therapy, but one third of them will spontaneously resolve within 6 months. If repeated ablation is needed, success rates are high.

Late AF Recurrence

Approximately 15% of patients have late recurrence of AF. It is postulated that incomplete isolation of the PV, triggers outside the PV, and persistence of substrate in the LA may be responsible for late AF recurrence and failure of the therapy. Risk factors for AF recurrence include old age, dilated LA, persistent form of AF, hypertension, and LV dysfunction.

Very Late AF Recurrence

Recurrence of AF >1 year after initial ablation may occur in 5% to 10% of patients. Reconnected PVs and ectopic foci in the RA appear to be responsible for most very late recurrences AF.

Patients should be closely followed for AF recurrence postprocedure. According to the HRS/EHRA/ECAS 2007 Expert Consensus Statement, patients should be seen in follow-up (and have an ECG done) at a maximum of 3 months following the ablation procedure, then every 6 months for at least 2 years. Event monitoring is indicated in patients who complain of palpitations during follow-up. Recurrence postablation is recognized if an atrial fibrillation/flutter/tachycardia episode that lasts at least 30 seconds is documented by ECG. Changes in autonomic tone (eg, higher resting heart rate, decreased heart rate variability) have been reported post–AF ablation. These changes frequently resolve in the first month postprocedure. Persistent sinus tachycardia may be the cause of palpitations in patients postablation who have no documented recurrence of AF.

10

■ Outcomes and Further Management

There are presently no data from large, randomized, multicenter trials on the safety and efficacy of catheter ablation of AF. Current knowledge comes from small randomized trials, nonrandomized trials, observational studies, single-center experience, and meta-analyses. These studies have major limitations, which include different end points (freedom from symptoms vs freedom from AF vs decreased burden of AF), short follow-up, variations in patient populations, AF type, and RFA techniques. In the absence of hard end points of AF therapy (eg, survival or stroke rate), symptomatic improvement (QoL), decreased hospitalization, and possibly cost of therapy are the main beneficial outcomes in the available trials.

Freedom from recurrent AF (or atrial arrhythmias) in the absence of antiarrhythmic therapy is currently defined as a primary end point of AF ablation. This definition excludes early and frequently transient recurrence of atrial arrhythmias up to 3 months postablation. Based on results of multiple studies, the success rate (with limited follow-up period) is currently estimated to be between 65% and 75%. The success rate of catheter ablation is higher for paroxysmal AF than for longstanding, persistent AF.

Approximately 20% to 30% of patients will require a second procedure, which may be successful in one third of patients in whom the initial procedure failed. Other therapeutic options in symptomatic patients with AF include reinitiation of chronic antiarrhythmic therapy or surgical procedures. Previously ineffective AADs may control AF postablation, since even a failed procedure can significantly influence substrate and/or reduce triggers for the condition.

■ Comparison of Catheter Ablation With Antiarrhythmic Therapy

The same limitations in the assessment of the efficacy of catheter ablation for AF apply to any comparison of catheter ablation to antiarrhythmic therapy. The small size of randomized trials, the observational nature of the relatively larger studies, limited follow-up, variations in patient populations and RFA techniques, and nonuniform end points make appropriate comparison difficult. However, findings from these studies consistently suggest superiority of catheter ablation over pharmacologic therapy. Results of randomized clinical trials comparing efficacy of catheter ablation and AADs are presented in **Table 10.15**.

The relative safety and efficacy of catheter ablation compared with AAD therapy was examined in the recently published meta-analysis of 63 RFA and 34 AADs studies. This analysis showed a 71% success rate for the repeated catheter ablation strategy vs 52% for AADs. In particular, the single-procedure success rate of ablation without AAD therapy was 57%, the multiple-procedure success rate without AADs was 71%, and the multiple-procedure success rate on AADs or with unknown cotherapy was 77% (**Figure 10.9**). Major complications of catheter ablation occurred in 4.9% of patients. Adverse events for AADs were less severe but more common (30% vs 5%).

The initial results regarding the efficacy of the novel ablation technique using a cryoablation balloon catheter compared with antiarrhythmic therapy were presented recently. In the Sustained Treatment of Paroxysmal Atrial Fibrillation (STOP-AF) trial, 245 relatively young and low-risk patients with two or more episodes of AF within 2 months or evidence of failure with at least one AAD were randomized in a 2:1 ratio to cryoablation or AAD therapy. In the first 3 months of the study (blanking period), repeating of ablation procedure was allowed and was performed in 19% of patients in the cryoablation group. After 12 months of follow-up, 69.9% of patients treated with cryoablation were free from AF and did not require therapy with a nonstudy drug or an interventional procedure for treatment of AF compared with only 7.3% of patients in the AAD-therapy group. Although the advantage of this novel technique appears to be striking, the results of the study are difficult to interpret because of a high rate of treatment crossovers from the drug-therapy arm to the cryoablation arm, which drove the study outcome and could have represented a bias of the investigators. Serious adverse events associated with cryoablation therapy included five cases of pulmonary vein stenosis. Additionally, 13.5% of patients had phrenic nerve paralysis, which in the vast majority of patients resolved within a 12-month follow-up period.

The more definitive data on the role of catheter ablation in AF management should be delivered with the results of the ongoing trials such as the Catheter Ablation Versus Anti-arrhythmic Drug Therapy for Atrial Fibrillation (CABANA) trial. The multicenter, prospective, randomized CABANA trial (with a planned recruitment of 3000 patients) aims to provide data on effectiveness, mortality, safety, QoL, and long-term outcome of ablative therapy in comparison to pharmacotherapy in AF. This trial will enroll patients >65 years old with paroxysmal or persistent AF (with no exclusions) or <65 years with more than one risk factor for CVA (eg, hypertension, low LVEF, prior stroke, or prior transient ischemic attack). Patients will be randomized to catheter ablation (technique at operator discretion) or pharmaco-

TABLE 10.15 — Randomized Clinical Trials of Catheter Ablation vs AADs or No Treatment in AF

Study	N	Age (y)	Type of AF	Previous Use of AAD	Ablation Technique	Repeat Ablation: Ablation Group	Crossed to Ablation: AAD Group	AF Free at 1 Year Ablation	AF Free at 1 Year AAD
Krittayaphong et al, 2003[1]	30	Ablation: 55 ± 10 AAD: 47 ± 15	Paroxysmal, persistent	≥1[a]	PVI+LA lines + CTI ablation + RA lines	Not stated	Not stated	79%	40%
Wazni et al, 2005[2] (RAAFT)	70	Ablation: 53 ± 8 AAD: 54 ± 8	Mainly paroxysmal	No	PVI	12%[b]	49%[c]	87%	37%
Stabile et al, 2005[3] (CACAF)[d]	245	Ablation: 62 ± 9 AAD: 62 ± 10	Paroxysmal, persistent	≥2	PVI+LA lines ±CTI ablation	No exact data	57%	56%	9%
Oral et al, 2006[e,4]	245	57 ± 9	Persistent	≥1 (mean 2.1 ± 1.2)	CPVA	AF: 26% LA flutter: 6%	77%	74%	4%
Pappone et al, 2006[5] (APAF)	198	Ablation: 55 ± 10 AAD: 57 ± 10	Paroxysmal	≥2 (mean 2 ±1)	CPVA+CTI ablation	AF: 6% Atrial tachycardia: 3%	42%	86%	22%
Jais et al, 2008[6] (A4 study)	112	51 ± 11	Paroxysmal	≥1	PVI±LA lines ±CTI ablation	Mean: 1.8 ± 0.8 Median: 2/patient	63%	89%	23%
Forleo et al, 2008[f,7]	70	Ablation: 63 ± 9 AAD: 65 ± 6	Paroxysmal, persistent	≥1	PVI±LA lines ±CTI ablation	Not stated	Not stated	80%	43%

Wilber et al, 2010[8] (Thermocool)[g]	167	Ablation: 55.5 AAD: 56.1	Paroxysmal	≥1 (mean 1.3)[h]	PVI±LA lines ±CFAEs±CTI ablation±RA lines	12.6% within 80 days after first procedure[i]	59%[c]	66%	16%
Packer et al, 2010[9] (STOP-AF)[j]	245	Ablation: 56.7 AAD: 56.4	Paroxysmal	≥1[b]	Cryo-PVI±LA lines	19% within 90 days after first procedure	79%	69.9%	7.3%

[a] No previous use of amiodarone, but 'failed' drugs include β-blockers, calcium channel antagonists, and digitalis, in addition to class IA and IC agents.

[b] Excluding amiodarone.

[c] After 1 year; not allowed during formal 1-year follow-up.

[d] All patients in the ablation arm were treated with AADs.

[e] Patients in the control group received amiodarone and had up to two electrical cardioversions if required during the first 3 months; amiodarone was discontinued if patients were in sinus rhythm after 3 months.

[f] With type 2 diabetes mellitus.

[g] Follow-up 9 months.

[h] Patients who received amiodarone in the previous 6 months were excluded.

[i] Considered treatment failure.

[j] Presented at the 59th Annual Scientific Session of the American College of Cardiology; March 15, 2010.

Continued

10

TABLE 10.15 — *Continued*

[1] Krittayaphong R, et al. *J Med Assoc Thai.* 2003;86(suppl 1):S8-S16.

[2] Wazni OM, et al. *JAMA.* 2005;293:2634-2640.

[3] Stabile G, et al. *Eur Heart J.* 2006;27(2):216-221.

[4] Oral H, et al. *N Engl J Med.* 2006;354(9):934-941.

[5] Pappone C, et al. *J Am Coll Cardiol.* 2006;48:2340-2347.

[6] Jais P, et al. *Circulation.* 2008;118:2498-2505.

[7] Forleo GB, et al. *J Cardiovasc Electrophysiol.* 2009;20(1):22-28.

[8] Wilber DJ, et al. *JAMA.* 2010;303:333-340.

[9] Packer D, et al. Cryoballoon ablation of pulmonary veins for paroxysmal atrial fibrillation. First results of the North American arctic front STOP-AF pivotal trial (abstract). Paper presented at the 59th Annual Scientific Session of the American College of Cardiology; March 15, 2010; Atlanta, GA.

Modified from the Task Force for the Management of Atrial Fibrillation of the European Society of Cardiology (ESC), *Eur Heart J.* 2010;31:2369-2429.

FIGURE 10.9 — Efficacy of Catheter Ablation in Patients With AF

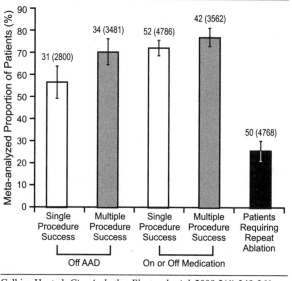

Calkins H, et al. *Circ Arrhythm Electrophysiol.* 2009;2(4):349-361.

logic therapy (rate or rhythm control). The results of the pilot phase of this trial were recently reported. Based on the findings from the pilot study, the different techniques used for ablation and the crossovers between the two arms may be a potential concern in the interpretation of CABANA results.

■ Indications

The role of catheter ablation in the maintenance of NSR has not been fully determined. Lack of large, randomized trials proving the benefit of catheter ablation on hard end points of AF therapy (eg, mortality, stroke rate) justify using catheter ablation only for treating symptomatic patients with the goal of improving QoL.

Based on the ACC/AHA/ESC 2006 Guidelines for the Management of AF, catheter ablation is accepted as a second-line rhythm-control therapy for AF in symptomatic patients who have little or no left atrial enlargement and in whom therapy with at least one AAD has failed.

These recommendations have been continuously expanding. The HRS/EHRA/ECAS 2007 Expert Consensus Statement on Catheter and Surgical Ablation for AF recommended that referral for AF ablation should be considered in:

- Patients with symptomatic AF in whom therapy with at least one AAD (Class I or III) has failed
- Selected patients as a first-line strategy
- Selected symptomatic patients with HF and/or reduced EF.

Furthermore, based on the efficacy and relative safety of catheter ablation in patients with paroxysmal AF and minimal or no heart disease, recent 2010 ESC Guidelines for the Management of AF state that catheter ablation may be considered in selected highly symptomatic patients with paroxysmal AF and minimal or no heart disease even without previous trials of AADs. 2010 ESC recommendations regarding the choice between catheter ablation and AADs based on the presence (or absence) of structural heart disease are presented in **Figure 10.10**.

Referral for an ablation procedure in the elderly and in patients with long-standing AF and dilated LA is controversial. Catheter ablation is contraindicated in patients with an LA thrombus.

Data on efficacy and safety of catheter ablation for AF are derived from the studies performed by experienced cardiac electrophysiologists. Operator experience should be an important factor when considering referral for catheter ablation of AF.

Surgical Options

Surgical ablation (eg, the Cox-Maze procedure) is the most definitive rhythm-control therapy for patients with AF. Approximately 90% of patients with AF achieve long-term maintenance of NSR after the Cox-Maze procedure (reports vary from 75% to 98%). However, due to its invasive nature, technical complexity, and significant risk of complications, it is usually not used as first-line AF therapy.

The classic Maze procedure was invented by Dr. James Cox and it has been continuously improved over the past 2 decades (currently, Cox-Maze III is performed by most of the operators). Several small incisions are made along both the left and right atria. The created scar tissue disrupts the reentrant pathways (required for AF maintenance) and facilitates electrical-impulse conduction from the SA node to the AV node in order to maintain atrial contraction.

It is assumed that elimination of AF with surgery requires ablation of the following lesions: a PV lesion; a lesion across the isthmus between the inferior PV and the mitral annulus; a right atrial isthmus lesion between the coronary sinus and the tricuspid valve annulus; and a lesion in the coronary sinus (**Figure 10.11**). Furthermore, several variations of the Cox-Maze procedure may influence its outcome, including biatrial vs the left atrial approach, and modifications to limit sinus node injury.

During the procedure, the LA appendage is also excised. This may be the main reason for an impressive reduction of thromboembolic risk reported postsurgery. In a series of 306 patients with AF in whom medical therapy failed and who were then treated with surgery, perioperative stroke rate was 0.7%. During 11.5 years of follow-up, only one patient had a subsequent stroke.

Although these results may prompt one to stop anticoagulation postprocedure, there are no data from large, randomized trials proving safety of this approach. Long duration of AF prior to surgery is a predictor of procedural failure. However, unlike with catheter RFA, the pattern of AF, ie, paroxysmal or persistent, does not seem to impact the outcome of Cox-Maze surgery.

Despite excellent long-term AF outcomes of Cox-Maze surgery when performed by an experienced operator, this procedure is associated with serious risks compared with pharmacologic or other invasive approaches. Benefits vs risks and complications of surgery are presented in **Table 10.16**.

Based on above data, it is accepted that the surgical Cox-Maze III procedure may be appropriate for some patients with AF, such as:

FIGURE 10.10 — 2010 ESC Recommendations on Choice Between Catheter Ablation and AADs Based on the Presence (or Absence) of Structural Heart Disease

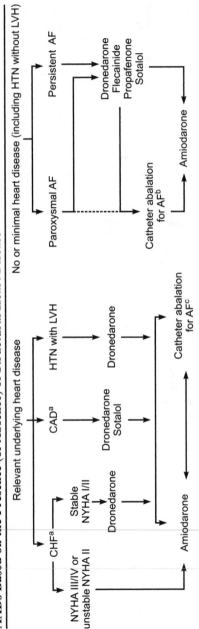

Antiarrhythmic agents are listed alphabetically within each treatment box. Note that LA ablation as first-line therapy (dashed line) is a Class IIb recommendation for patients with paroxysmal AF and no or minimal heart disease, who remain highly symptomatic, despite rate control, and who reject AAD therapy.

[a] Dofetilide, which is used in the United States in AF patients with HF or CAD, was not considered in the ESC Guidelines.

[b] Usually PVI is appropriate.

[c] More extensive LA ablation may be needed.

The Task Force for the Management of Atrial Fibrillation of the European Society of Cardiology (ESC). *Eur Heart J.* 2010;31:2369-2429.

10

FIGURE 10.11 — Standard Cox-Maze III Surgical Procedure for AF

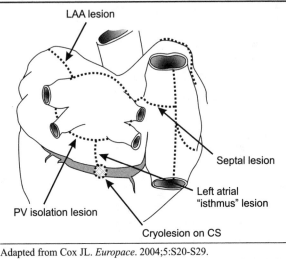

LAA lesion

Septal lesion

Left atrial "isthmus" lesion

PV isolation lesion

Cryolesion on CS

Adapted from Cox JL. *Europace*. 2004;5:S20-S29.

TABLE 10.16 — Benefits vs Risks and Complications of the Cox-Maze III Procedure

Benefits
- Excellent long-term outcome (90% success rate reported)
- May allow stopping anticoagulation in patients with contraindications to antithrombotic therapy
- Feasible and beneficial in patients undergoing mitral valve surgery

Risks
- Complex and technically difficult (outcomes and complications very operator dependent)
- Mortality rates 1% to 2%
- Cardiopulmonary bypass for 1.5 to 3 hours
- Reoperation rate up to 7% due to bleeding
- Postoperative hospital stay >1 week frequently reported
- Sinus node dysfunction, including brady- and tachy-arrhythmias (10% to 15% of the patients required post-operative pacemakers)
- Risk of left atrial dysfunction (complete isolation of the right and left pulmonary veins may destroy mechanical function of posterior left atrium)

- Significantly symptomatic young patients in whom antiarrhythmic and ablation therapy has failed
- Those with a contraindication to systemic anticoagulation or a history of stroke on therapeutic doses of warfarin
- Those with any valvular heart disease, who are a candidate for valve repair or tissue valve replacement (ie, would not need lifelong anticoagulation)
- Patients undergoing mitral valve surgery (resolution of AF postoperatively improves long-term prognosis in patients with mitral valve disease)
- Those with persistent or permanent AF undergoing any cardiac surgery by an operator experienced in Cox-Maze procedure.

The complexity and significant complications of Cox-Maze III, along with the expanding role of RFA therapy for AF, have led to attempts to simplify this procedure while preserving benefit of the surgical treatment of AF. As such, creating scar tissue with extensive cutting and sewing was replaced by lines of ablation made by various energy sources, such as radiofrequency, cryoablation, or laser (**Figure 10.12**).

This technique is commonly named Cox-Maze IV procedure (although term "Maze" should be applied only when the extensive lesion set of Cox-Maze III procedure is ablated). The Cox-Maze IV procedure is associated with several benefits compared with traditional Cox-Maze III surgery (**Table 10.17**).

Bipolar RFA is used to ensure a transmural effect, although some operators still prefer the "cut and sew" Cox-Maze technique to secure full thickness isolation of the PVs. Many operators modified the incisions of the Cox-Maze III and IV procedures. This makes results of these procedures difficult to interpret, since recurrence of AF may be due to either inadequate ablation or an insufficient lesion set. Long-term data are not yet available for the Cox-Maze IV procedure. However, freedom from AF is initially reported to be similar to that with the Cox-Maze III (approximately 90%). Further development of the Cox-Maze procedure is expected, with the goal of

10

**FIGURE 10.12 — Bipolar Radiofrequency:
Modified Cox-Maze IV Procedure**

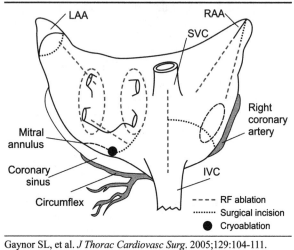

Gaynor SL, et al. *J Thorac Cardiovasc Surg*. 2005;129:104-111.

**TABLE 10.17 — Possible Benefits of the
Cox-Maze IV Procedure**

• Technical simplicity
• Decreased time of surgery
• Shorter hospitalization
• Feasible for off-pump surgery
• Feasible for minimally invasive approaches
• Decreased bleeding complications
• Improved atrial contractility (posterior left atrial wall
 remains intact)

ablation using a minimally invasive, epicardial approach performed on a beating heart.

SUGGESTED READING

Abi-Mansour P, Carberry PA, McCowan RJ, Henthorn RW, Dunn GH, Perry KT. Conversion efficacy and safety of repeated doses of ibutilide in patients with atrial flutter and atrial fibrillation. Study Investigators. *Am Heart J.* 1998;136(4 Pt 1):632-642.

Alboni P, Botto GL, Baldi N, et al. Outpatient treatment of recent-onset atrial fibrillation with the "pill-in-the-pocket" approach. *N Engl J Med.* 2004;351(23):2384-2391.

d'Avila A, Ruskin JN. Nonpharmacologic strategies: the evolving story of ablation and hybrid therapy. *Am J Cardiol.* 2008;102(6A):20H-24H.

Arnsdorf MF, Ganz LI, Manning WJ. Restoration of sinus rhythm in atrial fibrillation: Recommendations. In: Basow DS, ed. *UpToDate.* Waltham, MA: UpToDate; 2010.

Arnsdorf MF, Podrid PJ, ManningWJ. Restoration of sinus rhythm in atrial fibrillation: Therapeutic options. In: Basow DS, ed. *UpToDate.* Waltham, MA: UpToDate; 2010.

Boriani G, Biffi M, Capucci A, et al. Conversion of recent-onset atrial fibrillation to sinus rhythm: effects of different drug protocols. *Pacing Clin Electrophysiol.* 1998;21(11 Pt 2):2470-2474.

Boriani G, Diemberger I, Biffi M, et al. How, why, and when may atrial defibrillation find a specific role in implantable devices? A clinical viewpoint. *Pacing Clin Electrophysiol.* 2007;30(3):422-433.

Calkins H, Brugada J, Packer DL, et al; Heart Rhythm Society; European Heart Rhythm Association; European Cardiac Arrhythmia Society; American College of Cardiology; American Heart Association; Society of Thoracic Surgeons. HRS/EHRA/ECAS expert consensus statement on catheter and surgical ablation of atrial fibrillation: recommendations for personnel, policy, procedures and follow-up. A report of the Heart Rhythm Society (HRS) Task Force on Catheter and Surgical Ablation of Atrial Fibrillation developed in partnership with the European Heart Rhythm Association (EHRA) and the European Cardiac Arrhythmia Society (ECAS); in collaboration with the American College of Cardiology (ACC), American Heart Association (AHA), and the Society of Thoracic Surgeons (STS). Endorsed and approved by the governing bodies of the American College of Cardiology, the American Heart Association, the European Cardiac Arrhythmia Society, the European Heart Rhythm Association, the Society of Thoracic Surgeons, and the Heart Rhythm Society [erratum appears in *Europace.* 2009;11(1):132]. *Europace.* 2007;9(6):335-379.

10

Calkins H, Reynolds MR, Spector P, et al. Treatment of atrial fibrillation with antiarrhythmic drugs or radiofrequency ablation: two systematic literature reviews and meta-analyses. *Circ Arrhythm Electrophysiol.* 2009;2(4):349-361.

Cappato R, Calkins H, Chen SA, et al. Prevalence and causes of fatal outcome in catheter ablation of atrial fibrillation. *J Am Coll Cardiol.* 2009;53(19):1798-1803.

Cheng J, Arnsdorf MF. Radiofrequency catheter ablation to prevent recurrent atrial fibrillation. In: Basow DS, ed. *UpToDate.* Waltham, MA: UpToDate; 2010.

Conway E, Musco S, Kowey PR. New horizons in antiarrhythmic therapy: will novel agents overcome current deficits? *Am J Cardiol.* 2008;102(6A):12H-19H.

Cotter G, Blatt A, Kaluski E, et al. Conversion of recent onset paroxysmal atrial fibrillation to normal sinus rhythm: the effect of no treatment and high-dose amiodarone. A randomized, placebo-controlled study. *Eur Heart J.* 1999;20(24):1833-1842.

Cox J. Surgical treatment of atrial fibrillation: a review. *Europace.* 2004;5(suppl 1):S20-S29.

Cox JL, Ad N, Palazzo T. Impact of the maze procedure on the stroke rate in patients with atrial fibrillation. *J Thorac Cardiovasc Surg.* 1999; 118:833-840.

Crandall MA, Bradley DJ, Packer DL, Asirvatham SJ. Contemporary management of atrial fibrillation: update on anticoagulation and invasive management strategies. *Mayo Clin Proc.* 2009;84(7):643-662.

Ehrlich JR, Nattel S. Novel approaches for pharmacological management of atrial fibrillation. *Drugs.* 2009;69(7):757-774.

European Heart Rhythm Association; European Association for Cardio-Thoracic Surgery, Camm AJ, Kirchhof P, Lip GY, et al. Guidelines for the management of atrial fibrillation: the Task Force for the Management of Atrial Fibrillation of the European Society of Cardiology (ESC). *Eur Heart J.* 2010;31(19):2369-2429.

Fuster V, Rydén LE, Cannom DS, et al; American College of Cardiology/American Heart Association Task Force on Practice Guidelines; European Society of Cardiology Committee for Practice Guidelines; European Heart Rhythm Association; Heart Rhythm Society. ACC/AHA/ESC 2006 Guidelines for the Management of Patients with Atrial Fibrillation: a report of the American College of Cardiology/American Heart Association Task Force on Practice Guidelines and the European Society of Cardiology Committee for Practice Guidelines (Writing Committee to Revise the 2001 Guidelines for the Management of Patients With Atrial Fibrillation): developed in collaboration with the

European Heart Rhythm Association and the Heart Rhythm Society [erratum appears in *Circulation.* 2007;116(6):e138]. *Circulation.* 2006;114(7):e257-e354.

Gaita F, Caponi D, Pianelli M, et al. Radiofrequency catheter ablation of atrial fibrillation: a cause of silent thromboembolism? Magnetic resonance imaging assessment of cerebral thromboembolism in patients undergoing ablation of atrial fibrillation. *Circulation.* 2010;122(17):1667-1673.

Galve E, Rius T, Ballester R, et al. Intravenous amiodarone in treatment of recent-onset atrial fibrillation: results of a randomized, controlled study. *J Am Coll Cardiol.* 1996;27(5):1079-1082.

Kim SS, Knight BP. Electrical and pharmacologic cardioversion for atrial fibrillation. *Cardiol Clin.* 2009;27(1):95-107.

Kowey PR, Gan-Xin Y, Crijns H. Anthiarrhythmic drugs. In: Fuster V, O'Rourke R, Walsh R, Poole-Wilson P, eds. *Hurst's The Heart.* 12th ed. New York, NY: McGraw-Hill Professional; 2008.

Lévy S, Camm J. Implantable atrial defibrillators for the treatment of atrial fibrillation. In: Basow DS, ed. *UpToDate.* Waltham, MA: UpToDate; 2010.

Lubitz SA, Fischer A, Fuster V. Catheter ablation for atrial fibrillation. *BMJ.* 2008;336(7648):819-826.

Miller J, Zipes D. Therapy for Cardiac Arrhythmias. In: Libby P, Bonow R, Mann D, Ziper D, eds. *Braunwald's Heart Diseases.* 8th ed. Philadelphia, PA: Saunders Elsevier; 2008:779.

Mokadam NA, McCarthy PM, Gillinov AM, et al. A prospective multicenter trial of bipolar radiofrequency ablation for atrial fibrillation: early results. *Ann Thorac Surg.* 2004;78(5):1665-1670.

Noheria A, Kumar K, Wylie JV, Josephson ME. Catheter ablation vs antiarrhythmic drug therapy for atrial fibrillation: a systematic review. *Arch Intern Med.* 2008;168(6):581-586.

Oral H, Souza JJ, Michaud GF, et al. Facilitating transthoracic cardioversion of atrial fibrillation with ibutilide pretreatment. *N Engl J Med.* 1999;340(24):1849-1854.

Page RL, Kerber RE, Russell JK, et al; BiCard Investigators. Biphasic versus monophasic shock waveform for conversion of atrial fibrillation: the results of an international randomized, double-blind multicenter trial. *J Am Coll Cardiol.* 2002;39(12):1956-1963.

Peuhkurinen K, Niemelä M, Ylitalo A, Linnaluoto M, Lilja M, Juvonen J. Effectiveness of amiodarone as a single oral dose for recent-onset atrial fibrillation. *Am J Cardiol.* 2000;85(4):462-465.

Reiffel JA. Cardioversion for atrial fibrillation: treatment options and advances. *Pacing Clin Electrophysiol.* 2009;32(8):1073-1084.

10

Saltman AE, Gillinov AM. Surgical approaches for atrial fibrillation. *Cardiol Clin*. 2009;27(1):179-188.

Shen J, Bailey MS, Damiano RJ Jr. The surgical treatment of atrial fibrillation. *Heart Rhythm*. 2009;6(8 suppl):S45-S50.

Singh S, Zoble RG, Yellen L, et al. Efficacy and safety of oral dofetilide in converting to and maintaining sinus rhythm in patients with chronic atrial fibrillation or atrial flutter: the symptomatic atrial fibrillation investigative research on dofetilide (SAFIRE-D) study. *Circulation*. 2000;102(19):2385-2390.

Stambler BS, Wood MA, Ellenbogen KA, Perry KT, Wakefield LK, VanderLugt JT. Efficacy and safety of repeated intravenous doses of ibutilide for rapid conversion of atrial flutter or fibrillation. Ibutilide Repeat Dose Study Investigators. *Circulation*. 1996;94(7):1613-1621.

Timmermans C, Luz-Maria R, Crigns H. Cardioversion. In: Kowey PR, Naccarelli GV, eds. *Atrial Fibrillation*. New York, NY: Marcel Dekker; 2005:159-180.

11
Antiarrhythmic Drugs for Maintenance of Sinus Rhythm

Introduction

Patients with AF in whom rhythm-control therapy is chosen usually require prophylactic treatment with AADs to maintain sinus rhythm postcardioversion. Although intuitively desirable, maintenance of sinus rhythm with AADs has not been shown to lower mortality in large clinical trials when compared with a rate-control strategy. It is widely accepted that proarrhythmic and toxic side effects of AADs counterbalance the possible benefit of maintaining NSR. Additionally, since stroke rates appear similar whether rhythm- or rate-control strategy is chosen, AAD therapy does not decrease the need for anticoagulation. The use of AADs for maintenance of sinus rhythm in patients with AF requires understanding of goals, benefits, and risks of AAD therapy.

General Principles of AAD Therapy for Maintenance of Sinus Rhythm in AF

■ Goals of AAD Therapy

While initiating chronic rhythm-control strategy, one has to consider that chronic AAD therapy does not prevent recurrences of AF in the majority of patients. As such, marked reduction in the frequency and duration of symptomatic AF may be a reasonable clinical goal. Additionally, the prevention of AF recurrences with AADs may regress atrial remodeling, which has been shown to perpetuate the arrhythmia ("AF begets AF"). AAD therapy may be then used in young and symptomatic patients with paroxysmal and persistent AF as a goal to prevent establishing a permanent symptomatic arrhythmia. Effective prevention of AF should be associated with low toxicity and proarrhythmia risks.

191

■ Indications

A rhythm-control strategy with chronic AAD therapy to maintain sinus rhythm may be considered in the following scenarios:

- Failure to achieve rate control in patients with AF and rapid ventricular response
- Symptomatic AF patients despite sufficient rate control
- HF patients with a history of decompensation with paroxysmal or persistent AF
- AF patients who prefer rhythm-control therapy.

A rhythm-control strategy is also preferred in patients with AF secondary to reversible causes (eg, postoperatively) and in young subjects with a first episode of AF. However, cardioversion to sinus rhythm is not routinely followed by long-term AAD therapy in the majority of these patients.

The relative lack of efficacy and the unfavorable safety profile of classic AADs have spurred the development of new agents. If these new drugs are more effective in the maintenance of sinus rhythm and are shown not to be associated with significant adverse effects, this may widen the indications for antiarrhythmic therapy for AF.

■ Efficacy

The use of an AAD after successful cardioversion reduces the 71% to 84% baseline 1-year risk of AF recurrence by 30% to 50%. In the AFFIRM trial, maintenance of sinus rhythm was higher and was achieved in 80% of patients at 1 year whether the patient was kept on the same AAD vs using a different AAD postcardioversion.

The efficacy of AADs in maintaining sinus rhythm should always be considered in the context of their potential side effects. For example, although amiodarone is the most effective agent in maintaining sinus rhythm, the risk of a variety of side effects associated with chronic treatment favors initial therapy with other AADs in many patients.

■ Safety Considerations of Antiarrhythmic Therapy for AF

Potential side effects of AADs are the major limiting factor in using antiarrhythmic therapy for maintenance of sinus rhythm. Possible lethal complications, such as proarrhythmia and organ toxicity, are major concerns. Bradyarrhythmias and worsening of hemodynamics may also complicate antiarrhythmic therapy, especially in patients with underlying heart disease. Although not associated with major morbidity, bothersome drug intolerance (eg, diarrhea, photosensitivity) is the main reason for discontinuation or noncompliance.

Proarrhythmia

AADs used to suppress AF may potentially cause a new ventricular arrhythmia or worsen preexisting atrial tachyarrhythmia, or even a bradyarrhythmia. Proarrhythmia is more common in patients with underlying structural heart disease, although drug interactions (especially with agents causing QT prolongation), abnormal metabolism (due to renal or liver insufficiency), or electrolyte imbalance may contribute. As such, proarrhythmia is generated as an interaction of a drug's electrophysiologic action with structural functional changes in the myocardium and/or "unfavorable" extracardiac conditions.

Ventricular Proarrhythmias

Ventricular proarrhythmias in AF patients treated with AADs can be divided into two groups:

- Monomorphic ventricular tachycardia
- TdP (type of polymorphic ventricular tachycardia).

Both of them can be lethal or hemodynamically destabilizing. Mechanisms of ventricular proarrhythmias are presented in **Figure 11.1**.

Monomorphic ventricular tachycardia requires the presence of an anatomic reentrant circuit. Increased heterogeneity of the myocardium associated with the presence of unidirectional block may create reentry circuits leading to incessant wide-complex tachycardia. In

FIGURE 11.1 — Major Proarrhythmic Mechanisms

Class IA and III Agents: Torsades de Pointes

Class IC Agents: Wide-Complex VT

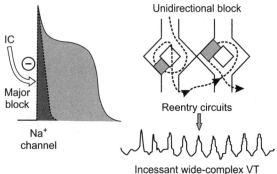

Class IA and Class III agents widen the action potential duration and, in the presence of an early after depolarization, can give rise to triggered activity TdP *(top)*. Note major role of QT prolongation *(bottom)*. Class IC agents have as their major proarrhythmic mechanism a powerful inhibition of the sodium channel, particularly in conduction tissue. Increasing heterogeneity together with unidirectional block sets the stage for reentry circuits and monomorphic wide-complex ventricular tachycardia (VT).

Opie LH, Gersh BJ. *Drugs for the Heart.* 7th ed. Philadelphia, PA: Saunders; 2009.

such a milieu, any AAD that slows conduction more than the effective refractory period may facilitate reentrant VT, which often terminates in VF. This proarrhythmia is typically associated with the use of Class IC agents in patients with CAD or LV dysfunction.

Action potential and QT interval prolongation is the key factor in the genesis of TdP. A prolonged QTc is defined as a QT corrected for patient's heart rate exceeding 440 msec. Early after depolarizations in the presence of a long QT can give rise to triggered activity and initiate TdP. Class IA and III AADs that block I_{Kr} and/or increase late I_{Na} may widen the action potential duration, prolong the QT interval, and facilitate TdP. Certain AADs (eg, amiodarone and sotalol) exert their beneficial effect by increasing action potential duration. As such, QT prolongation may be both therapeutically beneficial and potentially proarrhythmic.

As bradycardia prolongs the action potential duration, sotalol carries a relatively high risk of TdP because of its reverse use dependency (higher efficacy with slower high rates). In contrast, although amiodarone significantly prolongs the QT interval, it rarely triggers TdP (unless the patient has preexisting significant QTc prolongation or profound electrolyte imbalance). It is hypothesized that a multichannel mechanism of action (including sodium and calcium channel inhibition and β-blockade) may offset the propensity of amiodarone to produce TdP. Dronedarone, which has even more pronounced antiadrenergic activity and potent multichannel effects, has not been shown to increase the risk of TdP.

Any condition or drug therapy leading to prolongation of the QT interval may further increase the risk of TdP in AF patients treated with class IA and III AADs. Congenital long–QT syndrome, bradycardia, ventricular hypertrophy, and electrolyte imbalance (eg, hypokalemia, hypomagnesemia, hypocalcemia) are the major clinical states associated with QTc prolongation. Common non-AAD drugs associated with QTc prolongation are presented in **Table 11.1**. These agents may directly prolong the QT interval, slow metabolism of AADs, or cause proarrhythmic electrolyte abnormalities.

Atrial Proarrhythmia

Class IC agents (flecainide and propafenone) can convert AF into atrial flutter with a slower rate. Atrial flutter may then be associated with 1:1 AV nodal conduction with accelerated ventricular rates (150-200 BPM). As such, patients treated with IC agents might require AV nodal–blocking drugs to prevent high ventricular rates associated with 1:1 AV conduction. A vagolytic effect

TABLE 11.1 — Major Classes of Non-antiarrhythmics That Prolong QT Interval and Should Be Avoided in AF Patients Treated With AADs (Classes IA and III)

- Psychotropic agents (eg, phenothiazines, thioridazine, haloperidol, risperidone), tricyclic antidepressants, SSRIs, methadone
- Antimicrobial drugs (eg, macrolides,[a] quinolones,[a] pentamidine, chloroquine, mefloquine)
- Antifungal (eg, ketoconazole, voriconazole)
- Antihistamines (eg, terfenadine and astemizole)
- Thiazide and loop diuretics (risk of hypomagnesemia and hypokalemia)
- HIV protease inhibitors (eg, ritonavir)
- Antimotility drugs (eg, cisapride, domperidone)
- Other (eg, ranolazine, droperidol)

[a] Not all agents among the class exert same effect on QT interval.

---

of class IA agents may also occasionally lead to rapid conduction through the AV node. Shortening the atrial effective refractory period by adenosine or digoxin may promote the development of AF in some patients. There are other forms of atrial proarrhythmia, including atrial torsade presumed to be due to profound extension of the atrial refractory period (with agents such as I_{Kur} blockers).

Bradyarrhythmia

Sinus bradycardia or AV nodal block due to AAD therapy is relatively common. Complete AV nodal block as an initial presentation is uncommon. Sotalol causes bradycardia in 10% to 15% of patients, while amiodarone causes this in approximately 5% of patients. However, advanced bradyarrhythmias requiring PPM implantation are more common with amiodarone than with sotalol. Dronedarone causes bradycardia in approximately 3.5% of patients. Propafenone and flecainide may rarely worsen sinus node dysfunction or cause AV blocks. Patients treated with any of these agents should be monitored for bradyarrhythmias, especially if new symptoms of low cardiac output are noted or bradycardia is found on electrocardiographic monitoring *(see below)*.

■ Interference With Implanted Device Function by AADs

AF patients treated with rhythm-control strategies frequently have PPMs and/or implanted defibrillators. AF associated with sinus node dysfunction may require implantation of a pacemaker for excessive bradycardia caused by antiarrhythmic therapy. Also, patients with AF and advanced HF commonly have an implanted ICD for primary or secondary prevention of sudden cardiac death. AADs can impact thresholds for pacing and arrhythmia termination. AADs, by slowing ventricular tachycardia rate, can interrupt detection and termination algorithms of the ICD.

The effects on the ICD threshold of commonly used AADs is presented in **Table 11.2**.

TABLE 11.2 — Threshold Effects of AADs Used in AF

| | Threshold | |
Drug	Pacing	Defibrillation
Disopyramide	Increase	No change
Flecainide	Increase	Increase
Propafenone	Increase	No change
Ibutilide	No change	Decrease
Amiodarone	Variable	Increase
Dronedarone	No change	No change
Sotalol	No change	Decrease
Dofetilide	No change	Decrease

Modified from Fuster V, et al, eds. *Hurst's The Heart.* 12th ed. New York, NY: McGraw-Hill Companies, Inc; 2007:1077-1094, and Reiffel JA, et al. *Pacing Clin Electrophysiol.* 1985;8(3 Pt 1):369-373.

■ Hemodynamic Effects

AADs may exert significant hemodynamic effects that may limit their use in AF patients with LV dysfunction or HF. Class I drugs, such as propafenone, and flecainide (IC) and disopyramide (IA), have negative inotropic activity and may cause decompensated HF. Class III AADs are generally well tolerated. Amiodarone and dofetilide can be safely used and are the agents of choice in patients with severe LV dysfunction. Dronedarone, which exerts stronger antiadrenergic activity than amiodarone, is contraindicated in patients with advanced HF. Also sotalol, which has potent β-adrenergic–blocking activity, should be used cautiously in HF patients.

■ **Organ Toxicity**

Organ toxicity of AADs may be defined as a noncardiac effect associated with potentially fatal outcomes. This should be differentiated from drug intolerance (eg, GI upset), which may cause poor compliance and discontinuation of the therapy but does not result in increased morbidity and mortality. Organ toxicity is highest with amiodarone (eg, thyroid, pulmonary, hepatic, ocular, neuropathy). Chronic therapy with amiodarone carries a risk of organ toxicity even when low doses are used. The annual risk of pulmonary fibrosis was reported to average 2% with daily doses of ≥200 mg. Rare cases of severe liver toxicity caused by dronedarone have been reported. Class IA agents, such as quinidine and procainamide, may be associated with organ toxicity, which is lower with sotalol, dofetilide, propafenone, and flecainide.

Monitoring of Antiarrhythmic Therapy

Close follow-up is required for patients receiving antiarrhythmic therapy. The goal of monitoring is to prevent complications, particularly potential lethal ones such as proarrhythmias, bradyarrhythmias, and serious organ toxicity. The extent of monitoring depends on the AAD used, possible interactions with concomitant therapies, and the presence of other comorbidities. In general, AADs should be started at a low dose and titrated based on desired response and possible presence of side effects. Recommended tests for monitoring the safety of AADs are presented in **Table 11.3**.

A focused history and physical examination to screen for side effects of antiarrhythmic therapy are mandated on every follow-up visit. Concomitant pharmacologic therapies should always be reviewed and monitored closely for possible drug interactions.

All patients taking AADs should have renal function, potassium, and magnesium levels assessed periodically.

Patients on sotalol and dofetilide may require frequent assessments. Presence of renal insufficiency warrants dose reduction or discontinuation of these drugs. Class III agents (amiodarone and dronedarone) are metabolized by the liver. Biannual liver function tests are required in patients on amiodarone, and therapy is discontinued if liver dysfunction is caused by these agents. Liver function tests should be performed periodically (especially during first 6 months of therapy) in patients taking dronedarone. Dronedarone should not be used in patients who developed liver dysfunction on amiodarone. Amiodarone mandates monitoring of thyroid function twice a year and ocular examinations once a year. For patients taking amiodarone, baseline chest x-ray and pulmonary function tests with diffusing capacity are recommended or if unexplained dyspnea or cough develops. Since Class IC drugs propafenone and flecainide are also mostly metabolized by the liver, they may also require occasional evaluation of liver function.

An ECG should be performed at least every 6 months (and always when the dose is changed). Therapy with dronedarone is an exception and requires an ECG at least every 3 months (electrocardiographic evidence of AF mandates cardioversion or discontinuation of dronedarone).

All components of the ECG should be analyzed with special focus on particular elements based on the agent used:

- Heart rate and PR interval when flecainide, propafenone, sotalol, amiodarone, or dronedarone are used
- QRS duration if the patient is treated with propafenone or flecainide
- QT interval when any of Class III and IA agents is used.

If the QRS duration increases >50% from baseline, the dose of the Class IC agent needs to be reduced or the drug discontinued. A corrected QT interval >500 msec should be avoided in patients on Class IA or Class III AADs (please see below for detailed diagrams of sotalol and dofetilide dosing based on the QTc interval). Amiodarone

TABLE 11.3 — Recommended Tests for Monitoring Chronic Antiarrhythmic Therapy Based on the Drug Used

Test	Class 1A — Disopyramide	Class 1C — Propafenone, Flecainide	Class III — Amiodarone	Dronedarone	Sotalol	Dofetilide
Renal function, electrolytes (K, Mg)	Baseline and as necessary	Baseline and as necessary	Baseline and as necessary	Baseline, periodically after initiation of therapy, and as necessary	Baseline, then every 3 mo or more often if clinically indicated	Baseline, then every 3 mo or more often if clinically indicated
Other laboratory tests	LFTs, baseline, and as necessary	LFTs, baseline, and as necessary	Thyroid and LFTs, baseline and every 6 mo	Check LFTs periodically (especially during first 6 months of therapy)		
ECG or continuous ECG recording	Baseline and every 6 mo, any drug dose or clinical status change Watch QTc	Baseline and every 6 mo, any drug dose or clinical status change Watch PR and QRS (QRS should not increase >50% from baseline)	Baseline and every 6 mo, any drug dose or clinical status change Watch HR, PR, and QTc	Baseline and every 3 mo, any drug dose or clinical status change Watch rhythm, HR, PR, and QTc Discontinue or cardiovert if AF	Every 3 mo, drug dose or clinical status change Watch HR, PR, and QTc; discontinue if >520 msec	Baseline and every 3 mo, drug dose, or clinical status change Watch QTc; discontinue if >500 msec

			present Discontinue if sinus with QTc >500 ms)	
Echocardiogram	Consider in every patient prior to therapy initiation and if clinical status changes	Consider in every patient prior to therapy initiation and if clinical status changes	Consider in every patient prior to therapy initiation and if clinical status changes	Consider in every patient prior to therapy initiation and if clinical status changes
Stress test		Consider at baseline, then periodically if risk factors for CAD or symptoms that are concerning for ischemia		
Other			ICD interrogation; once initial loading completed, then when indicated Chest x-ray: baseline and every year Pulmonary function test: baseline and if clinically indicated	

201

is the exception, as longer QT intervals are not associated with increased risk of proarrhythmia. All tracings should also be evaluated for electrocardiographic signs of electrolyte disturbances (eg, hypokalemia).

Continuous electrocardiographic recording is a convenient and effective method of rhythm and conduction abnormalities monitoring when AADs are initiated outside of the hospital for maintenance of sinus rhythm in AF. ECG monitoring is recommended with new symptoms suggestive of tachy- or bradyarrhythmia (eg, lightheadedness, shortness of breath, fatigue) or when significant bradycardia is detected on the 12-lead ECG.

Exercise testing should be considered in patients receiving Class IC drugs to screen for ischemic heart disease, the presence of which generally precludes their use. Exercise also helps detect QRS widening that may occur only with rapid heart rates (use-dependent conduction slowing) and is useful to detect exercise-induced proarrhythmia.

Echocardiographic assessment of LV function is indicated in patients taking Class IA, IC, and certain Class III agents (eg, dronedarone and sotalol). LV dysfunction, LVH, or a scar due to a clinically silent MI all increase the risk of proarrhythmia and may warrant a reevaluation. An echocardiogram is generally indicated in patients who develop new symptoms of HF.

Choice of AAD

Antiarrhythmic therapy may prevent AF recurrences via different mechanisms:
- Interruption of reentrant pathways (eg, prolongation of refractoriness, slowing conduction)
- Inhibition of initiating ectopy
- Elimination of tachyarrhythmias that can degrade into AF (atrial flutter, SVT).

AADs may also affect the autonomic nervous system and prevent adrenergic or vagally mediated AF. However, the choice of an AAD is not only determined by its electrophysiologic mechanism but also by potential side effects in particular patients. As such, antiarrhythmic therapy should always be individualized. Currently available AADs for maintenance of sinus rhythm in AF according to the Vaughan-Williams classification are presented in **Table 11**.**4**.

Current ACC/AHA/ESC Guidelines also conclude that there is no evidence that digitalis and nondihydropyridine CCBs (eg, diltiazem and verapamil) prevent recurrence of paroxysmal AF.

The ideal drug should have a low risk of serious side effects, convenient dosing, and affordable cost to maximize patient's compliance and decrease the risk of side effects associated with inappropriate use. An algorithmic approach to limit excessive (or inappropriate) therapy with an AAD and lower risk of associated side effects is presented in **Figure 11**.**2**. The selection of a specific agent is usually based on the presence or absence of underlying cardiac disease. This determines the risk of proarrhythmia and the risk-benefit ratio of using AADs. An algorithm presenting the choice of an antiarrhythmic agent based on the presence or absence of structural heart disease appears in the recently published 2011 Update of ACCF/AHA/HRS Guidelines on the Management of Patients With Atrial Fibrillation and is presented in **Figure 11**.**3**.

11

■ **Patients With No or Minimal Heart Disease**

β-Blockers are only modestly effective in preventing recurrence of AF. Since β-blockers are generally not associated with risk of proarrhythmia or severe drug toxicity, they may be tried first in selected patients with lone AF. When initiating AAD, long-term benefits of maintaining NSR should outweigh the potential risks from proarrhythmia in these patients. Class IC agents (propafenone and flecainide), dronedarone, and sotalol have an acceptable low risk of proarrhythmia and are associated with minimal noncardiac toxicity.

Drugs associated with a high risk of organ toxicity (amiodarone) and a higher risk of proarrhythmia (dofetilide) are used as second-line therapy. Low-dose amiodarone therapy is still associated with significant risk of organ toxicity. As such, current guidelines do not recommend the use of amiodarone (even at a low dose) as a first-line agent in AF patients without structural heart disease.

TABLE 11.4 — AADs Recommended for Maintenance of Sinus Rhythm in AF According to the Vaughan-Williams Classification

Drug	Mechanism of Action	Daily Dosing (mg)	Major Adverse Effect
Class I			
Disopyramide (1A)	Sodium channel blockade; delays phase 0 of action potential	400-750	Proarrhythmia (TdP) Negative inotropic effect (HF), hypotension Anticholinergic effect (glaucoma, urinary retention, constipation, dry mouth)
Flecainide (1C)	Sodium channel blockade; strongly delays phase 0 of action potential	200-300	Proarrhythmia (ventricular tachycardia, conversion to atrial flutter with rapid conduction through the AV) Bradycardia, AV blocks, decompensated HF CNS symptoms (eg, dizziness, unsteady gait), >GI upset
Propafenone (1C)	Sodium channel blockade; strongly delays phase 0 of action potential	450-900	Proarrhythmia (ventricular tachycardia, conversion to atrial flutter with rapid conduction through the AV) Bradycardia, AV blocks, decompensated HF GI upset (eg, nausea, abnormal taste), ?CNS symptoms Bronchospasm

Class III			
Sotalol	Potassium channel blockade (mainly I_{Kr}), β-receptor blockade	160-320	Proarrhythmia (TdP) Side effects caused by potent β-blockade activity (eg, fatigue, HF, bradycardia, bronchospasm)
Amiodarone	Multichannel blockade (predominantly Class III but also Class I, β-blocking, and calcium channel blocking activity)	100-400	Intolerance (eg, GI upset, photosensitivity) Organ toxicity (thyroid, pulmonary, hepatic, ocular, neuropathy) Proarrhythmia (TdP [rare], QT prolongation) Bradycardia, hypotension
Dronedarone	Multichannel blockade (comparing with amiodarone, this drug is a more potent inhibitor of peak sodium and I_{K-Ach} currents and has stronger antiadrenergic activity)	800	Intolerance (GI side effects are common) Hepatic toxicity (rare) Bradycardia, HF QT prolongation (TdP [extremely rare])
Dofetilide	Potassium channel blockade (mainly I_{Kr})	0.5-1	Proarrhythmia (TdP), QT prolongation

Due to risk of proarrhythmia and extracardiac side effects, the Class IA agents quinidine and procainamide are no longer recommended for maintenance of sinus rhythm in AF.

FIGURE 11.2 — Stepwise Approach to Reduce Inappropriate Use of AADs for Maintenance of Sinus Rhythm in AF

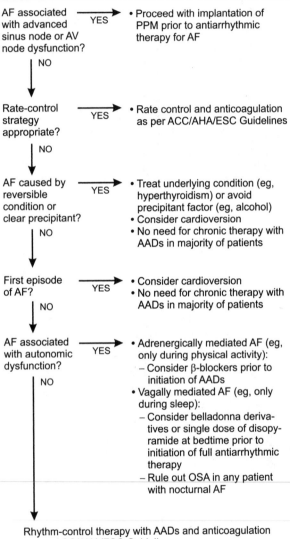

AF associated with advanced sinus node or AV node dysfunction? — **YES** →
- Proceed with implantation of PPM prior to antiarrhythmic therapy for AF

NO ↓

Rate-control strategy appropriate? — **YES** →
- Rate control and anticoagulation as per ACC/AHA/ESC Guidelines

NO ↓

AF caused by reversible condition or clear precipitant? — **YES** →
- Treat underlying condition (eg, hyperthyroidism) or avoid precipitant factor (eg, alcohol)
- Consider cardioversion
- No need for chronic therapy with AADs in majority of patients

NO ↓

First episode of AF? — **YES** →
- Consider cardioversion
- No need for chronic therapy with AADs in majority of patients

NO ↓

AF associated with autonomic dysfunction? — **YES** →
- Adrenergically mediated AF (eg, only during physical activity):
  - Consider β-blockers prior to initiation of AADs
- Vagally mediated AF (eg, only during sleep):
  - Consider belladonna derivatives or single dose of disopyramide at bedtime prior to initiation of full antiarrhythmic therapy
  - Rule out OSA in any patient with nocturnal AF

NO ↓

Rhythm-control therapy with AADs and anticoagulation as per ACC/AHA/ESC Guidelines

FIGURE 11.3 — 2011 ACCF/AHA/HRS Recommendations on Choice of AAD for Maintenance of Sinus Rhythm According to Underlying Pathology

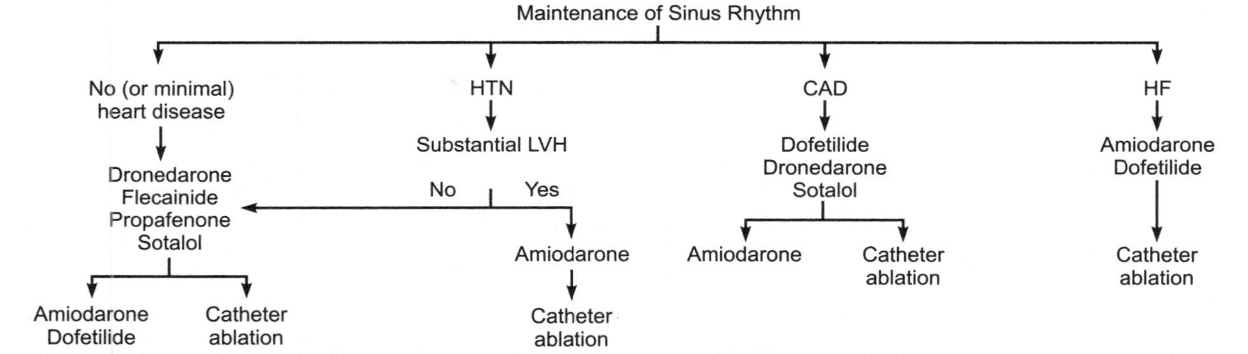

Maintenance of Sinus Rhythm

No (or minimal) heart disease

Dronedarone
Flecainide
Propafenone
Sotalol → Catheter ablation

Amiodarone
Dofetilide

HTN → Substantial LVH

No / Yes

Yes: Amiodarone → Catheter ablation

CAD

Dofetilide
Dronedarone
Sotalol → Catheter ablation

Amiodarone

HF

Amiodarone
Dofetilide → Catheter ablation

Therapy to maintain sinus rhythm in patients with recurrent paroxysmal or persistent AF. Drugs are listed alphabetically and not in order of suggested use. The seriousness of heart disease progresses from left to right, and selection of therapy in patients with multiple conditions depends on the most serious condition present.

Modified from 2011 ACCF/AHA/HRS Focused Update on the Management of Patients With Atrial Fibrillation (Updating the 2006 Guideline) [published online ahead of print December 20, 2010]. *J Am Coll Cardiol.* doi:10.1016/j.jacc.2010.10.001.

When AF is mediated by autonomic dysfunction in patients without structural heart disease, physiologic approaches modulating vagal or adrenergic activity should be attempted.

β-Blockers are the first-line therapy (followed by sotalol and dronedarone) in patients with adrenergically mediated AF, such as that occurring during stress or physical exercise.

For patients with vagally induced AF (eg, occurring with slow heart rates during sleep or in young athletes), the long-acting anticholinergic activity of disopyramide makes it an attractive AAD. Flecainide is a second-line agent. Propafenone should not be used in this setting because its weak intrinsic β-blocking activity may facilitate vagally mediated AF.

■ Hypertensive Patients With or Without LVH

In the absence of substantial LVH (wall thickness ≥1.4 cm), AF patients with hypertension are treated according to the same algorithm as patients without structural heart disease. Advanced LVH is associated with increased action potential duration, early ventricular after depolarizations, and subendocardial ischemia. This increases the risk of proarrhythmia of most AADs other than amiodarone, such that amiodarone is the agent of choice in the presence of significant LVH. Dronedarone may also be considered in AF patients with significant LVH, but definitive safety data are needed.

■ Patients With Coronary Artery Disease

Myocardial ischemia or scar tissue increases the risk of proarrhythmia in patients with CAD. Safety of AADs in CAD has been demonstrated for sotalol, dofetilide, and amiodarone. Dronedarone also appears to be safe in patients with coronary disease and paroxysmal or persistent AF. We recommend sotalol as a preferred first-line agent in patients with CAD who do not have HF or significant LVH. Amiodarone should be used with caution in elderly patients post-MI due to increased risk of bradycardia. Class IC agents should not be used in patients with coronary disease based on findings from CAST. In this trial, the use of flecainide or encainide to

208

suppress ventricular premature beats in patients post-MI was associated with increased mortality, presumably due to ventricular proarrhythmia. Although propafenone was not studied in CAST, it may carry similar risk of proarrhythmia due to its mechanism of action and, as such, is not recommended in patients with CAD.

■ Heart Failure Patients

Myocardial vulnerability, fibrotic ischemia changes, electrolyte imbalance, and presence of dilated or hypertrophic left ventricles in patients with HF contribute to the risk of proarrhythmia. In patients with an EF ≤40% or decompensated HF, amiodarone is the preferred AAD, due to its lack of significant proarrhythmic or negative inotropic effects. Organ toxicities with chronic therapy may be limited by using as low a dose as possible. Dofetilide was shown to be a well-tolerated and safe alternative to amiodarone in the DIAMOND study. Dofetilide does not have rate-control properties and should be used in conjunction with rate-lowering agents other than verapamil. Dronedarone is contraindicated in patients with NYHA Class IV or Class II-III HF with a recent decompensation. Class I agents should be avoided as well.

Initiation of Therapy

Initiation of antiarrhythmic therapy for AF is associated with an up to 10% to 15% risk of adverse cardiac events. This risk is highest in the first 24 hours, with ventricular proarrhythmia and severe bradycardia being the major concerns.

Many advise a 48- to 72-hour inpatient monitoring period to assess for major CV side effects of certain AADs. However, the risk of major cardiac side effects remains elevated for the duration of dosing (especially in high-risk patients on amiodarone). As such, frequent outpatient follow-up is generally recommended.

Current drug labeling mandates in-hospital monitoring for initiation of therapy with dofetilide and sotalol. The risk of TdP is approximately 2.5% for sotalol and 3%

for dofetilide but is higher in the presence of other risk factors, such as associated heart disease, renal dysfunction, and electrolyte abnormalities.

Rarely used Class IA AADs also require inpatient monitoring for institution of therapy.

In low-risk patients, prophylaxis against recurrent AF episodes may be started with certain AADs as outpatient therapy under careful observation and close follow-up.

In patients without structural heart disease who are in sinus rhythm, Class IC drugs (propafenone and flecainide) may be initiated in an out-hospital setting. Additional doses of medications can be then self-administrated for AF recurrences (booster dosing). This strategy was proven to be safe and effective in AF patients without sinus or AV node dysfunction, bundle-branch block, QT-interval prolongation, or structural heart disease, who underwent at least one attempt of in-hospital pharmacologic cardioversion. For reliable patients who do not want to use drugs all of the time and who have highly sporadic arrhythmia, these agents may be also used as a "pill-in-the-pocket" strategy for cardioversion of AF (see *Chapter 10*).

Amiodarone carries a low risk of proarrhythmia or hemodynamic compromise. As such, amiodarone can usually be initiated safely without an inpatient evaluation in patients without conduction abnormalities or risk factors for TdP (eg, hypokalemia, hypomagnesemia). The same applies to initiation of dronedarone. However, therapeutic anticoagulation should be achieved prior to initiation of these agents.

Although drug labeling recommends hospitalization for starting sotalol therapy, ACC/AHA/ESC Guidelines allow initiation of sotalol outside of the hospital in AF patients who meet all of the following criteria:
- Baseline uncorrected QT <450 msec
- No structural heart disease
- Serum electrolytes normal
- Other risk factors for proarrhythmia are considered.

In the outpatient setting, sotalol should be started at a low dose. The patient should have an ECG, looking for prolongation of the QT interval 24 to 48 hours after drug initiation and after any dose increase. Based on a patient's risk profile, more frequent follow-up visits may be necessary with other AADs initiated in an outpatient setting. Alternatively, continuous ECG surveillance may be used to monitor for cardiac rhythm and conduction disturbances, realizing that this does not provide the capacity to resuscitate the patient should a proarrhythmia occur (see *Chapter 6* and **Table 6.2** for options of continuous ECG recording).

The ICD provides protection against bradyarrhythmias or ventricular tachyarrhythmias, as well as providing monitoring of the therapy. As such, strict requirements of inpatient initiation of certain AADs may not always apply to carefully selected patients with ICDs.

The choice of AAD based on initiation setting is presented in **Table 11.5**.

TABLE 11.5 — Hospitalization Requirements for Initiation of AAD Therapy for Maintenance of Sinus Rhythm in AF

Hospitalization Required
- Dofetilide
- Sotalol[a]

Hospitalization Not Required in Majority of Patients
- Amiodarone
- Dronedarone[b]
- Flecainide
- Propafenone

[a] Allowed by ACC/AHA/ESC Guidelines for initiation out of the hospital in very carefully selected patients who can be strictly followed in an outpatient setting.
[b] Dronedarone is designed for initiation in an outpatient setting.

Combination Therapy

■ Combination of AADs With Preventive Therapies
Growing evidence supports the role of RAAS inhibition in the prevention of atrial remodeling. However, ACE inhibitor or ARB postcardioversion have not been

shown to have added benefit to AADs alone in the maintenance of NSR (see *Chapter 7*). ACE inhibitors or ARBs should be used in all AF patients with compelling indications for RAAS inhibition (eg, HF, LV systolic dysfunction, diabetes). The low risk of interaction with AADs and a possible role in the prevention of AF may make ACE inhibitors and ARBs first-choice agents for hypertensive patients with AF.

■ Combination of AAD With Rate-Control Agents

In patients with a history of AF associated with rapid ventricular response, rate-lowering agents are frequently added to AADs (Class IC or III) to prevent a rapid ventricular rate with paroxysms of AF. Additionally, AV nodal blockers may lower the risk of 1:1 AV conduction in patients who convert from AF to atrial flutter.

■ Combination of AADs

The combination of AADs in patients who either fail a single AAD or who develop side effects on doses necessary to prevent AF is not recommended and should be used only in certain circumstances. There are only limited data supporting efficacy of this approach. Additionally, even low doses of AADs used in combination have higher risk of proarrhythmia or drug toxicity. As such, alternative single-drug therapy, nonpharmacologic therapy, (eg, radiofrequency ablation), or a rate-control strategy should be considered.

Anticoagulation

Antiarrhythmic therapy to maintain NSR does not change the indication for anticoagulation in patients with AF. Importantly, a rhythm-control strategy should not be used with the goal of reducing embolic risk if there are contraindications to warfarin. In the AFFIRM and RACE trials, embolic risk was similar for patients treated with rate- and rhythm-control strategies. Asymptomatic recurrences of AF in patients treated with AAD therapy are presumably the reason for the embolic risk, and may be a major factor responsible for requiring anticoagulation in such patients.

Key characteristics of recommended AADs are presented below. Only properties related to chronic therapy for maintenance of sinus rhythm in AF are considered (characteristics of these agents relevant to pharmacologic cardioversion of AF are discussed in *Chapter 10* and **Tables 10.9** through **10.12**).

Review of each AAD is followed by a discussion of selected trials to support evidence-based characteristics of particular drugs.

■ **Amiodarone for Maintenance of Sinus Rhythm**
  General and Electrophysiologic Characteristics
  - Complex AAD, predominantly Class III drug, but also has Class I, II, and IV activity
  - Causes sinus bradycardia, increased PR and QRS duration, and QT prolongation

  Pharmacokinetics
  - Metabolized by the liver; no dose adjustment necessary in patients with renal failure because not renally eliminated
  - Highly lipophilic compound with a very large volume of distribution (involving multiple compartments) and very long half-life, usually >50 days (on average t½ 25-110 days)
  - Oral amiodarone has a slow onset of action (usually >48 hours) compared with IV amiodarone (1-12 hours)
  - Delayed effect of oral therapy necessitates oral or IV loading
  - Therapeutic serum level 1.0-2.5 mcg/mL (occasionally used in monitoring of therapy)

  Role in Maintenance of Sinus Rhythm
  - Most effective drug available for maintenance of sinus rhythm in patients with paroxysmal or persistent AF *(see trials 1-4 below)*

11

- Agent of choice in AF patients at increased risk of proarrhythmia, ie, advanced HF or structural heart disease *(see trial 5 below)*
- Highly effective for prevention of AF after cardiac surgery *(see trial 6 below)*
- Significant risk of extracardiac toxicity makes it a second-line choice in the majority of patients with AF
- Provides rate control during breakthrough episodes of AF
- Chronic therapy associated with increased efficacy of electrical cardioversion for recurrence of AF
- Low-dose therapy may be started in outpatient settings in patients who do not have underlying heart disease, marked bradycardia, signs of sinus node disease, or a prolonged QTc

Dosing

- There is no uniformly accepted dosing recommendation for amiodarone loading and maintenance therapy. Most commonly used protocols are presented below
- Oral loading dose of 800 mg/day in two divided doses for 2 weeks, followed by maintenance dose of 200 to 400 mg/day and lowered at 3 to 6 months to 100 to 300 mg/day
- IV loading dose of 150 mg (over 10 minutes) or 300 mg (over 30 minutes) boluses, followed by continuous infusion of 1 mg/minute over 6 hours, then 0.5 mg/minute (up to 1.2 g in the first 24 hours a day). Then continue infusion at 0.5 mg/hour (720 mg/day) or change to oral loading/maintenance as above. Supplemental infusions of 150 mg may be necessary
- Total dose of ~8 g to 10 g of amiodarone usually required for full loading
- Higher daily loading doses often associated with increased risk of side effects: GI upset when given orally, or hypotension and phlebitis when given IV
- A new, captisol-based formulation of IV amiodarone (Nexterone) may be easier to administer and appears to be devoid of hypotensive effect

- Maintenance therapy with low-dose amiodarone (≤200 mg daily) is more effective than other AADs for maintenance of sinus rhythm and may be associated with fewer side effects than higher doses of amiodarone

Adverse Effects

- Most of the side effects are dose dependent; however, even at low doses (mean 152 to 330 mg/day), amiodarone was shown to be associated with discontinuation rates 50% higher than placebo
- Causes clinically significant bradycardia in about 5% of patients, which may require pacing or discontinuation of therapy in about 2% of patients
- Low risk of TdP (unless used in combination with other QT-prolonging drugs)
- Extracardiac side effects associated with chronic therapy lead to discontinuation of amiodarone in up to 20% of patients. Almost all organ systems may be affected:
  - Pulmonary: risk is about 1% per year and requires discontinuation of therapy. Toxicity may present as interstitial pneumonitis (potentially leading to pulmonary fibrosis), bronchiolitis obliterans, adult respiratory distress syndrome (ARDS), or a solitary pulmonary mass
  - Endocrine: amiodarone-induced hypothyroidism occurs in about 8 % of patients, hyperthyroidism in about 2%. The former may be treated with thyroid replacement but the latter is potentially fatal and requires discontinuation of therapy. Testicular dysfunction may also develop with chronic amiodarone therapy
  - GI: very rarely, amiodarone may induce potentially fatal hepatitis. Commonly, an asymptomatic transient elevation of hepatic enzymes is noted. This may be dose related at initiation of therapy and may not preclude a rechallenge with a lower dose. GI intolerance is also frequent (eg, nausea can occur in up to 25% of patients with CHF treated with amiodarone)

11

- Neurologic: peripheral neuropathy and myopathy causing abnormal gait (usually improves with lowering the dose). Tremors are frequently noted
- Ocular: optic neuritis (potentially causing blindness) requires immediate discontinuation of therapy. Corneal microdeposits do not reduce visual acuity and do not require does adjustment or discontinuation of therapy
- Skin: photosensitivity of the skin is common with chronic therapy with amiodarone and may be alleviated by avoidance of sun exposure and use of a sunblock. Blue-gray skin discoloration occurs in up to 3% of patients, is dose dependent, and requires dose reduction or discontinuation of the therapy
- Causes partial inhibition of tubular transport of creatinine, which leads to increases in serum creatinine concentration that is not related to reduced glomerular filtration
- Due to risk of adverse events, patients treated with amiodarone should have follow-up visits and laboratory testing at least every 3 months for the first year, then every 6 months

Contraindications

- Advanced sinus node disease or AV conduction disease greater than first-degree AV block
- Severe chronic lung disease or advanced liver failure

Major Drug or Device Interactions

- Increases risk of bleeding in patients on warfarin (dose of warfarin needs to be decreased by one third initially with INR surveillance). It also increases serum digoxin level, predisposing to digitalis toxicity (dose of digoxin usually needs to be decreased by one half initially). The combination of amiodarone with simvastatin in doses >20 mg is not recommended because of an increased risk of myopathy and rhabdomyolysis

- May have additive proarrhythmic effects with other drugs that prolong the QT interval (eg, should not be used together with sotalol unless an ICD is in place) and increases risk of bradyarrhythmias if used with other AV nodal agents. However, its antiarrhythmic activity is potentiated by β-blockers
- In patients with an ICD, amiodarone may increase the defibrillation threshold and requires device interrogation prior to discharge from the hospital or upon completion of the loading dose

Amiodarone for Maintenance of Sinus Rhythm: Results of Selected Studies

1. A systematic review of 44 randomized trials (11,322 patients) with at least 6 months follow-up examined the safety and efficacy of Class IA (disopyramide, quinidine), Class IC (flecainide, propafenone), and Class III (amiodarone, dofetilide, sotalol) AADs for the treatment of AF. All AADs reduced recurrence of AF, and amiodarone was found to be the most effective AAD. All AADs were associated with an increased risk of discontinuation due to adverse events, and all except amiodarone and propafenone had a proarrhythmic effect. Class IA agents were associated with an increased mortality.

2. In SAFE-T, amiodarone was more effective than sotalol and placebo for maintaining sinus rhythm in patients with AF. The recurrence rates of AF at 1 year were 48% with amiodarone, 68% with sotalol, and 87% in the placebo group. A higher incidence of minor bleeding episodes was noted in the amiodarone group, likely because of interaction with warfarin (for detailed discussion on SAFE-T study, please the section entitled *Sotalol for Maintenance of Sinus Rhythm: Results of Selected Trials*).

3. In a substudy of the AFFIRM trial, patients in the rhythm-control arm were randomly assigned to initial antiarrhythmic therapy with amiodarone, sotalol, or a Class I drug. The primary end point was defined as patients being alive, in sinus rhythm, without need for

11

cardioversion, and still taking the same drug at 1 year. At 1 year, the likelihood of the primary end point was significantly higher with amiodarone compared with sotalol (60% vs 38%) or amiodarone compared with a Class I drug, (62% vs 23%).

4. The CTAF was a prospective, multicenter trial designed to test the hypothesis that low doses of amiodarone would be more effective in preventing recurrent AF than sotalol or propafenone. Amiodarone was given in a dose of 10 mg/kg of body weight daily for 14 days, followed by 300 mg/day for 4 weeks, after which a daily maintenance dose of 200 mg was given. Of the 403 patients in the study, 201 were assigned to amiodarone, and 202 to either sotalol (101 patients) or propafenone (101 patients). After a mean follow-up of 16 months, the recurrence rate was lowest in the amiodarone group, 35% vs 63% in the sotalol or propafenone groups. Similarly, the median time to recurrence of AF was longer for amiodarone than for sotalol or propafenone (>468 vs 98 days). Adverse events requiring the discontinuation of drug therapy were more common in the amiodarone group (18% vs 11%) (**Figure 11.4**).

FIGURE 11.4 — Kaplan-Meier Estimates of the Percentage of Patients Remaining Free of Recurrence of AF in CTAF

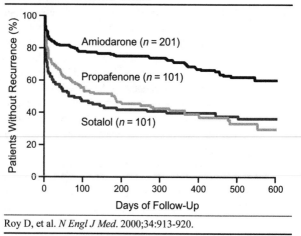

Roy D, et al. *N Engl J Med.* 2000;34:913-920.

5. In a post hoc analysis of the Veterans Affairs Congestive Heart Failure: Survival Trial of Antiarrhythmic Therapy, amiodarone facilitated conversion to and maintenance of sinus rhythm in patients with LV systolic dysfunction and NYHA Class II to IV symptoms of HF. Furthermore, the subset of patients who were maintained in sinus rhythm on amiodarone had a lower overall mortality compared with those who did not convert to sinus rhythm. Amiodarone did not lead to worsening of HF.

6. In a small, double-blind, randomized study, amiodarone was evaluated as a prophylactic therapy to prevent AF after cardiac surgery. Compared with placebo, amiodarone (dosed at 600 mg/day for 7 days prior to surgery, then 200 mg/day until the day of discharge from the hospital) significantly decreased the incidence of postoperative AF (53% vs 25%) and the duration of hospital stay (7.9 vs 6.5 days), as well as reducing hospitalization costs. No significant increase in postoperative complications was noted in the amiodarone group.

■ Dronedarone for Maintenance of Sinus Rhythm
General and Electrophysiologic Characteristics

- Amiodarone derivative, structurally modified by removal of the iodine moiety (to reduce organ toxicity) and the addition of a methylsulfonamide group (to decrease lipophilicity and reduce half-life and tissue accumulation)
- Multichannel blocking properties similar to those of amiodarone, more potent blocker of peak sodium current and I_{K-Ach} current, stronger anti-adrenergic effect compared with amiodarone

Pharmacokinetics

- Metabolized by the liver with a half-life elimination of 24 hours
- No dose adjustment needed in renal failure, although caution should be used at very low GFRs of <30
- Absorption increases 2- to 3-fold when it is taken with food

- Steady-state plasma concentrations reached in 7 days
- Has reverse dose effect on rhythm control such that using higher than recommended doses decreases its efficacy in maintenance of sinus rhythm *(see trial 1 below)*

Role in Maintenance of Sinus Rhythm
- Proven to reduce symptomatic and asymptomatic recurrences of AF *(see trial 2 below)*
- First AAD shown to reduce death and CV hospitalizations in patients with paroxysmal and persistent AF *(see trial 5 below)*
- Contraindicated in patients with permanent AF (ie, who will not or cannot be cardioverted into normal sinus rhythm). In this subset of patients with AF, dronedarone doubles the risk of death, stroke, and hospitalization for heart failure *(see trial 9 below)*
- Associated with increased mortality when used with advanced HF and severe LV dysfunction *(see trial 4 below)*
- Reduces ventricular rate during AF recurrence
- Not as effective as amiodarone for maintenance of sinus rhythm in patients in AF but associated with less adverse events and lower discontinuation rates *(see trial 7 below)*
- Comparative efficacy against other AADs (except amiodarone) not yet available
- In the contrast to other AADs, initiation of dronedarone within <48 hours after discontinuation of amiodarone (in patients without significant bradycardia or prolonged QTc) appears to be safe and not associated with increased risk of proarrhythmia. Dronedarone may be the agent of choice for patients who stop amiodarone due to serious side effects (with exception of liver toxicity) but need prompt therapy for prevention of AF. However, more prospective data are needed at this point *(see trial 8 below)*

Recommended Dosing

- Available only for oral administration at 400 mg twice daily
- Dose adjustment or titration is not recommended

Adverse Effects

- Adverse reactions leading to discontinuation of therapy most commonly include GI side effects (eg, diarrhea, nausea, abdominal pain) in up to 25% of patients, and asthenia, rash, and bradycardia in 3% *(see trials 1-5 below)*
- Rare cases of liver toxicity (including acute liver failure requiring liver transplant) have been reported
- Not associated with other significant risks of organ toxicity with maximum follow-up of 30 months *(see trials 1-5 below)*
- Causes dose-dependent prolongation of QTc interval in 30% of patients, but TdP is rare *(see trials 1-5 below)*
- May increase serum creatinine level by ~0.1 mg/mL due to partial inhibition of tubular secretion of creatinine. This effect peaks ~7 days, is reversible, and is not associated with reduced renal function *(see trials 1-5 below)*. More pronounced but also reversible increases of creatinine (with or without BUN elevation) have been recently reported

Contraindications

- Permanent AF
- Patients with NYHA Class IV HF or NYHA Class II-III HF with recent decompensation requiring hospitalization or referral to a specialized HF clinic. Discontinuation of dronedarone should be considered in patients who develop any new or worsening symptoms of HF *(see trial 4 below)*
- Severe liver impairment, history of liver toxicity with amiodarone use, bradycardia (<50 BPM), sick sinus syndrome, marked first-degree (PR interval >280 msec) or higher AV block, prolong

11

QTc ≥500 msec at baseline, or coadministration with other agents prolonging QT interval
- Women who are or may become pregnant (pregnancy category X). Effective birth control is recommended in premenopausal woman treated with this agent

Major Drug Interactions

- Metabolized by the CYP3A4 isoenzyme system and should not be used together with potent CYP3A4 inhibitors (eg, antifungals, macrolide antibiotics, or protease inhibitors). Dronedarone requires dose reduction to avoid bradyarrhythmias when coadministered with moderate CYP3A4 inhibitors (verapamil and diltiazem). Dronedarone results in a 2- to 4-fold increase in simvastatin levels (CYP3A4 substrate), which may lead to statin-induced myopathy
- Causes ~2.5-fold increase in serum digoxin concentration, necessitates digoxin level monitoring, and digoxin dose reduction by half
- May increase tacrolimus or sirolimus levels in post- transplant patients; requires dose monitoring and adjustment during therapy with these agents

Dronedarone for Maintenance of Sinus Rhythm: Results of Selected Studies

1. The Dronedarone Atrial Fibrillation Study After Electrical Cardioversion (DAFNE) was a double-blind, randomized, placebo-controlled study conducted to determine the appropriate dose of dronedarone for maintenance of AF after cardioversion. Two hundred seventy patients with persistent AF were randomized to therapy with 800, 1200, or 1600 mg dronedarone daily vs placebo and were then followed for 6 months. Compared with placebo, dronedarone delayed the time to first AF recurrence but only at the lowest dose of 800 mg daily (60 days vs 5.3 days). At 6 months, 35% of patients treated with 800 mg of dronedarone daily were in sinus rhythm compared with 10% in the placebo group. No signs of organ toxicity (eg, pulmo-

nary, thyroid, ocular, hepatic) were seen in any of the dronedarone groups during 6 months of follow-up. GI side effects were the main reason for discontinuation of dronedarone. Importantly, although therapy with dronedarone led to dose-dependent prolongation of the QT interval, no proarrhythmic effects (particularly TdP) were observed.

2. The European Trial in Atrial Fibrillation or Flutter Patients Receiving Dronedarone for the Maintenance of Sinus Rhythm (EURIDIS) and the American-Australian-African Trial with Dronedarone in Atrial Fibrillation or Flutter Patients for the Maintenance of Sinus Rhythm (ADONIS) further studied the efficacy of dronedarone at a dose of 400 mg twice a day. Time to first AF or atrial flutter recurrence over 12 months was a primary end point, and mean the ventricular rate during AF or atrial flutter recurrences was a secondary end point. Both trials enrolled a total of 1237 patients in sinus rhythm with a history of at least one episode of AF or atrial flutter during the previous 3 months. The patients were randomized in a 2:1 ratio to dronedarone 400 mg twice daily or placebo. The mean age of the study population was 63 years. Although up to 40% patients in both trials had evidence of structural heart disease, the majority of patients had normal LVEF (mean EF 58%) and only a mildly dilated LA (mean 4.2 cm). Patients with mild HF (NYHA I or II) comprised 17% of the study population. Patients with NYHA Class III or IV were excluded from the study.

In the combined results from the two trials, the median time to the first recurrence of AF was 116 days in the dronedarone group compared with 53 days in the placebo arm. Dronedarone reduced the ventricular rate during AF recurrence by a mean of 12 to 15 BPM. A post hoc analysis of these studies showed a 27% reduction of RR of hospitalization and death with dronedarone therapy. Therapy with dronedarone 400 mg twice a day resulted in a similar rate of cardiac and noncardiac adverse events as placebo. A mild increase in serum creatinine in 2.4% of the patients treated with dronedarone was noted.

3. The Efficacy and Safety of Dronedarone for the Control of Ventricular Rate (ERATO) study showed that in patients who had symptomatic permanent AF, dronedarone significantly reduced both resting (by 12 BPM) and maximal exercise heart rates (25 BPM) compared with placebo. However, based on data from the recently terminated PALLAS trial *(see below)*, dronedarone is contradicted in patients with permanent AF.

4. The Antiarrhythmic Trial With Dronedarone in Moderate-to-Severe Congestive Heart Failure Evaluating Morbidity Decrease (ANDROMEDA) was a double-blind, placebo-controlled study evaluating the effect of dronedarone on mortality in high-risk patients who had CHF and ventricular dysfunction. This was not a study of patients with AF, although about a third of patients had AF and suppression of AF was included as a secondary end point of the trial. The primary end point of the study was death or hospitalization for HF. Eligible patients with an EF ≤35% and a history of NYHA class III or IV symptoms within a month were randomized to receive dronedarone 400 mg twice a day or placebo. At the time of randomization, 98% of patient were classified as NYHA class II and III and only 2% were Class IV. The study enrolled 627 patients (310 in the dronedarone group and 317 in the placebo group). After median therapy duration of 2 months, the trial was prematurely stopped. During this relatively short follow-up, a total of 25 patients in the dronedarone arm (8.1%) and 12 patients in the placebo group (3.8%) died. Deaths were predominantly due to worsening HF; there was no evidence of an increased incidence of proarrhythmia or sudden cardiac death in dronedarone group. The risk of death and hospitalization was highest in patients with the most advanced LV systolic dysfunction. Possible causes of increased mortality in patients with advanced HF have not been fully elucidated but may have been contributed to by withdrawal of HF therapy.

5. A trial called Assess the Efficacy of Dronedarone for the Prevention of Cardiovascular Hospitalization or Death From Any Cause in Patients With Atrial Fibrillation/Atrial Flutter (ATHENA) was a placebo-controlled,

double-blind, parallel-arm study to determine whether dronedarone would decrease the rate of hospitalization due to CV events or death in patients with AF. A total of 4628 patients with a history of paroxysmal or persistent AF/atrial flutter and at least one CV risk factor (age >70, hypertension, diabetes mellitus, prior CVA or transient ischemic attack, LA >50 mm, EF ≤40%) were randomized to dronedarone 400 mg twice a day or placebo. Only 21% of patients had a history of NYHA Class II or III HF symptoms, and 12% had an LVEF ≤45%. Patients with unstable hemodynamic conditions, ie, decompensated HF within the previous 4 weeks and NYHA Class IV CHF, were excluded from the study. The mean follow-up period was 21 ± 5 months.

The primary outcome (all-cause mortality and first CV hospitalization) occurred in 734 patients (31.9%) in the dronedarone arm and in 917 patients (39.4%) in the placebo arm. All-cause mortality was lower with dronedarone, 5.0% vs 6.0%. First hospitalization due to CV events occurred less often in the dronedarone arm, 29.3% vs 36.9%. Death and hospitalization due to HF were similar in the treatment groups, but interestingly, there were significantly less hospitalizations for an ACS in the dronedarone group. **Figure 11.5** presents the cumulative incidence of the primary and secondary outcomes in the ATHENA trial. Premature discontinuation of the study drug was high in both groups at about 30%. GI side effects were the main reason for drug discontinuation. Treatment with dronedarone was not associated with a significant risk of thyroid or pulmonary disorders. Significant QT prolongation was reported in 1.7% of patients treated with dronedarone but was not associated with more documented proarrhythmia. As noted in other trials, a mild increase in creatinine level was noted in 5% of patients treated with dronedarone and was not associated with deterioration of renal function.

6. Post hoc analysis of ATHENA *(see below)* showed a reduction in stroke in patients who were randomized to dronedarone therapy and were otherwise receiving usual care, including antithrombotic therapy and heart rate control. In the ATHENA study, the baseline risk

225

FIGURE 11.5 — Kaplan-Meier Cumulative Incidences of the Primary and Secondary Outcomes in the ATHENA Trial

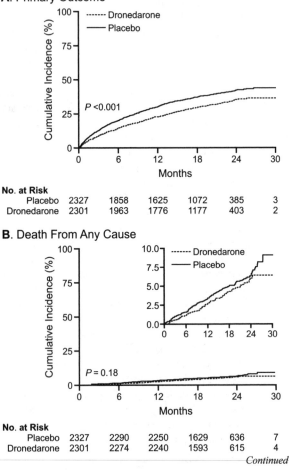

A. Primary Outcome

No. at Risk

Placebo	2327	1858	1625	1072	385	3
Dronedarone	2301	1963	1776	1177	403	2

B. Death From Any Cause

No. at Risk

Placebo	2327	2290	2250	1629	636	7
Dronedarone	2301	2274	2240	1593	615	4

Continued

FIGURE 11.5 — *Continued*

C. Death From Cardiovascular Causes

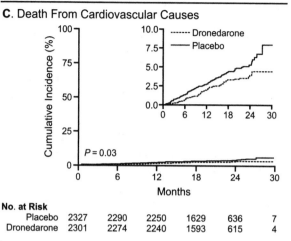

No. at Risk

Placebo	2327	2290	2250	1629	636	7
Dronedarone	2301	2274	2240	1593	615	4

D. First Hospitalization Due to Cardiovascular Events

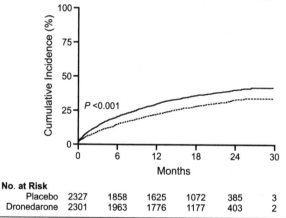

No. at Risk

Placebo	2327	1858	1625	1072	385	3
Dronedarone	2301	1963	1776	1177	403	2

Treatment with dronedarone significantly reduced the occurrence of the composite primary outcome of first hospitalization due to cardiovascular events or death from any cause (hazard ratio [HR] 0.76) *(A)*, secondary outcomes of death from cardiovascular causes (HR 0.71) *(C)*, and first hospitalization due to cardiovascular events (HR 0.74) *(D)*. There was no difference in all-cause mortality (HR 0.84) *(B)*.

Modified from Hohnloser SH, et al. *N Engl J Med.* 2009;360:668-678.

factors for stroke were equally balanced between the placebo and dronedarone arms. The mean CHADS2 score was 2 in both groups and the initial use of either oral anticoagulant therapy or an antiplatelet agent alone was 60%. The risk of stroke was 1.2% per year in the dronedarone group compared with 1.8% per year in the placebo arm. The cumulative risks of stroke and composite outcome of stroke, ACS, or CV death are shown in **Figure 11.6**.

FIGURE 11.6 — Cumulative Risk of Stroke *(A)* and Composite Outcome of Stroke, Acute Coronary Syndrome, or Cardiovascular Death *(B)*

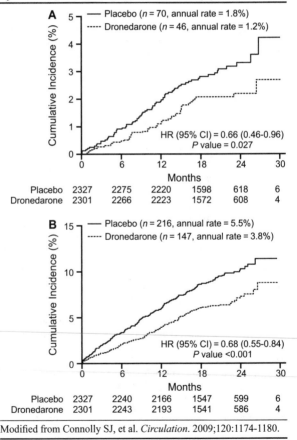

Modified from Connolly SJ, et al. *Circulation*. 2009;120:1174-1180.

The risk reduction was independent of whether patients were receiving oral anticoagulant therapy and was more pronounced in patients with a higher CHADS2 score. Until confirmed by further studies, these results of the post hoc analysis, although intriguing, should not lead to the conclusion that dronedarone prevents strokes in patients with AF.

7. A meta-analysis of four placebo-controlled trials of dronedarone, four placebo-controlled trials of amiodarone and one trial of dronedarone vs amiodarone (the DIONYSOS study) evaluated the efficacy and safety of both agents for the prevention of recurrences of AF. This analysis concluded that amiodarone is superior to dronedarone for the prevention of recurrent AF, but that amiodarone showed a trend toward all-cause mortality and a greater overall adverse-event rate requiring drug discontinuation.

   It was estimated that for every 1000 patients treated with dronedarone instead of amiodarone, there are approximately 228 more recurrences of AF in exchange for 9.6 fewer deaths and 62 fewer adverse events requiring discontinuation of drug.

8. Post hoc analysis of the EURIDIS and ADONIS trials examined the safety of starting dronedarone in patients being previously treated with amiodarone. Ninety-eight patients started dronedarone within 48 hours of stopping amiodarone. Dronedarone's efficacy for reducing the rate of AF recurrence was the same for those who received amiodarone within 48 hours of study initiation and those who did not. Rates of serious side events, including bradyarrhythmia, were similar in the groups. Adverse events, especially bradyarrhythmias, leading to drug discontinuation were slightly higher for patients treated with dronedarone compared with placebo regardless of time since amiodarone withdrawal. No episodes of TdP were reported.

9. PALLAS (Permanent Atrial Fibrillation Outcome Study Using Dronedarone on Top of Standard Therapy) trial was designed to evaluate the effectiveness of dronedarone in patients with permanent AF and additional risk factors for thromboembolism (CAD, prior stroke or TIA, symptomatic HF, LVEF <40%, PAD, or age

11

>75 with hypertension and diabetes mellitus). After enrollment of 3236 patients (who were randomized to placebo vs dronedarone 400 mg twice daily) and a median follow-up of <4 months, the study was terminated because of a significantly higher number of CV events in the dronedarone-treated group. During this short follow-up period, 25 patients died in dronedarone group vs 13 in placebo group (HR 1.94, CI 0.99-3.79) with the majority of deaths in the dronedarone group due to arrhythmia/sudden death (HR 3.26, CI 1.06-10.0). Stroke occurred in 23 patients in dronedarone vs 10 in placebo group (HR 2.32, CI 1.11-4.88). The increased risk of stroke with dronedarone was observed in the first 2 weeks of therapy and majority of dronedarone-treated patients did not have an INR of 2.0-3.0. Hospitalizations for heart failure were also higher in the dronedarone group (HR 1.81, CI 1.10-2.99). Based on these striking results, dronedarone is contraindicated in patients with permanent AF.

■ Sotalol for Maintenance of Sinus Rhythm
General and Electrophysiologic Characteristics

- Racemic mixture of d-isomer (blocks I_{Kr}) and l-isomer (prolongs repolarization and exhibits β-blocking activity)
- Combined Class II (β-blocking) and Class III activity (present in doses >160/mg/day)
- Noncardioselective, hydrophilic β-blocker without intrinsic sympathomimetic activity
- Effect on the action potential duration shows reverse-use dependence (QT interval prolongs as the heart rate slows), with decreased antiarrhythmic efficacy at higher heart rates
- Electrocardiographic effects include sinus bradycardia (sinus rate decreases by about 25%), and prolonged PR and QT intervals in a dose-dependent manner. QRS duration is not altered (increase in the QT interval results solely from the JT interval). Doses between 160-640 mg/day show an increased in QTc interval (which is corrected for the heart rate) by 10-40 msec

Pharmacokinetics
- Plasma half-life ~12 hours
- Not metabolized by liver; excreted solely by the kidneys

Role in Maintenance of Sinus Rhythm
- Drug of choice for maintenance of sinus rhythm in AF patients with CAD *(see trial 1 below)*
- Reasonable alternative for patients with postoperative AF in whom β-blockers have failed but cannot tolerate amiodarone *(see trial 3 below)*
- Useful for monotherapy in highly symptomatic patients with lone AF (β-blocking activity contributes to decreased heart rate and symptoms with paroxysmal AF)

Recommended Dosing
- Preferably to be initiated in-hospital and requires 3 days of monitoring while the dose is titrated based on QTc and renal function
  - Initial dose 80-160 mg/day
  - Therapeutic response usually with 160 to 320 mg/day
- Dosing intervals depend on creatinine clearance (CrCl)
  - CrCl >60 mL/minute (2-3 times a day)
  - CrCl 40-60 mL/minute (once daily)
  - CrCl <40 mL/minute (contraindicated)

Adverse Effects
- Well tolerated; major causes of discontinuation include fatigue (especially in younger patients), bradycardia, and proarrhythmia
- Cardiac side effects include sinus bradycardia (10% to 15%), advanced AV block (<1%), decompensation of HF (1.5% to 3%), and TdP (~2.5%)
- Abrupt discontinuation may cause side effect related to β-blocking withdrawal
- Increased risk of TdP with doses >320 mg/day (0.3% with 320 mg/day, up to 3.2% with higher doses), serum creatinine >1.4 mg/dL (women)

and >1.6 mg/dL (men), bradycardia, baseline QTc >450 msec, severe LV dysfunction, female gender

Contraindications

- Reduced CrCl <40 mL/minute, QTc >500 msec, significant LVH (>1.4 cm), advanced HF, or LV systolic dysfunction (EF <40%)
- Contraindications to β blockade (eg, sick sinus syndrome, advanced AV block, severe asthma)

Major Drug Interactions

- Because of risk of TdP, cotherapy with other QT-prolonging drugs has to be avoided
- Initiation of therapy requires previous AAD to be discontinued for >2 to 3 half-lives (after stopping amiodarone, sotalol should not be started until the QTc normalizes)

Sotalol for Maintenance of Sinus Rhythm: Results of Selected Studies

1. In the Sotalol Amiodarone Atrial Fibrillation Efficacy Trial (SAFE-T), 665 patients with persistent AF were randomized to receive amiodarone, sotalol, or placebo. Electrical cardioversion was performed if sinus rhythm was not restored by 28 days. Interestingly, therapy with amiodarone and sotalol were equally efficient and more so than placebo by 28 days in converting to NSR (27.7% and 26.5% vs 0.8%, respectively). Patients were then continued on the same drug regimen and followed for 1 to 4.5 years. Recurrence rates at 1 year were 48% with amiodarone, 68% with sotalol, and 87% in the placebo group. The median time to recurrence beginning after day 28 was 487 days (amiodarone group), 74 days (sotalol group), and 6 days (placebo). Among patients with ischemic heart disease (approximately 25% in the trial), the median time to recurrence of AF was not significantly different for amiodarone and sotalol (569 vs 428 days) (**Figure 11.7**).
2. Results of CTAF suggest that sotalol is inferior to amiodarone but equally effective as propafenone in maintenance of sinus rhythm (for detailed discus-

FIGURE 11.7 — Kaplan-Meier Estimates of the Time to Recurrence of AF in SAFE-T

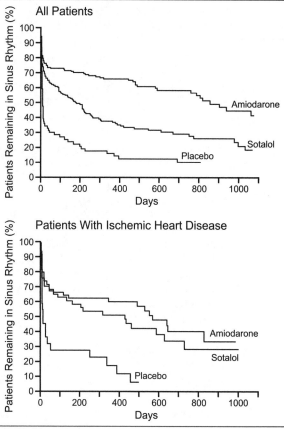

Modified from Singh BN, et al. *New Engl J Med.* 2005;352:1861-1872.

sion on CTAF, see section entitled *Amiodarone for Maintenance of Sinus Rhythm: Results of Selected Trials*).

3. A systematic review of 52 randomized trials of β-blockers, sotalol, amiodarone, or pacing for prevention of AF in patients undergoing cardiac surgery showed that all drugs and pacing were effective in preventing AF. All of these therapies also decreased

11

length of hospital stay but did not reduce postoperative risk of stroke.

■ Dofetilide for Maintenance of Sinus Rhythm

General and Electrophysiologic Characteristics

- Class III AAD; selectively blocks I_{Kr}
- Increases atrial and ventricular effective refractory period, prolongs repolarization (increases QT interval without changing PR or QRS interval)
- Exhibits reverse-use dependency (greater prolongation of repolarization and refractory period with slower heart rates)
- Favorable hemodynamic profile (ie, does not exert inotropic negative effect)

Pharmacokinetics

- Plasma concentrations peak in 2 to 3 hours after oral dosing
- About 80% of dofetilide is excreted by the kidney (cationic renal secretion), while 20% is metabolized by the liver (via the CYP3A4 isoenzyme) and the metabolites are then excreted by the kidney
- Elimination half-life of 8 to 10 hours after oral or IV administration

Role in Maintenance of Sinus Rhythm

- Effective in maintenance of sinus rhythm in AF and not associated with organ toxicity with chronic use; however, risk of proarrhythmia (TdP) limits its use in the majority of patients with AF *(see trial 1 below)*
- Safe when used cautiously in post–MI and HF patients with no effect on mortality *(see trial 2 below)*
- Recommended as a first-line agent in AF patients with severe LV dysfunction or HF and second-line agent for AF patients with ischemic heart disease *(see trial 2 below)*
- Does not exert rate-control activity
- Initiation of the therapy restricted only to registered hospital and medical personnel *(see trials 1-2 below)*

Recommended Dosing, Adverse Effects, and Contraindications

- TdP may occur in up to 4% of patients and initiation of dofetilide is contraindicated if baseline QTc is >440 msec or CrCl <20 mL/min
- Majority of TdP occurs within 3 days of starting therapy and patients must be hospitalized for drug initiation for 3 days with dosing based on CrCl and QTc interval (**Figure 11.8**)
- If at any point QTc is ≥500 msec (550 msec in patients with ventricular conduction abnormalities), therapy should be stopped and patients should be monitored until QTc returns to baseline level
- Due to risk of proarrhythmia, cotherapy with various agents increasing dofetilide levels is contraindicated *(see below)*
- Chronic therapy requires follow-up with renal function and QTc assessment every 3 to 6 months

Major Drug Interactions

- Use of other QTc-prolonging drugs with dofetilide is contraindicated
- Previous antiarrhythmic therapy has to be discontinued for ≥3 plasma half-lives prior to starting dofetilide
- Due to unpredictable pharmacokinetics of amiodarone, dofetilide cannot be initiated <3 months after discontinuation of amiodarone or until amiodarone plasma level is ≤0.3 mcg/mL
- Thiazide diuretic (alone or in combination) should be avoided due to increased risk of proarrhythmia with electrolyte imbalance
- Risk of TdP with dofetilide has to be considered during cotherapy with drugs that potentially cause significant bradycardia (reverse-use dependence)
- Verapamil may increase peak plasma levels of dofetilide by almost 40% and therefore should not be used in patients treated with dofetilide
- Concomitant use of cation transport system inhibitors in the kidney, eg, cimetidine, trimethoprim,

11

FIGURE 11.8 — Initiation of Dofetilide Therapy With Dosing Based on CrCl and QTc

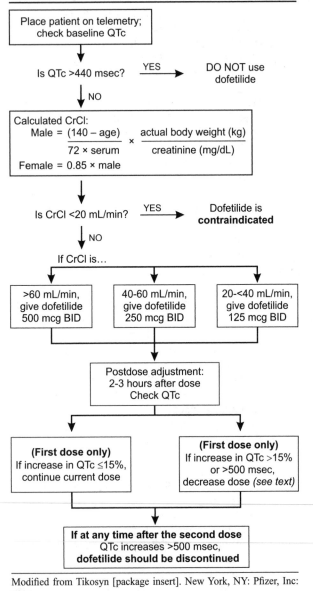

Modified from Tikosyn [package insert]. New York, NY: Pfizer, Inc: 2006.

ketoconazole, prochlorperazine and megestrol, and potent inhibitors of the CYP3A4 system, including cimetidine and ketoconazole, may significantly raise serum dofetilide level and are contraindicated

Dofetilide for Maintenance of Sinus Rhythm: Results of Selected Studies

1. The Symptomatic Atrial Fibrillation Investigative Research on Dofetilide (SAFIRE-D) was a double-blind, multicenter, placebo-controlled study that examined the safety and efficacy of dofetilide for conversion of AF or atrial flutter to sinus rhythm and for maintenance of sinus rhythm for 1 year. Three hundred twenty-five patients who had persistent AF or atrial flutter were randomized to 125-, 250-, or 500-mcg dofetilide or placebo twice daily. Dofetilide dosing was reduced for impaired renal function and for prolongation of the QTc over 15% of baseline. Pharmacologic cardioversion rates for placebo and 125-, 250-, and 500-mcg dofetilide twice daily were 1.2 % vs 6.1%, 9.8%, and 29.9%, respectively. The probability of remaining in sinus rhythm at 1 year was 25% vs 40%, 37%, and 58% for placebo and 125-, 250-, and 500-mcg dofetilide, respectively. The all-cause mortality was similar in all four groups and a lower incidence of TdP (0.8%) compared with the DIAMOND studies was reported.

Similar results were reported in the European and Australian Multicenter Evaluative Research on Atrial Fibrillation and Dofetilide (EMERALD) trial. In this study, AF patients were randomized to either three doses of dofetilide (125, 250, or 500 mcg twice daily), sotalol (80 mg twice daily), or placebo. At 1 year, among patients who entered the maintenance phase of the study, 16% of the placebo group, 38% of the sotalol group, and 30%, 45%, and 51% of the 125-mcg, 250-mcg, and 500-mcg dofetilide twice daily, respectively, remained in sinus rhythm. Higher dosing of dofetilide appeared to be associated with an increased risk of TdP.

2. The Danish Investigations of Arrhythmia and Mortality on Dofetilide (DIAMOND) study group in two large randomized control trials (DIAMOND-CHF and

DIAMOND-AF) examined the safety of dofetilide in HF patients.

In DIAMOND-CHF, 1518 patients with severe symptomatic LV dysfunction (NYHA Class III and IV) were randomized to dofetilide or placebo. After a median of 18 months of follow-up, there was no difference in the primary end point of all-cause mortality in both groups (41% vs 42%). Therapy with dofetilide significantly reduced the risk of hospitalization for decompensation of HF. There was a 3.3% incidence of TdP in the dofetilide group. The peak increase in the corrected QT interval occurred within the first 2 days of treatment and 76% of TdP cases occurred within 3 days of initiation of dofetilide. Dose reduction based on CrCl decreased the incidence of TdP.

The DIAMOND-AF substudy examined the use of dofetilide in AF or atrial flutter patients with LV dysfunction and either CHF or recent MI. Analysis of 506 individual (from DIAMOND studies database) with baseline AF or flutter showed that 44% of patients in the dofetilide group converted to sinus rhythm by 1 year compared with 14% in the placebo group. At 1 year, patients receiving dofetilide had a 79% probability of maintaining sinus rhythm vs 42% in the placebo arm. Dofetilide had no effect on all-cause mortality, but restoration and maintenance of sinus rhythm was associated with a significant reduction in mortality. TdP occurred in 1.6% of patients treated with dofetilide. All such cases were successfully treated. Compared with placebo, dofetilide therapy was associated with a significantly lower risk of rehospitalization.

3. Pooled analysis of randomized clinical trials of patients with supraventricular arrhythmias compared survival between patients taking dofetilide and placebo. A total of 1346 patients receiving dofetilide and 677 treated with placebo were analyzed. Therapy with dofetilide was not associated with an increase in mortality. However, since TdP is not common, the occurrence of proarrhythmia could not be adequately assessed in this small number of patients.

■ Propafenone and Flecainide for Maintenance of Sinus Rhythm

General and Electrophysiologic Characteristics

- Class IC agents; slow conduction in atrial, AV node, His-Purkinje system, ventricle and accessory pathways. Propafenone also has mild β-blocker activity (especially in doses >450 mg/day)
- Prolong PR and QRS interval; no significant effect on QT interval
- Have use-dependent effects on the sodium channels in the heart and their conduction-slowing effects are more pronounced at higher heart rates

Pharmacokinetics

- Metabolized mostly by the liver (dose has to be decreased in liver failure)
- Kidney excretion important with flecainide (dose has to be decreased by 50% if GFR is ≤50 mL/minute)
- Propafenone metabolism occurs by the hepatic cytochrome P-450 CYP2D6 isoenzyme system
- Up to 10% of patients treated with propafenone are poor metabolizers (isoenzyme is absent or less active) and have prolonged breakdown of drug that causes excess β-blocking effects
- Half-life: 20 hours for flecainide and 6 hours for propafenone (poor metabolizers—12 hours or longer)

Role in Maintenance of Sinus Rhythm

- Propafenone and flecainide show similar effectiveness in maintenance of sinus rhythm in AF *(see trial 1 below)*
- Moderately effective and generally safe for maintenance of sinus rhythm in AF patients without structural heart disease *(see trials 2-3 below)*
- May be initiated in outpatient settings, but presence of structural heart disease and CAD should be excluded
- Not very effective in AF prevention after CABG surgery *(see trial 6 below)*

11

Recommended Dosing

- Flecainide—start 100 mg every 12 hours; increase by 50 mg/day in 4 days; maximum dose: 300 mg/day
- Propafenone (immediate release)—start 150 mg every 8 hours, increase at 4-day intervals up to 300 mg every 8 hours
- Propafenone (extended release)—start 225 mg every 12 hours; increase at a minimum of 5-day intervals up to 425 mg every 12 hours

Adverse Effects

- Generally well tolerated with almost no risk of organ toxicity with chronic use
- Major potential CV side effects include proarrhythmia (ventricular tachycardia, conversion of AF to slow atrial flutter with 1:1 conduction causing rapid ventricular rates), bradycardia, AV blocks, and worsening HF
- To reduce risk of proarrhythmia
  - In patients who showed propensity to conduct very rapidly through the AV node, start AV nodal-blocking agent prior to initiation of Class IC AAD in order to decrease risk of conversion to atrial flutter with rapid conduction through the AV node
  - Consider stopping Class IC drugs if QRS duration increased by >50% from baseline in order to decrease the risk of ventricular arrhythmia
- Mild noncardiac side effects occur in 10% to 20% of patients and include CNS symptoms (eg, dizziness, blurred vision, difficulty in focusing, headache, and gait disturbances), GI upset, and rash. CNS symptoms are more common with flecainide. Propafenone more commonly causes GI symptoms (nausea, dysgeusia) and should be avoided in patients who have severe obstructive lung disease. Propafenone very rarely may cause lupus and neutropenia

Contraindications

- Patients with structural heart disease (especially post–MI) *(see trials 4 and 5 below)*
- Coronary disease, HF, severe sinus node dysfunction, severe conduction disease *(see trial 5 below)*

Major Drug Interactions

- Propafenone may increase the level of digoxin (by 40% to 60%), metoprolol, and warfarin. Carvedilol has the same hepatic metabolism involving the CYP2D6 pathway and may increase propafenone plasma levels
- Flecainide levels are increased by amiodarone, and flecainide should be given at half dose if patients are treated with both agents

Propafenone and Flecainide for Maintenance of Sinus Rhythm: Selected Studies

1. In a randomized, open-label, multicenter trial of 200 patients with paroxysmal AF and no history of heart disease, the relative safety, efficacy, and tolerance of flecainide ($n=97$) and propafenone ($n=103$) therapy was studied during 12 months of follow-up. Initial daily doses of 200 mg of flecainide and 450 mg of propafenone were used. These doses could be titrated up to a maximum of 300 mg/day flecainide and 900 mg/day propafenone after two or more episodes of paroxysmal AF. There was no statistically significant difference in the safety or efficacy between the two agents. An intention-to-treat analysis showed that the probability of effective and safe therapy after 12 months was 77% with flecainide and 75% with propafenone.

2. The Rythmol Atrial Fibrillation Trial (RAFT) was a randomized, double-blind, placebo-controlled study, designed to test the efficacy and safety of a sustained-release preparation of propafenone (propafenone SR) in reducing the frequency of symptomatic recurrences of AF. Five hundred twenty-three AF patients were assigned to receive placebo or propafenone SR 425, 325, or 225 mg, all twice daily. At the end of the 39-week follow-up period, recurrence rate of AF was

69% in the placebo group compared with 52%, 42%, and 30% in the propafenone groups (225 mg, 325 mg, and 425 mg, respectively). The median time to recurrence was 41 days in the placebo group, 112 days in the 225-mg group, 291 days in the 325-mg group, and >300 days in the propafenone SR 425-mg group. There was a significantly higher withdrawal rate in the patients receiving 425 mg twice daily.

Comparable efficacy of the sustained-release preparation of propafenone was found in the similarly designed European Rythmol/Rhythmonorm Atrial Fibrillation Trial (ERAFT); however, in this study, the risk of serious adverse event was similar in the propafenone SR treatment groups (10.0% with propafenone SR 325 mg twice daily and 11.2% with propafenone SR 425 mg twice daily).

3. In the CTAF, propafenone was equally effective as sotalol but inferior to amiodarone in preventing recurrence of AF (for detailed discussion of CTAF, see section on *Amiodarone for Maintenance of Sinus Rhythm: Results of Selected Trials*).

4. The Cardiac Arrhythmia Suppression Trial studied the hypothesis that suppression of ventricular ectopy or episodes of nonsustained ventricular tachycardia in asymptomatic patients 6 days to 2 years after an acute MI would reduce the incidence of sudden death. This was not a study of patients with AF. In this trial, use of Class IC agents (encainide, flecainide) was discontinued because of excess mortality. In fact, flecainide had an apparent proarrhythmic effect with a significantly increased incidence of mortality and nonfatal cardiac arrest compared with placebo (6.1% vs 2.3%).

Although propafenone was not studied in the CAST, results of this study are frequently extrapolated to all Class IC agents to prevent their use in patients with CAD.

5. In the analysis of 723 patients with new-onset AF from the CARAF cohort, 57% and 38% of subjects had contraindications and/or warnings at baseline that might prevent the use of flecainide and propafenone, respectively. Comorbid conditions were common, and 56% had structural heart disease, mostly CAD and LV

dysfunction. One third of patients were receiving these medications despite contraindications and/or warnings.

6. The Clinical Outcomes From the Prevention of Post-Operative Arrhythmia II (COPPA II) study tested the efficacy and safety of oral propafenone for the prevention of AF in patients who underwent CABG. Two hundred ninety-three patients were randomized to propafenone 450 mg/day, propafenone 675 mg/day, or placebo administered for the term of hospitalization. Compared with placebo, propafenone at a daily dose of 675 mg showed a nonstatistically significant reduction in incidence of AF but did not show a reduction in length of hospitalization.

■ Disopyramide for Maintenance of Sinus Rhythm
General and Electrophysiologic Characteristics
- Class IA sodium channel blocker; prolongs the QRS and QT intervals
- Exerts marked anticholinergic and negatively inotropic effects

Pharmacokinetics
- Hepatic metabolism (~50%); unchanged urinary excretion (~50%)
- Half-life ~8 hours (longer in patients with renal failure or HF)

Role in Maintenance of Sinus Rhythm
- May be preferred agent in patients with vagally induced AF
- Due to its negative inotropic effect, may be the agent of choice in patients with hypertrophic cardiomyopathy and AF
- Documented efficacy in prevention of AF but usually not indicated for majority of AF patients because of unfavorable side effect profile (see trials 1-2 below)

Recommended Dosing
- 100 mg to 200 mg 3 to 4 times per day (short-acting form) or 200 mg to 400 mg twice daily

11

(sustained preparation). The maximum dose should not exceed 800 mg/day
- In renal or hepatic failure, the initial dose of diso-pyramide should be decreased to 50 mg to 100 mg every 12 hours

Adverse Effects
- Related to electrophysiologic or hemodynamic action: TdP, HF, hypotension, rarely depressed conduction
- Related to anticholinergic activity: dry mouth, blurred vision, urinary retention, constipation, and worsening of glaucoma

Contraindications
- Prolonged QTc, LV dysfunction or HF, hypotension
- Glaucoma, history of urinary retention or prostate enlargement (problematic in middle-aged or elderly males)

Major Drug Interactions
- Carries increased risk of TdP when used with other drugs that prolong QTc
- Has to be used with caution with β-blockers and CCBs due to additively negative inotropic effects
- May increase effect of anticholinergic agents

Disopyramide for Maintenance of Sinus Rhythm for AF: Selected Studies
1. A systematic review of randomized controlled trials published by the American Academy of Family Physicians and the American College of Physicians stated that the strongest evidence for efficacy in main-tenance of sinus rhythm for AF exists for amiodarone, propafenone, disopyramide, and sotalol. Pooled analysis of two randomized trials of disopyramide for maintenance of sinus rhythm showed that this agent decreases risk of AF recurrence compared with placebo.
2. A small, randomized double-blind study comparing propafenone and disopyramide for maintenance of sinus

rhythm in AF showed equal efficacy for both agents. At 6 months, 55% of patients treated with propafenone and 67% of patients treated with disopyramide remained in sinus rhythm. However, therapy with propafenone was better tolerated. Side effects requiring drug discontinuation occurred in 16% of patients on propafenone and in 26% treated with disopyramide.

SUGGESTED READING

2011 ACCF/AHA/HRS Focused Update on the Management of Patients With Atrial Fibrillation (Updating the 2006 Guideline) [published online ahead of print December 20, 2010]. *J Am Coll Cardiol.* doi:10.1016/j.jacc.2010.10.001.

AFFIRM First Antiarrhythmic Drug Substudy Investigators. Maintenance of sinus rhythm in patients with atrial fibrillation: an AFFIRM substudy of the first antiarrhythmic drug. *J Am Coll Cardiol.* 2003;42(1):20-29.

Arnsdorf M. Antiarrhythmic drugs to maintain sinus rhythm in patients with atrial fibrillation: clinical trials. In: Basow DS, ed. *UpToDate.* Waltham, MA: UpToDate; 2010.

Arnsdorf M, Ganz L. Antiarrhythmic drugs to maintain sinus rhythm in patients with atrial fibrillation: recommendations. In: Basow DS, ed. *UpToDate.* Waltham, MA: UpToDate; 2010.

Chimienti M, Cullen MT Jr, Casadei G. Safety of long-term flecainide and propafenone in the management of patients with symptomatic paroxysmal atrial fibrillation: report from the Flecainide and Propafenone Italian Study Investigators. *Am J Cardiol.* 1996;77(3):60A-75A.

Connolly SJ, Crijns HJ, Torp-Pedersen C, et al; ATHENA Investigators. Analysis of stroke in ATHENA: a placebo-controlled, double-blind, parallel-arm trial to assess the efficacy of dronedarone 400 mg BID for the prevention of cardiovascular hospitalization or death from any cause in patients with atrial fibrillation/atrial flutter. *Circulation.* 2009;120(13):1174-1180.

Conway EL, Musco S, Kowey PR. Drug therapy for atrial fibrillation. *Cardiol Clin.* 2009;27(1):109-123.

Crijns HJ, Gosselink AT, Lie KI. Propafenone versus disopyramide for maintenance of sinus rhythm after electrical cardioversion of chronic atrial fibrillation: a randomized, double-blind study. PRODIS Study Group. *Cardiovasc Drugs Ther.* 1996;10(2):145-152.

Crystal E, Connolly SJ, Sleik K, Ginger TJ, Yusuf S. Interventions on prevention of postoperative atrial fibrillation in patients undergoing heart surgery: a meta-analysis. *Circulation.* 2002;106(1):75-80.

11

Daoud EG, Strickberger SA, Man KC, et al. Preoperative amiodarone as prophylaxis against atrial fibrillation after heart surgery. *N Engl J Med*. 1997;337(25):1785-1791.

Davy JM, Herold M, Hoglund C, et al; ERATO Study Investigators. Dronedarone for the control of ventricular rate in permanent atrial fibrillation: the Efficacy and safety of dRonedArone for the cOntrol of ventricular rate during atrial fibrillation (ERATO) study. *Am Heart J*. 2008;156(3):527.e1-527.e9.

Deedwania PC, Singh BN, Ellenbogen K, Fisher S, Fletcher R, Singh SN. Spontaneous conversion and maintenance of sinus rhythm by amiodarone in patients with heart failure and atrial fibrillation: observations from the veterans affairs congestive heart failure survival trial of antiarrhythmic therapy (CHF-STAT). The Department of Veterans Affairs CHF-STAT Investigators. *Circulation*. 1998;98(23):2574-2579.

Echt DS, Liebson PR, Mitchell LB, et al. Mortality and morbidity in patients receiving encainide, flecainide, or placebo. The Cardiac Arrhythmia Suppression Trial. *N Engl J Med*. 1991;324(12):781-788.

European Heart Rhythm Association; European Association for Cardio-Thoracic Surgery, Camm AJ, Kirchhof P, Lip GY, et al. Guidelines for the management of atrial fibrillation: the Task Force for the Management of Atrial Fibrillation of the European Society of Cardiology (ESC). *Eur Heart J*. 2010;31(19):2369-2429.

Fuster V, Rydén LE, Cannom DS, et al; American College of Cardiology/American Heart Association Task Force on Practice Guidelines; European Society of Cardiology Committee for Practice Guidelines; European Heart Rhythm Association; Heart Rhythm Society. ACC/AHA/ESC 2006 Guidelines for the Management of Patients with Atrial Fibrillation: a report of the American College of Cardiology/American Heart Association Task Force on Practice Guidelines and the European Society of Cardiology Committee for Practice Guidelines (Writing Committee to Revise the 2001 Guidelines for the Management of Patients With Atrial Fibrillation): developed in collaboration with the European Heart Rhythm Association and the Heart Rhythm Society. *Circulation*. 2006;114(7):e257-e354.

Hohnloser SH, Crijns HJ, van Eickels M, et al; ATHENA Investigators. Effect of dronedarone on cardiovascular events in atrial fibrillation. *N Engl J Med*. 2009;360(7):668-678.

Humphries KH, Kerr CR, Steinbuch M, Dorian P; Canadian Registry of Atrial Fibrillation investigators. Limitations to antiarrhythmic drug use in patients with atrial fibrillation. *CMAJ*. 2004;171(7):741-745.

Køber L, Torp-Pedersen C, McMurray JJ, et al; Dronedarone Study Group. Increased mortality after dronedarone therapy for severe heart failure. *N Engl J Med*. 2008;358(25):2678-2687.

Kowey PR, Gan-Xin Y, Crijns H. Antiarrhythmic drugs. In: Fuster V, O'Rourke R, Walsh R, Poole-Wilson P, eds. *Hurst's The Heart.* 12th ed. New York, NY: McGraw-Hill Companies, Inc; 2008.

Kowey PR, Yannicelli D, Amsterdam E; COPPA-II Investigators. Effectiveness of oral propafenone for the prevention of atrial fibrillation after coronary artery bypass grafting. *Am J Cardiol.* 2004;94(5):663-665.

Lafuente-Lafuente C, Mouly S, Longás-Tejero MA, Mahé I, Bergmann JF. Antiarrhythmic drugs for maintaining sinus rhythm after cardioversion of atrial fibrillation: a systematic review of randomized controlled trials. *Arch Intern Med.* 2006;166(7):719-728.

McNamara RL, Tamariz LJ, Segal JB, Bass EB. Management of atrial fibrillation: review of the evidence for the role of pharmacologic therapy, electrical cardioversion, and echocardiography. *Ann Intern Med.* 2003;139(12):1018-1033.

Meinertz T, Lip GY, Lombardi F, et al; ERAFT Investigators. Efficacy and safety of propafenone sustained release in the prophylaxis of symptomatic paroxysmal atrial fibrillation (The European Rythmol/ Rytmonorm Atrial Fibrillation Trial [ERAFT] Study). *Am J Cardiol.* 2002;90(12):1300-1306.

Opie LH, Dimarco JP, Gersh BJ. Antiarrhythmic drugs and strategies. In: Opie LH, Gersh BJ, eds. *Drugs for the Heart.* 7th ed. Philadelphia, PA: Saunders Elsevier; 2009:235-292.

Pedersen OD, Bagger H, Keller N, Marchant B, Køber L, Torp-Pedersen C. Efficacy of dofetilide in the treatment of atrial fibrillation-flutter in patients with reduced left ventricular function: a Danish investigations of arrhythmia and mortality on dofetilide (diamond) substudy. *Circulation.* 2001;104(3):292-296.

Piccini JP, Hasselblad V, Peterson ED, Washam JB, Califf RM, Kong DF. Comparative efficacy of dronedarone and amiodarone for the maintenance of sinus rhythm in patients with atrial fibrillation. *J Am Coll Cardiol.* 2009;54(12):1089-1095.

Pritchett EL, Page RL, Carlson M, Undesser K, Fava G; Rythmol Atrial Fibrillation Trial (RAFT) Investigators. Efficacy and safety of sustained-release propafenone (propafenone SR) for patients with atrial fibrillation. *Am J Cardiol.* 2003;92(8):941-946.

Pritchett EL, Wilkinson WE. Effect of dofetilide on survival in patients with supraventricular arrhythmias. *Am Heart J.* 1999;138(5 Pt 1):994-997.

Roy D, Talajic M, Dorian P, et al. Amiodarone to prevent recurrence of atrial fibrillation. Canadian Trial of Atrial Fibrillation Investigators. *N Engl J Med.* 2000;342(13):913-920.

Singh BN, Connolly SJ, Crijns HJ, et al; EURIDIS and ADONIS Investigators. Dronedarone for maintenance of sinus rhythm in atrial fibrillation or flutter. *N Engl J Med.* 2007;357(10):987-999.

11

Singh BN, Singh SN, Reda DJ, et al; Sotalol Amiodarone Atrial Fibrillation Efficacy Trial (SAFE-T) Investigators. Amiodarone versus sotalol for atrial fibrillation. *N Engl J Med*. 2005;352(18):1861-1872.

Singh S, Zoble RG, Yellen L, et al. Efficacy and safety of oral dofetilide in converting to and maintaining sinus rhythm in patients with chronic atrial fibrillation or atrial flutter: the symptomatic atrial fibrillation investigative research on dofetilide (SAFIRE-D) study. *Circulation*. 2000;102(19):2385-2390.

Torp-Pedersen C, Møller M, Bloch-Thomsen PE, et al. Dofetilide in patients with congestive heart failure and left ventricular dysfunction. Danish Investigations of Arrhythmia and Mortality on Dofetilide Study Group. *N Engl J Med*. 1999;341(12):857-865.

Touboul P, Brugada J, Capucci A, Crijns HJ, Edvardsson N, Hohnloser SH. Dronedarone for prevention of atrial fibrillation: a dose-ranging study. *Eur Heart J*. 2003;24(16):1481-1487.

Vorperian VR, Havighurst TC, Miller S, January CT. Adverse effects of low dose amiodarone: a meta-analysis. *J Am Coll Cardiol*. 1997;30(3):791-798.

12 Strategies for Rate Control

Introduction

With the acute onset of AF, rate control with AV nodal agents is the preferred initial strategy for most hemodynamically stable patients. Furthermore, large clinical trials suggest that a long-term rate-control strategy compares favorably with rhythm control with regard to both morbidity and mortality. A rate-control strategy works satisfactorily in many patients, especially in those who are asymptomatic or in mildly symptomatic elderly patients. In patients in whom maintenance of sinus rhythm is difficult or when successful therapy results in intolerable side effects, a rate-control strategy provides an alternative option for chronic management.

Effective use of a rate-control strategy demands an understanding of the physiology and sequelae of AF. Although easier to achieve than rhythm control, effective rate control may also prove difficult. For instance, a rate-control strategy requires, at least initially, frequent follow-up assessments in order to ensure effective heart-rate control both at rest and with exercise or other stress. It also requires frequent dose titration to achieve optimal rate control. A majority of patients require multiple-drug therapy. Anticoagulation must be addressed. See *Chapter 9* for a complete discussion of the choice between rate and rhythm control in AF.

Goals and Definitions in Rate-Control Strategy

In patients with underlying heart disease who present with new-onset AF, effective rate control may prevent hemodynamic instability as manifested by hypotension, decompensated HF, or myocardial ischemia (**Table 12.1**). Heart-rate control may often alleviate symptoms.

TABLE 12.1 — Goals of Rate-Control Therapy in AF

Acute Presentation
- Prevention of hemodynamic instability, eg:
  - Hypotension
  - Decompensated HF
  - Myocardial ischemia
- Symptomatic relief

Chronic Management
- Symptomatic relief
- Improvement of exercise tolerance and QoL
- Prevention of tachycardia-induced cardiomyopathy
- Avoidance of worsening of underlying HF
- Prevention of systemic effect of neurohormonal activation

A rapid ventricular rate in association with AF is mostly determined by conduction properties of the AV node, increased sympathetic tone, and decreased parasympathetic activity. As such, the interruption of AV conduction (and controlling ventricular response) with AV nodal agents is the major goal of rate-control therapy. AF is traditionally considered successfully controlled when the ventricular rate at rest is <80 BPM.

The ventricular rate may increase excessively during exercise in patients with AF, even if well controlled at rest. This may have a detrimental effect on patients with coronary disease (leading t o tachycardia-induced ischemia) and HF (due to decreased ventricular filling and stroke volume). A heart rate between 90 and 115 BPM during moderate exercise is generally accepted as a therapeutic goal.

In the AFFIRM trial, criteria for heart-rate control included an average heart rate ≤100 BPM, no heart rate >110% of the age-predicted maximum during 24-hour Holter monitoring, and heart rate ≤110 BPM in a 6-minute–walk test.

However, it remains unclear if these criteria may be applied to all patients. In the RACE trial, investigators set a higher goal for the resting heart-rate control (<100 BPM) and observed a similar clinical outcome. Additionally, a subanalysis of the AFFIRM study showed no significant relation between resting or exercise heart rate and the survival of patients with AF treated with a rate-control strategy. In this substudy, patients' heart rates from the rate-control arm were analyzed. After 2 months of drug titration, neither heart rate at rest nor achieved exercise heart rate predicted overall CV survival. The QoL, NYHA functional class, and 6-minute walking distance were similar among AF patients treated with different levels of heart-rate control. These data suggested that strict heart-rate control may not be essential in some subpopulations of AF patients (especially in those with normal LV function who are asymptomatic).

The Rate Control Efficacy in Permanent Atrial Fibrillation: A Comparison Between Lenient Versus Strict Rate Control II (RACE II) trial was a multicenter, prospective, randomized study designed to compare a lenient vs a moderately strict rate-control strategy in patients with permanent AF. The RACE II trial tested the hypothesis that lenient rate control is not inferior to strict rate control in preventing CV events in patients with permanent AF and a resting ventricular rate >80 BPM. A total of 614 patients enrolled in the RACE II trial were randomized to either lenient (<110 BPM at rest) or stricter control (<80 BPM at rest and <110 BPM with moderate exercise). The primary end point was a composite of CV death, HF, hospitalization, stroke, systolic embolism, bleeding, and life-threatening arrhythmia. Patients were followed for up to 3 years, with outpatient visits occurring every 2 weeks until the heart rate targets were reached. The mean age of patients enrolled in the study was 68 years old and 66% were men. The median duration of AF was 18 months before enrollment. The majority of patients had no structural heart disease or HF (65% of patients were NYHA class I). Approximately 54% of patients had symptoms at the time of enrollment (only 24% reported palpitations). β-Blockers, CCBs, and/or digoxin were used to achieve target heart rates. Almost 99% of patients in the study were receiving warfarin. At the end of the dose titration phase, the target heart rate was achieved by 98% of patients in the lenient-control group but only in 67% of patients in the strict rate-control group. The mean resting heart rate at the end of the dose

12

adjustment period was 93 BPM in the lenient group and 76 BPM in the stricter control group. After 1 and 2 years and at the end of the follow-up period, the median resting heart rate in the lenient rate-control group was approximately 85 BPM as compared with approximately 75 BPM in the strict rate-control group. The cumulative incidence of the primary end point at 3 years was not statistically significant (12.9% in the lenient rate-control group and 14.9% in the strict rate-control group). The frequencies of symptoms and adverse events were similar in the two groups. The investigators concluded that in patients with permanent AF, lenient heart rate-control appears to be as effective as strict rate control and was easier to achieve.

However, a number of study limitations need to be considered. There was an overlap in the achieved ventricular rate in the study. The mean heart rate of 75 BPM in the strict rate-control group was compared with mean of 85 BPM achieved in the lenient rate-control group rather than the highest resting heart rate (110 BPM) set by the study protocol. Additionally, it is possible that rapid ventricular rates could lead to negative outcomes with a longer follow-up period. Furthermore, patients enrolled in the study had permanent AF and approximately 90% of subjects in lenient rate-control group were taking rate-control agents. As such, the results may not apply to patients who are not taking any AV nodal blockers or to patients newly presenting with AF. These results should also not be extrapolated to highly symptomatic patients with AF or patients with other comorbidities (eg, advanced HF or CAD). Considering these limitations, the RACE II study suggests that practitioners may use less strict therapeutic rate-control targets. The heart rate target of 85 BPM reached in the lenient-control group appears to be safe in the majority of patients with AF.

With a rate-control strategy, symptoms attributable to bradycardia may be limiting. While there is no specific lower limit of heart rate, an asymptomatic resting heart <40 BPM and/or pauses >3.0 seconds (while awake) are accepted generally as concerning. Pauses of 2 to 3 seconds during sleep are usually related to increased vagal tone and are not an indication for pacing. Symptoms of dyspnea, easy fatigability, and exercise intolerance should prompt further evaluation with ambulatory ECG monitoring, especially in the elderly, who are at increased risk for conduction-system disease progression.

The lower limit of heart rate achieved during exercise may have clinical significance. The failure of heart rate to increase appropriately during exercise (chronotropic incompetence) not only carries associated risk of adverse cardiac events but also, in symptomatic patients, may be an indication for permanent pacing. However, pacemaker implantation in this setting should not be overutilized. Chronotropic incompetence can be defined as a heart rate <85% of predicted (220 BPM minus patient age) during exercise testing.

Regularization of ventricular response is hypothesized to have beneficial effects on cardiac hemodynamics, leading to increased cardiac output, decreased pulmonary capillary wedge pressure, and decreased right atrial pressure. However, exercise capacity decreases as heart period variability decreases. This suggests that excessive regularization of heart and blunting of rate variability might have a negative impact in AF patients. Since the benefits of regularization of heart rate are currently unknown, regularization cannot be recommended as a goal of rate-control therapy. A summary of clinical parameters used in the assessment of rate control is presented in **Table 12.2**.

Choice of Pharmacologic Agents for Rate-Control Therapy

Drugs that prolong the functional refractory period or decrease conduction velocity in the AV node and slow the ventricular response are the mainstay of a rate-control strategy. The three major therapeutic classes of drugs used for this purpose are:

- β-Blockers
- Nondihydropyridine CCBs (eg, verapamil and diltiazem)
- Digitalis glycosides.

TABLE 12.2 — Clinical Parameters Used in Rate-Control Management of AF

Heart Rate	Criterion	Limits
Resting	Upper limit	<80 to 90 BPM
	Lower limit	<60 BPM in symptomatic patient
		<40 BPM while awake and/or pauses >3 seconds in asymptomatic patient
With exercise	Upper limit	90 to 115 BPM (moderate exercise)
		≤110 BPM (6-minute–walk test)
		Hourly average <100 BPM and no rates >220 BPM minus the patient's age
	Lower limit	Heart rate <85% of predicted (220 BPM minus age) with symptoms during exercise testing

These drugs may be used as monotherapy or, if necessary, may be combined, always with careful dose titration. In selected patients in whom first-line agents have failed, AADs with rate-lowering properties (eg, dronedarone, amiodarone) may be useful.

■ β-Blockers

β-Blockers are first-line agents for acute and chronic control of ventricular rate in patients with AF. They are the most effective single therapeutic class for rate control, both at rest and with exercise. β-Blockers are particularly useful in states of high adrenergic tone (eg, postoperative AF, thyrotoxicosis) and should be used for rate control in all AF patients with compelling indications for β-blockade (eg, LV dysfunction, HF, post-MI). The rate-control activity of the different β-blockers appears to be generally similar. This is dependent mostly on β_1-adrenergic blockade. Nadolol and atenolol have the most evidence for effective rate control in AF. Labetalol has the least favorable data (see **Tables 12.3**, **12.4**, and **12.5** for characteristics of commonly used β-blockers).

TABLE 12.3 — Metoprolol for Rate Control of AF[a]

- IV and PO preparations available, convenient for both acute and maintenance therapy:
  - Acute rate control: 2.5-5.0 mg IV over 2 minutes; may repeat every 5 minutes up to 15 mg total
  - Chronic rate control: 50-200 mg/day PO in 2 to 3 divided doses
- Peak effect: 20 minutes (IV), 1.5 to 4 hours (PO)
- Plasma half-life 3 to 7 hours
- When switching from IV to PO form, equivalent β-blocking effect is achieved in a ratio of 1:2.5
- When switching from immediate-release metoprolol to extended-release, the same total daily dose of metoprolol should be used
- Mortality benefit of long-acting form (metoprolol succinate) in patients with concomitant HF
- Safe in patients with renal failure, but dose adjustment is needed in patients with liver disease

[a] Characteristics apply to the short-acting formulation of this drug.

TABLE 12.4 — Esmolol for Rate Control of AF

- Ultra short-acting IV selective β-blocker (half-life of 9 minutes)
- Full recovery from β-blockade within 30 minutes in most patients
- Useful in acute settings (eg, postoperatively) or when uncertain whether a β-blocker will be tolerated
- More likely than IV diltiazem to produce rapid conversion to SR in AF after noncardiac surgery (but impact on ventricular rates after 2 and 12 hours is similar)
- Loading dose of 500 mcg/kg IV bolus over 1 minute followed by maintenance infusion of 50 mcg/kg/minute for 4 minutes; if inadequate response, may titrate up in 50 mcg/kg/minute increments every 4 minutes to a maximum infusion rate of 200-300 mcg/kg/minute
- Metabolized by red blood cell esterase; safe in patients with renal or liver failure

12

TABLE 12.5 — Specific Characteristics of Other β-Blockers Related to Rate-Control Therapy

Atenolol
- Strongest evidence of efficacy for rate control of AF
- Twice-a-day dosing may be required for optimal rate control
- Less CNS side effects
- Avoid in patients with renal insufficiency/failure

Carvedilol
- Lowers ventricular rate at rest and during exercise
- Reduces ventricular ectopy in patients with AF
- Improves LVEF (with trend toward a decrease in the combined end point of death or hospitalization for HF) in AF patients with chronic HF and systolic dysfunction (US Carvedilol Trials Program)
- Increases plasma levels of propafenone

Acebutolol
- Exerts intrinsic sympathomimetic activity
- Less likely to worsen bradycardia in AF patients with sick sinus syndrome
- Well tolerated (in particular, does not aggregate erectile dysfunction)

β-Blockers should be used with caution in patients with decompensated HF, low BP, and AF with sick sinus syndrome, asthma, marked first-degree or higher-grade AV block, and in combination with other drugs that inhibit AV nodal conduction.

■ **Nondihydropyridine CCBs**

Compared with β-blockers, the nondihydropyridine CCBs (eg, verapamil and diltiazem) control ventricular rate equally at rest but less well with exercise. However, they are better tolerated than β-blockers and have been shown to improve QoL and exercise tolerance. These agents may be also preferred over β-blockers in patients with COPD and essential hypertension.

Nondihydropyridine CCBs are not recommended in certain groups of patients with AF. Diltiazem and verapamil have a negative inotropic effect (less pronounced with diltiazem) and should be avoided in patients with LV systolic dysfunction and HF, especially in HF patients already receiving other negative inotropic agents (eg, β-blockers). Verapamil should be used cautiously in AF patients with a previous history of MI. Nondihydropyridine CCBs should not be started in patients with marked first-degree or other degrees of AV block. The risk of worsening conduction abnormalities is particularly increased for the combination of verapamil and digoxin. Verapamil (in doses >240 mg/day) may increase the digoxin level, and diltiazem may increase the bioavailability of propranolol.

Although their effect on the SA node is variable, patients with sick sinus syndrome and AF may be especially susceptible to bradycardia, and CCBs should be avoided in these subjects. Verapamil and diltiazem should not be used in AF patients with pre-excitation since the use of these agents may facilitate conduction via the accessory pathway and potentially lead to ventricular fibrillation. Nondihydropyridine CCBs also have vasodilatory effects and should not be given to patients who are hypotensive. Verapamil is equally effective as diltiazem for rate control of AF but appears to be associated with more side effects in elderly patients (eg, constipation). Verapamil increases the pacing threshold but does not change the defibrillation threshold.

Similar to certain β-blockers, diltiazem and verapamil are available in IV and oral preparations, convenient for both acute and maintenance therapy. Dosing protocols for acute and chronic therapy with verapamil and diltiazem are presented in **Tables 12.6** and **12.7**.

■ Digoxin

Digoxin decreases the ventricular response in AF mostly by vagotonic inhibition of AV conduction. It is not better than placebo in conversion to NSR and has a limited role in controlling ventricular response in acute settings, especially in the presence of high sympathetic tone. Additionally, the therapeutic effect of IV digoxin is usually seen after 30 minutes, and the peak effect may not be observed for up to a few hours. As such, in acute settings, IV digoxin is only indicated in AF patients with associated hypotension and/or HF and in those who

TABLE 12.6 — Verapamil for Rate Control of AF[a]

Acute Rate Control
- Dosing (IV): 5-10 mg IV over 2 to 3 minutes (repeat every 15 to 30 minutes as needed)
- Bolus infusion must be slow to avoid hypotension
- Onset of action: 2 minutes
- Peak effect: 10 to 15 minutes
- Rate control effect is lost in ~90 minutes if bolus is not repeated or oral maintenance therapy is not initiated

Chronic Rate Control
- Dosing (PO): 40 mg 3 to 4 times/day to maximum of 480 mg/day in divided doses
- Peak effect: 2 hours
- Half-life: 3 to 7 hours
- Conversion to slow-release form in 1:1 ratio

[a] Characteristics apply to the short-acting formulation of this drug.

TABLE 12.7 — Diltiazem for Rate Control of AF[a]

Acute Rate Control
- Dosing (IV):
  - First bolus 0.25 mg/kg (or 10-20 mg) over 2 minutes
  - Second bolus of 0.35 mg/kg (or 15-25 mg) over 2 minutes (if heart rate in 15 minutes after first bolus is >100 BPM or decreased <20%)
  - Followed by continuous drip 5-15 mg/hour
  - Usually effective in 4 to 5 minutes
- Hypotension occurs in 13% (symptomatic in 4%); responds well to IV fluids

Chronic Rate Control
- Dosing (PO): 30 mg 3 to 4 times daily, to maximum of 480 mg
- Peak effect: 1 to 2 hours
- Half-life: 5 hours
- Conversion to sustained-release form in 1:1 ratio

[a] Characteristics apply to the short-acting formulation of this drug.

cannot tolerate β-blockers or CCBs. Digoxin may also be added in patients with an uncontrolled ventricular response despite therapy with other AV nodal drugs.

Digoxin is most commonly used in patients with LV systolic dysfunction and/or HF. Digoxin decreases the ventricular response of AF, improves symptoms, and decreases hospitalizations. However, β-blockers, which improve survival in HF patients, should be first-line therapy in these patients. Therefore, digoxin is recommended in AF patients with HF only if:

- Patients are hemodynamically unstable and do not tolerate β-blockers
- They are unable to achieve rate control with β-blockers
- When attempting to improve HF symptoms independent of AF.

Digoxin levels should be kept below 1.0 ng/mL in HF patients because in the DIG Trial, higher digoxin levels were associated with increased mortality. When used for heart-rate control in patients with AF and no HF or LV dysfunction, it is not required that the digoxin level be <1.0 ng/mL. In fact, obtaining digoxin levels routinely in patients with normal or rapid heart rates in AF is unnecessary. Recommended dosing of digoxin in acute and chronic settings is presented in **Table 12.8**.

Digoxin often provides effective rate control at rest but not during exercise (when vagal tone is low and sympathetic tone is high). As such, digoxin is more often used as a second-line agent. In the absence of LV dysfunction, monotherapy with digoxin is usually reserved for elderly, sedentary patients.

The Registry of Information and Knowledge About Swedish Heart Intensive Care Admissions (RIKS-HIA) analyzed 60,764 patients admitted to coronary care units with AF, CHF, or both and treated with and without digoxin. Among AF patients without CHF, the 1-year mortality was statistically higher for those taking digoxin (adjusted RR 1.42 [95% CI 1.29-1.56]). Study investigators concluded that long-term therapy with digoxin is an independent risk factor for death in patients with AF and no CHF and should be used with caution in this population.

12

TABLE 12.8 — Digoxin for Rate Control of AF

Acute Rate Control
- Initial dose: 0.25-0.5 mg IV, followed by 0.25 mg every 4 to 6 hours as required
- Total dose for IV digitalization: 0.75 to 1.5 mg
- Onset of action: 30 to 60 minutes
- Peak effect: 1 to 6 hours

Chronic Rate Control
- Rapid oral digitalization:
  - Initial dose: 0.5 mg PO, followed by 0.25 or 0.5 mg every 6 hours
  - Total dose for oral digitalization: 1 to 2 mg
  - Follow with maintenance dose of 0.125 to 0.25 mg daily
- Slow digitalization:
  - 0.125 to 0.25 mg PO daily
  - Steady state achieved after 7 to 10 days
- Half-life 36 to 48 hours in patients with normal kidney function

Correlation Between Digoxin Level and Ventricular Rate Control Poor
- Check serum digoxin level only if:
  - Low digoxin concentration suspected, which allows higher dosing
  - Patient at risk for or suspected of having digitalis toxicity

Digoxin has a complex mechanism of action and a variety of side effects. Digoxin should be avoided in patients with WPW syndrome with AF as it may accelerate antegrade conduction over the bypass tract and lead to ventricular tachyarrhythmias. Digoxin may also lead to symptomatic bradyarrhythmias, especially in the elderly, in those with underlying conduction-system disease, or in patients taking other AV nodal antagonists. Verapamil and some AADs (eg, propafenone, quinidine, dronedarone, amiodarone) may cause an elevation of digoxin levels and potentiate its toxic effect. Digoxin should also be used with caution in patients with renal insufficiency or electrolyte abnormalities (ie, hypokalemia, hypomagnesemia, hypercalcemia). With chronic kidney disease, the maintenance dose should be decreased. During pregnancy, with a larger volume of distribution, higher doses are often required. Digoxin decreases the pacing threshold and does not change or decreases the ventricular defibrillation threshold (**Table 12.8**).

Data From Comparative Studies of AV Nodal Agents for Rate Control of AF

In the AFFIRM trial, 2027 patients were randomized to the rate-control arm and followed for 3.5 ± 1.3 years. The investigators assessed the efficacy of different rate-control drug regimens. Adequate rate control was achieved in 70% of patients given β-blockers as the first drug (with or without digoxin), 54% with CCBs (with or without digoxin), and 58% with digoxin alone. More patients switched to β-blocker therapy compared with any other agent during the trial.

In a small, crossover, open-label study of patients with permanent AF, five different daily drug regimens (digoxin 0.25 mg, diltiazem CD 240 mg, atenolol 50 mg, digoxin + diltiazem, and digoxin + atenolol) were assessed by mean 24-hour heart rates, circadian rhythm, and exercise-induced changes of ventricular rate. Atenolol was the most potent and digoxin the least effective as monotherapy. The combination of atenolol and digoxin produced the most effective rate control (**Figure 12.1**). Interestingly, exercise duration was similar in all treatment groups.

A single-center study from France investigated the effects of β-blocker and digoxin on mortality in patients with both AF and HF. In this study, 1269 consecutive patients were retrospectively identified and followed for a mean of 881 days (±859 days). Two hundred sixty patients were treated with a β-blocker alone, 189 with a β-blocker plus digoxin, 402 with digoxin alone, and 418 without a β-blocker or digoxin (control group). During follow-up, 247 patients died. Compared with the control group, treatment with a β-blocker was associated with decreased mortality, either alone or in combination with digoxin. Monotherapy with digoxin showed a survival rate similar to that of patients without any rate-control treatment.

FIGURE 12.1 — Effect of Various Pharmacologic Regimens on Exercise-Induced Ventricular Rate in Patients With Chronic AF

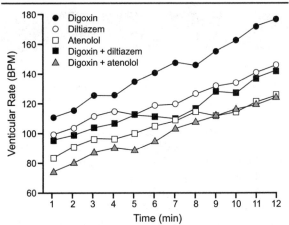

There was a linear trend in increases in ventricular rate on all five regimens. The mean ventricular rate on digoxin + atenolol treatment was the lowest and was significantly lower than those on digoxin, diltiazem, and digoxin + diltiazem.

Farshi R, et al. *J Am Coll Cardiol.* 1999;33(2):304-310.

Antiarrhythmic Drugs for Rate Control

Since many of these agents may cause pharmacologic cardioversion to sinus rhythm, anticoagulation must first be addressed.

■ Amiodarone

Amiodarone has both β-sympatholytic and calcium-antagonistic properties, which prolong AV nodal conduction and refractoriness. Rate-control properties of amiodarone are useful in critically ill patients with AF and a rapid ventricular response. In this setting, amiodarone is highly effective for rate control of AF resistant to therapy with β-blockers and CCBs. It also causes less systemic hypotension and is usually well tolerated. In patients with permanent AF, amiodarone may be considered as a last-line agent for chronic rate control when a combination of conventional agents fails. Amiodarone may raise the plasma level of digoxin. This may potentiate the rate-control effect in patients who receive both of these drugs. Due to the high risk of side effects associated with chronic therapy and the availability of nonpharmacologic approaches, the use of amiodarone as primary therapy for rate control is generally not recommended.

■ Sotalol

Sotalol is a nonselective β-blocking agent with type III antiarrhythmic characteristics. In fact, at doses of ≤160 mg, sotalol has primarily a β-blocking effect. There is a potential risk of proarrhythmia with higher doses of sotalol, which limits its use for purely a rate-control indication. Chronic rhythm control with sotalol in patients with paroxysmal AF may prevent a rapid ventricular response with recurrent AF.

■ Propafenone

Propafenone has mild β-blocking effects and slows conduction through the AV node. Up to 10% of patients are poor metabolizers of propafenone (see *Chapter 11*) and may experience a more pronounced β-blocking effect. Propafenone can raise digoxin levels by 40% to 60% and lead to decreased clearance of metoprolol. These interactions can additionally contribute to a slower ventricular response, and dose adjustment should be considered when propafenone is combined with other drugs. This agent is not usually used for rate control primarily. Because of its antiarrhythmic effect in the atrium, it may slow atrial rates and predispose to improved AV nodal conduction and an accelerated ventricular rate.

Other Agents

■ Clonidine

Clonidine, used mainly as an antihypertensive agent, has several characteristics that could contribute to ventricular rate control in AF. This drug is known to reduce peripheral sympathetic tone and acts directly at

α_2-receptors in the brainstem to suppress sympathetic outflow. Clonidine also stimulates parasympathetic outflow, resulting in prolongation of refractoriness of the AV node. Results of small studies suggest benefit of clonidine over placebo for rate control in patients presenting with acute-onset AF, as well as noninferiority of this drug when compared with standard agents.

In a study of 40 patients presenting to an emergency department with new-onset AF and a rapid ventricular response, the efficacy of clonidine (0.1 mg orally, dose repeated at 2 hours if heart rate >100 BPM) was compared with IV digoxin and verapamil IV followed by oral. At 6 hours, the mean reduction in heart rate was 44 BPM in the clonidine group, 52 BPM in the digoxin group, and 42 BPM in the verapamil group. The mean fall in systolic BP at 6 hours was 18 mm Hg with clonidine, compared with 2.1 mm Hg with digoxin and 7.2 mm Hg with verapamil.

Although large, perspective, randomized trials are needed to establish the role of clonidine for rate control, this agent is a second-line agent in AF patients with rapid ventricular response and hypertension. Bradycardia due to possible interaction with other AV nodal blocking agents has to be considered.

■ Magnesium Sulfate

The results of a small study of patients presenting acutely with AF and an uncontrolled ventricular response suggest that IV magnesium sulfate (2.5 g/20 minutes, then 2.5 g/2 hours) mildly increases the likelihood of achieving a ventricular rate <100 BPM and cardioversion to NSR. However, a meta-analysis of 10 small, randomized, controlled trials of 515 patients with acute-onset AF showed that when compared with calcium antagonists or IV amiodarone, magnesium was less effective in reducing the ventricular response. Only when added to digoxin did IV magnesium increase the proportion of patients with a ventricular response <100 BPM. The rate-lowering effect appears to be modest (12 BPM). An infusion of magnesium sulfate can lower BP and is associated with transient minor side effects (eg, flushing, tingling, dizziness) in 17% of patients.

Pacing may be required to prevent bradycardia in patients receiving AV nodal blocking agents. AV node ablation with pacemaker implantation is a nonpharmacologic approach for rate control in patients in whom medical therapy has failed. **Table 12.9** presents the current applications of nonpharmacologic therapy for rate control of AF.

TABLE 12.9 — Current Applications of Nonpharmacologic Therapy for Rate Control of AF

- Pacing in patients with sick sinus syndrome and paroxysmal AF
- Backup pacing in elderly patients with permanent AF and bradycardia
- AV node ablation and pacemaker implantation in patients who failed medical therapy
- AV nodal modification (rarely used) in patients in whom medical therapy fails

■ Pacemaker Implantation in Patients With AF

The presence of underlying sinus node dysfunction is frequent in patients with paroxysmal AF. The use of rate-lowering agents in these patients may uncover bradyarrhythmia. Sick sinus syndrome may also be associated with AV block.

Dual-chamber PPMs are most often implanted in the United States in patients with sick sinus syndrome and paroxysmal AF. This approach is in part based on analyses in which there was a 8.4% risk of AV block in patients with sick sinus syndrome during 34.2 months of follow-up.

In a Danish retrospective analysis of patients who received a single-chamber (AAI/AAIR) pacemaker for sick sinus syndrome, the annual risk of AV block requiring ventricular lead placement was much lower (1.7%). Additionally, rate-adaptive single-chamber atrial pacing (while compared with dual-chamber pacing) is known not only to decrease the risk of developing AF but also

12

may limit left atrial remodeling. Based on these data, implantation of a single-chamber atrial pacemaker is considered safe and is the preferred technique in Europe for treatment for AF patients with sick sinus syndrome and normal AV conduction.

Age-related degeneration of the conduction system frequently complicates the clinical course of patients with persistent or permanent AF treated with rate-lowering therapy. Simple dose adjustment of AV nodal agents may be sufficient. Occasionally, changing to a β-blocker with intrinsic sympathetic activity (eg, acebutolol) may lessen bradycardia. Eventually, most of these patients will need pacemaker implantation. A single-chamber, rate-responsive ventricular pacemaker is most often used. Rate-responsiveness algorithms permit changes in ventricular rate based on physiologic needs.

■ AV Nodal Ablation With Pacemaker Implantation

Radiofrequency ablation of the AV node and/ or the His bundle with implantation of a PPM is the most common and highly effective nonpharmacologic method for heart-rate control in patients with AF. Due to its invasive character and possible complications, it is recommended only for patients in whom a pharmacologic approach to heart-rate control fails. In the rate-control arm of the AFFIRM trial, 5% of patients required AV nodal ablation and PPM implantation after failure of medical therapy with a mean of 2.4 ($\pm$0.7) medications.

Choice of Implanted Pacemaker

Radiofrequency ablation usually leads to complete AV block and implantation of a PPM for ventricular rate support.

In patients with permanent AF and normal LV function, a single-chamber ventricular pacemaker is adequate. As ventricular rate will not spontaneously respond to exercise after AV nodal ablation, these devices should have rate-adaptive capabilities (ie, rate-responsive ventricular pacemaker), particularly in physically active patients.

Patients with paroxysmal AF who undergo AV nodal ablation should receive a dual-chamber pacemaker (eg, DDDR) with mode-switch capability. The latter feature enables the patient to maintain AV synchrony during periods of sinus rhythm.

In selected AF patients with HF, implantation of a biventricular pacemaker may be indicated at the time of AV nodal ablation. The Left Ventricular-Based Cardiac Stimulation Post AV Nodal Ablation Evaluation (PAVE) study prospectively compared chronic biventricular pacing to right ventricular pacing in patients undergoing AV nodal ablation for rate control of AF. At 6 months postablation, patients with EF ≤45% or with NYHA Class II or III symptoms who received a biventricular device had significant improvement in both the 6-minute–walk test and LVEF compared with the right-ventricular pacing group.

Clinical Benefit of Successful Rate Control

The procedural success rate of permanent AV nodal ablation is high with the initial procedure. Permanent ablation was achieved in 96% of patients in the PAVE trial and 97% in the NASPE (Prospective Catheter Ablation) Registry. A recurrence of AV nodal conduction that requires repeat ablation is generally estimated at 3.5% to 5%.

12

The beneficial effect of this therapy is contributed to by reinstitution of a regular and slow ventricular rate with improvement of LV function. A meta-analysis of 21 trials of 1181 patients showed significant improvement in functional capacity, cardiac symptoms, QoL, and ventricular function (EF). Although a decrease in health care use was noted, no survival advantage was noted.

Risks and Complications of AV Node Ablation

Ablation of the AV junction is irreversible. The patient becomes pacemaker dependent for life. It does not eliminate the need to address anticoagulation. The procedure is usually technically easy and carries low periprocedural risk. The most common complications include those associated with pacemaker implantation and vascular access. The risk of thromboembolism due to interruption of anticoagulation is low. The risk of worsening of LV function with pacing and lack of AV synchrony can be minimized with appropriate pacemaker selection.

Some reports have raised concerns about an increased short-term risk of death with AV nodal ablation and pacing therapy. However, in a meta-analysis of 21 trials of AV nodal ablation and pacing, the 1-year total-mortality and sudden-death rates were 6.3% and 2.0%, respectively. These rates are comparable to those in the general AF population treated with pharmacotherapy. Although a relationship between increased risk of sudden cardiac death and AV nodal ablation is not proven, the hypothesis is that bradycardia may induce repolarization abnormalities (leading to TdP) and activation of the sympathetic nervous system, particularly in patients with underlying structural heart disease. Programming the lower rate of the pacemaker to 90 BPM for the first month postimplantation and after ablation may decrease the risk of sudden cardiac death.

■ AV Nodal Modification

Partial ablation of inferior atrial inputs to the AV node reduces ventricular rate and improves symptoms in patients with AF. The hope was that modification could result in effective rate control without the need for PPM implantation. However, AV nodal modification has subsequently been found to have significant limitations. These include the development of complete AV block in 15% to 20% of cases, poor rate control during periods of increased sympathetic activity, and a tendency for the ventricular response to increase after the procedure.

In a small randomized trial that compared AV nodal ablation with PPM implantation vs AV nodal modification, there was better symptom control with complete ablation and pacing. As such, AV node modification is currently not recommended.

■ Regularization of Ventricular Response With Pacing

Ventricular rate regularization with pacing is conceptually desirable and has been shown to have beneficial hemodynamic effects in AF patients. However, studies to date have failed to show a significant benefit of this strategy. In the AF Symptoms Study, ventricular rate regularization had a beneficial effect on symptoms (less palpitations) but did not impact functional capacity or overall QoL.

Additionally, this technique does not appear to be practical in controlling ventricular response during exercise. Currently, there are no data to support ventricular pacing with regularization algorithms as a therapeutic modality in patients with permanent AF.

■ Chronic Atrioventricular Nodal Vagal Stimulation

Selective atrioventricular nodal vagal stimulation (AVN-VS) can be achieved by implantation of a nerve stimulator attached to the epicardial AVN fat pad. This technique was demonstrated in animal models to effectively control ventricular response in AF.

■ Gene Therapy

Preliminary studies in the animal model showed that modification of AV nodal conduction properties with gene therapy may be a future approach to the chronic control of ventricular response in AF.

Algorithms for Rate-Control Strategies Based on Clinical Presentation

Evaluation of a patient presenting with AF with a rapid ventricular response should always include:
- Urgency of need for therapy
- Previous history of AF and goals of therapy, rate vs rhythm approach
- Anticoagulation status.

In the hemodynamically stable patient with AF, a rate-control strategy is commonly chosen. However, the intensity of the therapy depends on the clinical presentation. Symptomatic patients presenting acutely with AF and a rapid ventricular response require urgent rate control with IV agents. Asymptomatic or mildly symptomatic patients with permanent AF whose ventricular response is only moderately increased usually require only titration or addition of oral AV nodal blocking drugs.

■ Acute Pharmacologic Rate Control

IV β-blockers or nondihydropyridine CCBs are the drugs of choice for rapid rate control in a symptomatic patient presenting acutely with AF and a rapid ventricular response. Therapies with AV nodal drugs are effective and safe in the majority of patients. The safety of this treatment should be assessed (prior to the initiation of therapy) by rapid clinical and electrocardiographic assessment and exclusion of patients who are hemodynamically unstable, have decompensated HF, or have ECGs suggestive of an accessory pathway. β-blockers are beneficial for acute rate control in AF associated with high catecholamine state (eg, postoperative AF, thyrotoxicosis, etc). CCBs are preferred in AF patients with wheezing due to reactive airway disease.

β-Blockers (esmolol) and CCBs (diltiazem) in IV preparations suitable for loading and maintenance are frequently used for acute rate-control management. However, there are only limited data directly comparing the efficacy of different agents. Other IV β-blockers (metoprolol and propranolol) and a nondihydropyridine CCB (verapamil) are suitable for loading but not for continuous infusion.

If a single drug fails, switching the β-blocker to a CCB or vice versa may be effective. A second IV agent may be added. However, the second drug should be titrated with caution since risk of common side effects when these agents are given acutely (ie, hypotension, heart block, worsening HF) is increased with combined therapy. **Table 12.10** presents factors favoring caution in using AV nodal agents for rate-control therapy in AF.

TABLE 12.10 — Factors Favoring Caution in the Titration of Rate-Control Therapy in AF

- Elderly
- Paroxysmal AF
- History of syncope
- Presence of any conduction abnormalities
- Patient already on other drugs with AV nodal blocking properties

As another approach, IV digoxin may be added as the second drug. This strategy may be especially useful in patients with borderline low BP or HF (**Table 12.10**). However, in a majority of patients, paroxysmal AF is precipitated by high sympathetic tone, and adding digoxin for rate control may be associated with only limited benefit. Additionally, the risk of conduction disturbances remains increased.

If the ventricular response remains uncontrolled with two AV nodal agents and dose has been maximized, a combination of β-blocker, CCB, and digoxin may be used.

Alternatively, in a patient who does not tolerate a combination of IV AV nodal agents or whose ventricular rate remains uncontrolled on these drugs, IV amiodarone may be considered. One must recognize the possible interaction of conventional AV nodal agents with amiodarone and the increased risk of stroke by unintended cardioversion with amiodarone.

Rarely, all pharmacologic measures for acute rate control fail. At this junction, either cardioversion or a rhythm-control strategy should be reconsidered or the patient should be evaluated for AV nodal ablation and pacemaker implantation as destination therapy for rate control.

The therapeutic approach to a patient presenting acutely with AF and an uncontrolled ventricular rate is showed in **Figure 12.2**.

Acute Rate Control in Special Populations
Decompensated Heart Failure

IV digoxin or/and amiodarone are preferred agents in the acute control of ventricular rhythm in a patient presenting with AF and decompensated HF. Urgent cardioversion may be required in unstable patients. In subjects with a history of HF or LV dysfunction on chronic β-blocker therapy who present with AF and decompensated HF, discontinuation of β-blockers is discouraged unless the patient is hemodynamically unstable. The use of a nondihydropyridine CCB in this setting is generally avoided.

FIGURE 12.2 — Initial Approach to a Patient Presenting Acutely With AF and an Uncontrolled Ventricular Response

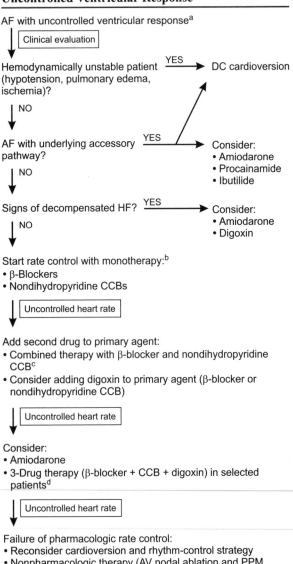

AF with uncontrolled ventricular response[a]

Clinical evaluation

Hemodynamically unstable patient (hypotension, pulmonary edema, ischemia)? — YES → DC cardioversion

NO

AF with underlying accessory pathway? — YES → Consider:
• Amiodarone
• Procainamide
• Ibutilide

NO

Signs of decompensated HF? — YES → Consider:
• Amiodarone
• Digoxin

NO

Start rate control with monotherapy:[b]
• β-Blockers
• Nondihydropyridine CCBs

Uncontrolled heart rate

Add second drug to primary agent:
• Combined therapy with β-blocker and nondihydropyridine CCB[c]
• Consider adding digoxin to primary agent (β-blocker or nondihydropyridine CCB)

Uncontrolled heart rate

Consider:
• Amiodarone
• 3-Drug therapy (β-blocker + CCB + digoxin) in selected patients[d]

Uncontrolled heart rate

Failure of pharmacologic rate control:
• Reconsider cardioversion and rhythm-control strategy
• Nonpharmacologic therapy (AV nodal ablation and PPM implantation)

Continued

FIGURE 12.2 — *Continued*

a Stroke-risk assessment and anticoagulation as per appropriate guidelines should always be an integral part of the initial assessment of a patient presenting with AF.

b IV preparation is usually recommended until rate controlled is achieved.

c Caution in elderly patients with borderline high BP and if AV-conduction disease suspected.

d Contraindicated in elderly or patients with SN or AV nodal disease.

Wolff-Parkinson-White (WPW) Syndrome

The use of IV nondihydropyridine CCBs, β-blockers, and digitalis is contraindicated in patient with AF and pre-excitation. These agents slow AV nodal conduction and can facilitate antegrade conduction over the accessory pathway during AF in patients with WPW. This may lead to acceleration of the ventricular rate and possibly to ventricular fibrillation. Rhythm-control strategy is a goal in these patients. The ventricular response in AF with pre-excitation may exceed 200 BPM and, if associated with hemodynamic instability, requires cardioversion. IV amiodarone, procainamide, or ibutilide may be used in a hemodynamically stable patient (these drugs may also slow conduction over the accessory pathway). After resolution of the acute event, ablation of the accessory pathway should be recommended.

Sick Sinus Syndrome or AV Block

Elderly patients with AF frequently have coexisting degeneration of the conduction system (eg, sick sinus syndrome, AV block). The use of IV AV nodal blocking agents for rate control of AF may lead to symptomatic bradycardia that requires placement of a temporary pacemaker. Permanent pacing is required in the majority of cases to allow effective but safe-rate pharmacotherapy. AV nodal ablation and implantation of PPM are reasonable options (**Figure 12.2**).

Chronic Pharmacologic Rate Control

Single or combination therapy with oral AV nodal blockers is used for long-term rate control in patients with persistent or permanent AF. A successful rate-control strategy requires close outpatient monitoring, appropriate medication adjustment, and heart rate assessment at rest and with exercise. Exercise stress testing without interruption of the treatment should be performed in all young, physically active individuals. A 6-minute–walk test or ambulatory ECG monitor may be a preferred modality in elderly patients with AF for assessment of rate-control efficacy.

β-Blockers or nondihydropyridine CCBs appear to be equally effective in controlling heart rate at rest, and there are no data suggesting a significant advantage of any particular agent. β-Blockers are more effective than CCBs for rate control in patients with an uncontrolled heart rate during exercise. Digoxin is less effective than β-blockers and CCBs and is best reserved for sedentary, elderly patients with underlying LV dysfunction and HF.

Occasionally, in patients who do not tolerate a single drug, consider smaller doses of two agents from different classes. Additionally, if an agent from one class fails, it may be prudent to try a drug from another class for combination therapy.

If the above strategies fail to control ventricular response, cautiously titrated combination therapy should be initiated. Digoxin with either a β-blocker or a CCB is frequently used in the chronic rate-control therapy of AF. In patients with an exercise-induced, uncontrolled ventricular response, a combination of digoxin with β-blockers is superior to digoxin with a CCB. If such regimens are ineffective, an oral β-blocker may be cautiously combined with a nondihydropyridine CCB. In dual therapy with β-blockers, diltiazem is preferred over verapamil because it has less negative inotropic and less vasoactive effects. This results in a lower risk of significant side effects when combined with β-blockers.

In patients who do not respond to therapy with two AV nodal blocking agents, ie, a combination of β-blockers and CCBs, digoxin may be considered.

In hypertensive patients with AF, adding clonidine has been shown to improve chronic rate control and may be a therapeutic option in selected patients. Some AADs may be used with the goal of rate control. Both amiodarone and sotalol have powerful AV nodal blocking properties. However, their use for chronic rate control is limited by side effects. One must introduce AADs cautiously in patients with AF. If not combined with an AV nodal blocking drug, certain AADs may slow the atrial rate enough to permit improved AV nodal conduction and acceleration of the ventricular rate. This is a particular hazard when Class IC AADs are used to treat AF that they convert to flutter.

Finally, with the failure of these drug strategies, AV nodal ablation with implantation of a PPM should be considered. This is a highly effective, invasive method for rate control which is mostly reserved for patients in whom pharmacologic therapies have failed.

The therapeutic approach to chronic rate control of AF is presented in **Figure 12.3**.

12

FIGURE 12.3 — Approach to Chronic Rate-Control Strategy in a Patient With Permanent AF

Assess ventricular response at rest and with exercise

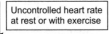

Initiate rate control therapy with first-line drugs:
- β-Blockers
- Nondihydropyridine CCB
- Digoxin (consider only in elderly and sedentary patients)

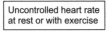

Add second agent:
- Add digoxin to β-blocker or to nondihydropyridine CCB
- Combine β-blocker with nondihydropyridine CCB[a]

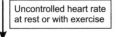

Consider:
- Combined therapy with β-blocker + CCB + digoxin
- Adding clonidine in hypertensive individuals

Uncontrolled heart rate at rest or with exercise

Failure of pharmacologic rate control:
- AV nodal ablation with PPM implantation
- Consider antiarrhythmic drugs with rate-control properties (sotalol, amiodarone)

---

[a] Diltiazem is preferred over verapamil due to lower risk of side effects (especially heart block) when used in combination with β-blocker.

SUGGESTED READING

Arnsdorf MF, Ganz LI. Control of ventricular rate in atrial fibrillation: pharmacologic therapy. In: Basow DS, ed. *UpToDate*. Waltham, MA: UpToDate; 2010.

Arnsdorf MF, Ganz LI. Control of ventricular rate in atrial fibrillation: nonpharmacologic therapy. In: Basow DS, ed. *UpToDate*. Waltham, MA: UpToDate; 2010.

Cooper HA, Bloomfield DA, Bush DE, et al; AFFIRM Investigators. Relation between achieved heart rate and outcomes in patients with atrial fibrillation (from the Atrial Fibrillation Follow-up Investigation of Rhythm Management [AFFIRM] Study). *Am J Cardiol*. 2004;93(10):1247-1253.

Davy JM, Herold M, Hoglund C, et al; ERATO Study Investigators. Dronedarone for the control of ventricular rate in permanent atrial fibrillation: the Efficacy and safety of dRonedArone for the cOntrol of ventricular rate during atrial fibrillation (ERATO) study. *Am Heart J*. 2008;156(3):527.e1-527.e9.

Doshi RN, Daoud EG, Fellows C, et al; PAVE Study Group. Left ventricular-based cardiac stimulation post AV nodal ablation evaluation (the PAVE study). *J Cardiovasc Electrophysiol*. 2005;16(11):1160-1165.

Epstein AE. Strategies for rate control. In: Kowey P, Naccarelli GV, eds. *Atrial Fibrillation*. New York: Marcel Dekker; 2005:121-134.

Farshi R, Kistner D, Sarma JS, Longmate JA, Singh BN. Ventricular rate control in chronic atrial fibrillation during daily activity and programmed exercise: a crossover open-label study of five drug regimens. *J Am Coll Cardiol*. 1999;33(2):304-310.

Fauchier L, Grimard C, Pierre B, et al. Comparison of beta blocker and digoxin alone and in combination for management of patients with atrial fibrillation and heart failure. *Am J Cardiol*. 2009;103(2):248-254.

Fuster V, Rydén LE, Cannom DS, et al; American College of Cardiology/American Heart Association Task Force on Practice Guidelines; European Society of Cardiology Committee for Practice Guidelines; European Heart Rhythm Association; Heart Rhythm Society. ACC/AHA/ESC 2006 Guidelines for the Management of Patients with Atrial Fibrillation: a report of the American College of Cardiology/American Heart Association Task Force on Practice Guidelines and the European Society of Cardiology Committee for Practice Guidelines (Writing Committee to Revise the 2001 Guidelines for the Management of Patients With Atrial Fibrillation): developed in collaboration with the European Heart Rhythm Association and the Heart Rhythm Society. *Circulation*. 2006;114(7):e257-e354.

12

Hallberg P, Lindbäck J, Lindahl B, Stenestrand U, Melhus H; RIKS-HIA group. Digoxin and mortality in atrial fibrillation: a prospective cohort study. *Eur J Clin Pharmacol*. 2007;63(10):959-971.

Hilliard AA, Miller TD, Hodge DO, Gibbons RJ. Heart rate control in patients with atrial fibrillation referred for exercise testing. *Am J Cardiol*. 2008;102(6):704-708.

Ho KM, Sheridan DJ, Paterson T. Use of intravenous magnesium to treat acute onset atrial fibrillation: a meta-analysis. *Heart*. 2007;93(11):1433-1440.

Kalahasty G, Ellenbogen K. The role of pacemakers in the management of patients with atrial fibrillation. *Cardiol Clin*. 2009;27(1):137-150.

Kristensen L, Nielsen JC, Mortensen PT, Pedersen OL, Pedersen AK, Andersen HR. Incidence of atrial fibrillation and thromboembolism in a randomised trial of atrial versus dual chamber pacing in 177 patients with sick sinus syndrome. *Heart*. 2004;90(6):661-666.

Kristensen L, Nielsen JC, Pedersen AK, Mortensen PT, Andersen HR. AV block and changes in pacing mode during long-term follow-up of 399 consecutive patients with sick sinus syndrome treated with an AAI/AAIR pacemaker. *Pacing Clin Electrophysiol*. 2001;24(3):358-365.

Opie LH. Calcium channel blockers (calcium antagonists). In: Opie LH, Gersh BJ, eds. *Drugs for the Heart: An Expert Consult*. 7th ed. Philadelphia, PA: Saunders Elsevier; 2009:59-87.

Opie LH, Horowitz JD. Beta blocking agents. In: Opie LH, Gersh BJ, eds. *Drugs for the Heart: An Expert Consult*. 7th ed. Philadelphia, PA: Saunders Elsevier; 2009:1-37.

Simpson CS, Ghali WA, Sanfilippo AJ, Moritz S, Abdollah H. Clinical assessment of clonidine in the treatment of new-onset rapid atrial fibrillation: a prospective, randomized clinical trial. *Am Heart J*. 2001;142(2):E3.

Sutton R, Kenny RA. The natural history of sick sinus syndrome. *Pacing Clin Electrophysiol*. 1986;9(6 Pt 2):1110-1114.

Van Gelder IC, Van Veldhuisen DJ, Crijns HJ, et al. Rate control efficacy in permanent atrial fibrillation: a comparison between lenient versus strict rate control in patients with and without heart failure. Background, aims, and design of RACE II. *Am Heart J*. 2006;152(3):420-426.

Wood MA, Brown-Mahoney C, Kay GN, Ellenbogen KA. Clinical outcomes after ablation and pacing therapy for atrial fibrillation: a meta-analysis. *Circulation*. 2000;101(10):1138-1144.

Wyse DG. Therapeutic considerations in applying rate control therapy for atrial fibrillation. *J Cardiovasc Pharmacol*. 2008;52(1):11-17.

13

Prevention of Thromboembolic Complications in AF

Pathophysiology of Thromboembolism in AF

The mechanism of thrombus formation in AF is complex and not completely understood. A previously accepted explanation of thrombus formation was blood stasis in the LA. Such an explanation appears to be over-simplified. Structural abnormalities in endothelium and endocardium, abnormal blood flow, and changes in blood content are all present in AF. Interactions between these abnormalities are likely responsible for a prothrombotic milieu in AF.

■ Structural Abnormalities in Endothelium and Endocardium

Endothelial damage is well documented in AF, evidenced by an elevated level of circulating endothelial cells in the blood. An elevated level of von Willebrand factor (vWF), a well established indicator of endothelial damage, is an independent risk factor for LAA thrombus formation with AF. Structural abnormalities in the endocardium, including inflammatory changes, myocyte hypertrophy, and necrosis, are documented in patients with AF, especially in the LA and LAA.

Extracellular matrix turnover and fibrosis not only contribute to conduction abnormalities, which may facilitate the establishment of AF circuits, but also promote prothrombotic effects. Various enzymes (eg, metalloproteinases) and growth factors (eg, transforming growth factor β) appear to stimulate thrombogenesis in AF.

Furthermore, complex atherosclerotic plaque of the thoracic aorta is an independent risk factor for stroke in patients with AF *(see below)*.

13

■ Blood Stasis

The LAA is a long, blind-ended structure with a narrow inlet attached to the LA. This promotes blood stasis and makes the LAA a major site of intra-atrial thrombus formation, not only in AF but also in sinus rhythm. Both the loss of atrial systole and left atrial dilatation in AF promotes blood stasis. Atrial stunning, the delay in recovery of atrial systolic function after successful cardioversion, is responsible for increased risk of thromboembolism after cardioversion. LV dilatation and impaired systolic function may additionally increase the risk of blood stasis and intracardiac thrombus formation in patients with AF. The presence of valvular heart disease strongly impacts thromboembolic risk. Mitral stenosis not only directly leads to LA dilatation but also, due to abnormalities in LA emptying and transmitral flow, increases the risk of thrombus formation in the LA and LAA.

An elevated hematocrit, due to volume depletion/overdiuresis, may increase the risk of thrombogenesis. Blood stasis is commonly seen in TEE as spontaneous echo contrast *(see below)*.

■ Hypercoagulable State

Markers of a prothrombotic state are increased in patients with both paroxysmal and permanent AF. These markers are even more elevated in AF patients after cardioversion, particularly electrical. Resolution of a prothrombotic state occurs to 2 to 4 weeks after restoration of NSR. AF affects thrombogenesis at different levels of the coagulation cascade. vWF is released due to endothelial damage/dysfunction and contributes to the prothrombotic state in AF. Increased fibrin turnover with elevated markers of thrombogenesis such as D-dimer and thrombin-antithrombin complexes are associated with AF and decrease with antithrombotic therapy. In patients with AF, the LA, and particularly the LAA endocardium, show reduced production of nitrous oxide (NO) and elevated levels of prothrombotic plasminogen activator inhibitor 1 (PAI-1). Platelet activation is also thought to contribute to the prothrombotic state in AF. Markers of platelet activation including thromboglobulin and platelet factor 4 are elevated in patients with AF. Left atrial thrombus and risk for thromboembolism have been associated with elevated levels of vWF and beta thromboglobulin.

Virchow's triad of thrombogenesis creates a useful framework to understand the prothrombotic state in AF. However, the exact mechanisms driving thrombogenesis and thromboembolic risk in AF are not established. An inflammatory state, as demonstrated by elevated levels of CRP and IL-6, extracellular matrix turnover, and release of prothrombotic growth factors, including VEGF, TGF β, and angiopoietin 2, is thought to play a role in perpetuating prothrombotic risk.

Clinical Presentation of Thromboembolism in AF

In a patient with a history of AF, thromboembolic events most often occur while the patient is in AF or in the first 10 days after conversion to sinus rhythm. Cardiac thromboembolism in AF classically presents with acute ischemic symptoms in the affected organs. The most common and feared complication of AF is cardioembolic stroke. Stroke is by far the most common cause of long-term disability and the third leading cause of death in patients with AF. Brain tissue is particularly vulnerable to ischemia and 80% mortality caused by thromboembolism in AF is attributed to stroke.

In AF, peripheral embolization to organs other than brain is much less common. In one study, about 7% of thromboembolic events were to other organs, but autopsy studies suggest that peripheral thromboembolism is frequently subclinical and underdiagnosed.

Immediate recognition of cardioembolic events is crucial as early implementation of appropriate therapy may prevent infarction and not only decrease mortality but also significantly limit long-term disability. Incidence, presentation, diagnosis, and outcomes of major thromboembolic complications of AF are presented below. Management of these conditions should follow appropriate treatment guidelines.

13

■ Ischemic Stroke and Transient Ischemic Attacks
Incidence

AF is associated with 5-fold increase in risk of embolic stroke. AF becomes a more powerful stroke hazard with advancing age. The annual incidence of stroke in AF patients increases from approximately 1.3% at age 50 to 59 years to 5.1% at age 80 to 89 years. The annual risk of stroke may exceed 10% in AF patients >80 years of age with multiple risk factors. Although it is estimated that cardioembolism due to AF is responsible for 15% to 20% of all ischemic strokes, it may cause approximately 35% of all strokes in patients >80 years of age.

Presentation

Cerebral thromboembolism may cause reversible ischemia or infarction of the dependent vascular territory. Two types of cerebral events are defined for risk stratification and management algorithms of stroke patients and are relevant to the discussion of cerebral thromboembolism in AF:

- TIAs: the neurologic deficit completely resolves in <24 hours (thrombus is lysed or defragmented rapidly)
- Ischemic stroke: neurologic deficit caused by irreversible ischemia is subsequently followed by cerebral infarction and causes focal neurologic deficit.

Cerebral infarction most commonly occurs due to an occlusion of a cerebral artery but rarely may also result in lacunar lesions (small noncortical infarcts). LAA/LA thrombus is the most common source of thromboembolism in patients with AF, although emboli from atheromatous proximal aorta and intrinsic cerebrovascular disease may be responsible for up to 25% of strokes in AF patients.

Cardioembolic strokes usually are of sudden onset, painless, and produce focal neurologic deficits, with symptoms and signs dependent mostly on the brain area affected (eg, supratentorium, cerebellum, or brainstem) and infarct size. AF causes more severe strokes and TIAs than other forms of ischemic stroke, most likely due to embolization of larger thrombi in AF. AF is also associated with silent strokes. In the SPINAF trial, CT scanning at presentation revealed silent areas of brain infarctions in 15% of AF patients. The estimated rate of new silent strokes was approximately 1.3 % per year during 3 years of follow-up. Interestingly, patients treated with warfarin and aspirin (ASA) in SPINAF had a similar rate of clinically silent strokes.

Diagnosis

The diagnosis of thromboembolic stroke is based on the clinical examination.

Brain CT without contrast is done initially to rule out intracranial hemorrhage (ICH) and make the critical distinction between ischemia and hemorrhage. Although nonspecific signs of ischemic stroke may be present on the CT scan as early as 2 hours after the onset of clinical symptoms, a reliable diagnosis may not be possible in the first 24 hours, even with the use of more sensitive contrast-enhanced CT.

Brain MRI is less feasible in the emergency room setting. However, an MRI (especially diffusion weighted) detects ischemic changes earlier than CT and may show ischemic penumbra, ie, the area of the brain that may be saved by immediate intervention. MRI is also superior to CT for the detection of small cortical infarcts and strokes in the posterior fossa, which are not well visualized by CT because of bone artifact. MRI is also better than CT in the detection of hemorrhagic transformation of an acute ischemic stroke.

Acute stroke in patients with AF is presumed to be caused by intracardiac thrombus. TEE, but rarely TTE, may confirm the diagnosis of residual thrombus in up to 45% of patients presenting with an acute thromboembolic event in the setting of new-onset AF. Once the diagnosis of cardioembolic stroke is made, further management should follow AHA/ASA guideline recommendations for therapy of acute ischemic stroke.

13

Outcome and Mortality

Cardioembolic stroke in the majority of AF patients is devastating and carries a higher risk of mortality and disability than other forms of ischemic stroke. Cerebral thromboembolism in patients with AF is associated with up to 30% mortality at 1 year. Approximately 15% to 30% of AF patients who survive become permanently disabled. AF patients with a prior history of embolic stroke are at the highest risk of a recurrent thromboembolic event. In the absence of anticoagulation, the risk of a subsequent event appears to be as high as 3% to 5% in the first few weeks and 12% per year in the 2 to 3 years after the initial event.

■ Other Thromboembolic Complications of AF

The most common sites of peripheral embolization are the lower and upper extremities, mesenteric arteries, aortoiliac, and renal arteries. Although cases of PE caused by RAA thrombus have been reported, the risk of clinically significant PE in AF patients with isolated RAA thrombus is unclear. Nonetheless, RAA thrombus may cause systemic emboli, such as stroke, in patients with patent foramen ovale and right to left shunt.

Although the vast majority of cardiac emboli in AF patients manifest in the brain (embolization to other vascular beds accounted for only 7% of events in one series), up to 20% of deaths related to thromboembolism are caused by peripheral embolization. This is partially caused by the fact that most of the peripheral emboli are subclinical (ie, revealed at autopsy) and that some relatively uncommon embolic complications of AF (eg, acute thromboembolic mesenteric ischemia) are associated with a very high mortality. In every patient with AF and new acute ischemic symptoms, a clinical suspicion of peripheral embolization should be high and followed by immediate diagnostic testing and therapy. The most common peripheral thromboembolic complications of AF are presented in **Table 13.1**.

Risk Stratification for Thromboembolism in AF

■ Background

The high mortality and morbidity associated with thromboembolic stroke has led to the investigation of stroke risk predictors in patients with AF. Thromboembolic risk in AF can be assessed using a single risk factor, eg, a patient's age. With respect to benefits vs risks of chronic anticoagulation, the ratio is greatest in patients with multiple embolic risk factors and low bleeding risk. Unfortunately, high stroke risk usually also predicts a high bleeding risk. Advanced models combining different risk factors for stratification have been developed. These complex risk stratification schemes are used to predict embolic risk and absolute benefit of therapeutic intervention with antithrombotic therapy. Prior to specific discussion of stroke risk stratification models in AF, general considerations are presented below.

■ Limitations of Stroke Risk Stratification Algorithms

The majority of current risk stratification schemes and their management implications are based on the results of randomized trials. However, these trials had relatively short-term follow-up (2 to 3 years on average), and their participants did not always represent the general cohort. Additionally, results of these trials could be biased as compliance to therapy is usually higher in randomized trials than in the general population. Using a supplementary risk model based on community cohorts *(see below)* may be preferable.

■ Type of AF

Most of the clinical trials enrolled patients with persistent or permanent AF; however, paroxysmal AF appears to carry a similar risk of stroke. Different forms of AF should be managed with antithrombotic therapy in a similar manner based on the presence or absence of risk factors.

TABLE 13.1 — Most Common Thromboembolic Complications of AF Other Than Stroke

Complication	Incidence in AF	Clinical Presentation	Diagnosis	Outcomes and Mortality
Acute thromboembolic limb ischemia	~0.4%/y for aorto-iliac and lower-extremity arteries emboli Lower-extremity emboli are twice more common than to upper extremities	'5 P'-pain, pallor, pulselessness, parethesia, paralysis in affected limb Symptoms depend on extent of embolic occlusion and collateral flow	Catheter-based angiography—gold standard Consider noninvasive imaging (CTA, MRA, US) based on the presentation	1-y mortality ~16% with lower-extremity and 5% with upper-extremity emboli
Acute thromboembolic mesenteric ischemia	~0.14%/y	Severe and unrelenting abdominal pain (out of proportion to the physical findings), nausea/vomiting, eventually peritonitis and shock	Contrast-enhanced CT is an initial modality of choice CTA—can show site of occlusion	Overall high mortality (~70%) due to frequent delay in diagnosis and surgery >24 h from presentation Generally good prognosis if diagnosed and treated <6 h from presentation

Splenic infarction	Rare (may be under-diagnosed) Thromboembolism is the most common cause of splenic infarct in patients >40 years old	No specific symptoms of left-upper abdominal pain, nausea/vomiting, fever, and chills	Contrast-enhanced CT	Usually resolves without clinical sequelae Rarely massive infarcts requiring splenectomy
Renal thromboembolism	Rare (may be under-diagnosed)	Nonspecific symptoms of flank or generalized abdominal pain, fever, vomiting	Renal angiography, renal scintigraphy, or contrast-enhanced CT	30-d mortality reported as high as 11% 25% of patients develop chronic renal failure 60% of patients normalize renal function

13

■ **Rhythm- vs Rate-Control Strategy**

Results of large clinical trials comparing rhythm vs rate control in AF showed equal risk of stroke regardless of strategy chosen, with most of the thromboembolic events having occurred if therapy with warfarin was inadequate (subtherapeutic INR) or had been stopped. Thus an antithrombotic strategy should be chosen regardless of rhythm- vs rate-control therapy of AF.

■ **Valvular vs Nonvalvular AF**

The risk of stroke in patients with coexisting valvular heart disease (valvular AF) is higher than in patients with nonvalvular AF. Patients with rheumatic mitral valve disease or with prosthetic heart valves (mechanical or bioprosthetic) are considered to be at very high risk of stroke and should be treated with anticoagulation therapy and without further risk stratification.

Clinical Risk Factors and Stratification Schemes

Multiple risk factors for stroke in AF have been identified. In the systematic review of risk factors for stroke in patients with AF by The Stroke Risk in Atrial Fibrillation Working Group, four clinical features (prior stroke or TIA, older age, hypertension, and diabetes mellitus) were found to be independent risk factors for stroke and thromboembolism. However, besides a previous history of stroke/TIA, absolute stroke rates associated with other individual risk factors are difficult to estimate from the available data in this analysis. Although advancing age by decade has been correlated with stroke rate, it is accepted that assessment of stroke risk in AF is improved by using risk-stratification models, which include a combination of clinical and echocardiographic risk factors.

The original, randomized stroke prevention trials in patients with nonvalvular AF (AFASAK, BAATAF, SPAF, CAFA and SPINAF) *(see* Pharmacologic Prevention of Stroke in AF *discussion below)* used their own combinations of risk factors for stroke prediction, but the results of the above trials did not provide a high degree of confidence. However, data from these trials were used for the development of more powerful risk stratification models: Atrial Fibrillation Investigators (AFI) and Stroke Prevention in Atrial Fibrillation III (SPAF III). These study risk stratification models were the precursors of the most popular contemporary model, the CHADS2 score.

■ CHADS2 Score and Risk Stratification Based on ACC/AHA/ESC 2006 Guidelines

Based on analysis and compilation of AFI and SPAF risk stratification models, the CHADS2 scheme was proposed, wherein C stands for recent congestive heart failure, H for hypertension, A for age 75 or older, D for diabetes, and S for prior stroke or transient ischemic attack. Each risk factor receives 1 point, with the exception of stroke (or TIA), which was assigned 2 points because of its high association with stroke. This risk stratification model was then tested on patients in the National Registry of Atrial Fibrillation which consisted of 1733 Medicare beneficiaries aged 65 to 95 years who had nonrheumatic AF and were not prescribed warfarin at hospital discharge. After a mean of 1.2 years of follow-up, the predictive value of the CHADS2 score to estimate stroke risk in patients with AF was estimated using statistical analysis (**Table 13.2**).

TABLE 13.2 — Risk of Stroke in National Registry of AF Participants, Stratified by CHADS2 Score

CHADS2 Score	Adjusted Stroke Rate (%/y)[a] (95% CI)	Patients (N=1733)
0	1.9 (1.2 to 3.0)	120
1	2.8 (2.0 to 3.8)	463
2	4.0 (3.1 to 5.1)	523
3	5.9 (4.6 to 7.3)	337
4	8.5 (6.3 to 11.1)	220
5	12.5 (8.2 to 17.5)	65
6	18.2 (10.5 to 27.4)	5

[a] The adjusted stroke rate was derived from multivariate analysis assuming no aspirin usage.

Gage BF, et al. *JAMA*. 2001;285:2864-2870.

13

The adjusted stroke rate per 100 patient-years (essentially equal percent per year) increased as the CHADS2 score increased (ranging from 1.9 with a score of 0 to 18.2 with a score of 6). The stroke rate increased by a factor of 1.5 for each 1-point increase in the CHADS2 score (P <0.001). Use of ASA was associated with a hazard rate of 0.8 resulting in a statistically insignificant 20% relative reduction in the rate of stroke. The predictive value of CHADS2 model was subsequently validated in a large (>11,000 patients) community-based cohort. In this clinical practice-based cohort, patients who were taking warfarin had lower risks in all CHADS2 groups. Although several risk stratification models (with generally similar predictive value) have been developed, the CHADS2 score is the most frequently used and was incorporated into the ACC/AHA/ESC 2006 Guidelines for the Management of Patients with Atrial Fibrillation.

In addition, the 2012 ACCP Guidelines reviewed some of the limitations of the CHADS2 Score but opted to use this score as the principal approach for its risk-based treatment recommendations. They did so because the CHADS2 score has been extensively validated and is easy for clinicians to remember. This is different than other recent recommendations (eg, 2010 ESC Guidelines for the management of atrial fibrillation, 2012 HRS/EHRA/ECAS Expert Consensus Statement on Catheter and Surgical Ablation of Atrial Fibrillation) which underlines importance of CHA2DS2-VASc score in further assessment of thromboembolic risk in patients with CHADS2 score of 1.

Antithrombotic therapy for patients with AF according to 2012 ACCP Guidelines is outlined in **Table 13.3**. In patients with nonvalvular AF and a low-risk CHADS2 score of 0, aspirin (81 to 325 mg/day) or no therapy is recommended. Patients with nonvalvular AF and a moderate-risk CHADS2 score of 1, either anticoagulation (dabigatran, rivaroxaban, or warfarin) or aspirin (81 to 325 mg/day) can be considered. In patients with nonvalvular AF and a high-risk CHADS2 score (≥2), anticoagulation (dabigatran, rivaroxaban, or warfarin) is preferred.

TABLE 13.3 — Antithrombotic Therapy for Patients With AF

1. Nonvalvular Paroxysmal to Permanent AF
   - CHADS2 Score is compiled by assigning one point for CHF, hypertension, age ≥75 years, and diabetes mellitus, and by assigning two points for previous stroke or TIA.
   - Other risk factors, female gender, CAD, and age 65-74 years are also given a point in the CHA2DS2-VASc scheme *(see text)*.

Risk Category	CHADS2 Score	Recommended Therapy
Low Risk	0	Aspirin (81-325 mg/d) or no therapy
Moderate Risk	1	Dabigatran, rivaroxaban, or warfarin (INR 2-3, target 2.5) or aspirin (81-325 mg/d)
High Risk	≥2	Dabigatran, rivaroxaban, or warfarin (INR 2-3, target 2.5)
2. Mitral Stenosis	—	Warfarin (INR 2-3, target 2.5)
3. Prosthetic Valve	—	Warfarin (INR >2.5)

Modified from You JJ, et al. *Chest.* 2012;141(suppl 2):e531S-e5375S.

13

The 2011 ACC/AHA/HRS Focused Update on the Management of Patients with Atrial Fibrillation gave dabigatran a Class I indication as an acceptable alternative to warfarin for the prevention of stroke or thromboembolism in patients with paroxysmal to permanent AF and risk factors for stroke or systemic embolization who do not have a prosthetic valve or hemodynamically significant valve disease, severe renal failure (creatinine clearance <15 mL/min), or advanced liver disease (impaired baseline clotting function).

In patients with mitral stenosis and prosthetic valves, the choice of oral anticoagulation should remain limited to warfarin unless future study provides other acceptable alternatives. In the patient with nonvalvular AF and moderate or high embolic risk (CHADS2 score $\geq$1), the anticoagulation options now include warfarin, the direct thrombin inhibitor, dabigatran, and the factor Xa inhibitor, rivaroxaban. These agents are individually discussed later in this chapter. The decision to switch a patient from warfarin to a new agent or to institute therapy with a specific agent requires consideration of multiple factors. These may include stability and compliance in monitoring of INR with prior warfarin use, availability and willingness to participate in an anticoagulation management program, twice daily dosing, stability of renal function, concomitant drug use, patient preferences, cost, and other factors.

Although the CHADS2 score is a simple, effective and useful tool in the clinical setting for risk stratification for stroke in AF, it has a few major disadvantages. It does not account for newly established risk factors for stroke. A relatively large group of patients have an intermediate risk for stroke based on this scoring method without a clear indication for anticoagulation strategy. Additionally, it defines an annual risk of stroke <2% as a low risk (which does not mandate anticoagulation therapy); however, controversies exist as some of these "low-risk" patients are destined to suffer from strokes without anticoagulation therapy.

Recently published studies suggest that some of the other risk factors (recognized as less valid by 2006 ACC/AHA/ESC Guidelines) should be considered in a stroke risk stratification scheme and may improve its modest predictive value. It is now generally accepted that female gender increases thromboembolic risk. Additionally, there is increasing data that atherosclerotic vascular disease (eg, MI, peripheral artery disease, and complex aortic plaque) increase thromboembolic risk in AF. Furthermore, results of some studies suggest that oral anticoagulation is clearly superior to ASA in thromboprophylaxis of the elderly (≥75 years), and undertreatment occurs because of fear of bleeding in this population.

An alternative to the CHADS2 model is the 2009 Birmingham scheme, which was incorporated into UK National Institute for Health and Clinical Excellence (NICE) guidelines on AF management. This novel method divides risk factors into definitive (previous stroke/TIA/thromboembolism and age ≥75 years) and combinational risk factors (heart failure/moderate to severe LV dysfunction, hypertension, diabetes, vascular disease, female gender, and age 65 to 74 years). This model uses CHA2DS2-VASc acronym with high risk defined as one definitive or two or more combination risk factors (score ≥2), intermediate risk as one combination risk factor (score=1), and low risk as an absence of any risk factors (score=0). A score of ≥2 (as in the revised CHADS2 scheme) warrants therapy with warfarin (**Table 13.4**).

This scheme was validated and compared with other risk stratification models such as CHADS2 and Framingham *(see below)* in a cohort of 1084 patients from the Euro Heart Survey for AF. They were not anticoagulated at baseline and were followed for 1 year. Although all schemes showed modest predictive value for thromboembolism, this novel model appears to be more accurate. Using a CHADS2 score model, almost 35% of patients were categorized into the intermediate-risk

13

TABLE 13.4 — The 2009 Birmingham Schema Expressed as a Point-Based Scoring System (CHA2DS2-VASc)

Risk Factor	Score[a]
CHF/LV dysfunction	1
Hypertension	1
Age ≥75 years	2
Diabetes mellitus	1
Stroke/TIA/TE	2
Vascular disease (prior MI, peripheral artery disease, or aortic plaque)	1
Age 65-74 years	1
Sex category (ie, female gender)	1

[a] High risk ≥2, intermediate risk = 1, low risk = 0. Score ≥2 warrants oral anticoagulation.

Lip GY, et al. *Chest.* 2010;137(2):263-272.

group, compared with 15% based on the Birmingham 2009 schema. The Birmingham 2009 schema classified only 9% as low risk (compared with 48% using Framingham scheme and 20% using CHADS2 model). Patients classified as low risk by the CHA2DS2-VASc scoring system did not have any thromboembolic events during 1 year of follow-up, whereas thromboembolism occurred in 1.4% of patients stratified as a low-risk by CHADS2. Furthermore, using CHADS2-VASc scoring system, 75% of patients were categorized into the high-risk category, which warrants anticoagulation with warfarin (compared with 45% by CHADS2 score). Although this system needs further validation, it improves predictive value for thromboembolism over the CHADS2 scoring system and may better identify AF patients who would benefit from anticoagulation.

Assessment of Stroke Risk in Community Patients With New-Onset AF

The assessment of stroke risk in patients with new-onset AF appears to be more applicable to clinical practice than the results of studies on selected participants in the randomized trials. A thromboembolic risk scheme based on a community cohort was developed using data from the Framingham Heart Study. This prospective, community-based study followed an observational cohort of 705 participants with new-onset AF who were not treated with warfarin at baseline. Patients who suffered an ischemic stroke, TIA, or death within 30 days of AF diagnosis were excluded. Patients in whom warfarin was initiated during the study were excluded from the warfarin-censored analysis. During a mean follow-up of 4 years, 83 patients had a stroke (2.9% per year) and 382 had a stroke or died (13.4% per year). Using five risk factors (advancing age, female sex, increasing systolic BP, prior stroke or TIA, and diabetes mellitus), the 5-year stroke risk may be predicted (**Figure 13.1**). Based on this scoring system, patients may be classified into low- (0 to 7), intermediate- (8 to 15) or high-risk groups (16 to 31). Using this model, 30.6% of patients were classified at a low-risk (annual rate of stroke ≤2%). Applying the Framingham risk score to predict the 5-year risk for stroke in patients with newly diagnosed AF may not only help to make treatment decisions but may also allow patients to understand the need for initiation of anticoagulation therapy.

Risk of Stroke Based on Echocardiographic Assessment

13

■ Transthoracic Echocardiogram (TTE)

TTE is usually obtained in AF patients in the evaluation of an etiology for diagnosis of associated structural heart disease or for an assessment of likelihood of maintenance of sinus rhythm before a decision regarding rhythm vs rate-control strategy is chosen. Assessment of the left ventricular systolic function in TTE is also used in thromboembolic risk stratification of AF patients. Moderate to severe LV dysfunction is a strong risk factor for thromboembolism in patients with AF (RR 2.5) and is currently incorporated into 2006 ACC/AHA/ESC management guidelines risk stratification. Left atrial size, as measured by diameter in the long-axis parasternal view, has yielded inconsistent results as a risk factor for

FIGURE 13.1 — Framingham Risk Score for Predicting the 5-Year Risk of Stroke in Patients With AF

STEP 1

Age (y)	Points
55-59	0
60-62	1
63-66	2
67-71	3
72-74	4
75-77	5
78-81	6
82-85	7
86-90	8
91-93	9
>93	10

STEP 2

Sex	Points
Men	0
Women	6

STEP 3

Systolic BP (mm Hg)	Points
<120	0
120-139	1
140-159	2
160-179	3
>179	4

STEP 4

Diabetes	Points
No	0
Yes	5

STEP 5

Prior Stroke or TIA	Points
No	0
Yes	6

STEP 6

- Add up points from Steps 1 through 5
- Look up predicted 5-y risk of stroke in table

Predicted 5-Year Risk of Stroke

Total Points	5-y Risk (%)
0-1	5
2-3	6
4	7
5	8
6-7	9
8	11
9	12
10	13
11	14
12	16
13	18
14	19
15	21
16	24
17	26
18	28
19	31
20	34
21	37
22	41
23	44
24	48
25	51
26	55
27	59
28	63
29	67
30	71
31	75

Wang TJ, et al. *JAMA*. 2003;290(8):1049-1056.

thromboembolism. Transthoracic echocardiogram is an insensitive modality for detection of left atrial appendage thrombus.

■ Transesophageal Echocardiogram (TEE)

In contrast to TTE, TEE is very sensitive and specific in the evaluation for a cardiac source of embolism and is the imaging modality of choice to exclude a cardiac source of embolism prior to cardioversion (see below). Thrombus, dense spontaneous echocontrast in the LA/LAA, and decreased LAA flow velocity (<20 cm/s) are well-documented TEE-derived risk factors for stroke. The sensitivity and specificity of TEE for the detection of left atrial thrombi are 95% and 99%, respectively. Additionally, the detection by TEE of complex atheromatous plaque in the thoracic aorta (defined as mobile, pedunculated, ulcerated, or >4 mm in thickness) is associated with a 12% yearly risk of stroke. Although oral anticoagulation effectively limits the risk of stroke in AF patients with the above TEE risk factors, they are not incorporated into risk stratification schemes. As such, TEE is not recommended purely for risk stratification purposes, but high-risk TEE findings, eg, from TEE obtained prior to cardioversion, may be used to identify patients who would benefit from anticoagulation, even though standard risk stratification placed them in a low-risk group. Key echocardiographic predictors of stroke are presented in **Table 13.5**.

13

TABLE 13.5 — Main Echocardiographic Predictors of Stroke in AF

Transthoracic ECG
- Moderate and severe LV systolic dysfunction

Transesophageal ECG
- Abnormalities in LA/LAA:
  - Thrombus
  - Reduced velocity of blood flow in the LAA (<20 cm/sec)
  - Dense spontaneous echo contrast
- Complex atheromatous plaque in the thoracic aorta

Although the exact pathogenesis of stroke in AF is not fully understood and may involve more complex mechanisms beyond thrombus embolization, anticoagulation with vitamin K antagonists has proven to be extremely effective in primary and secondary stroke prevention, decreasing stroke severity, and lowering mortality in patients with AF.

Newer anticoagulants, such as direct thrombin inhibitors (DTIs) or factor Xa inhibitors *(see below)*, do not require monitoring, appear to have a better safety profile than warfarin, and may become alternatives to warfarin in the near future. The efficacy of antiplatelet therapy for stroke prevention is less validated. ASA may be beneficial in some subsets of low-risk AF patients who may not have sufficient benefit from anticoagulation to outweigh side effects and risks. The benefit of ASA for stroke prevention may differ based on the type of risk factors present. The combination of ASA and clopidogrel for stroke prevention in AF is clearly inferior to warfarin. Although it may confer some protection from stroke, its use is associated with a higher risk of bleeding complications compared with ASA alone. Strategies for pharmacologic stroke prevention in AF are presented in **Figure 13.2**.

Oral Anticoagulation

■ Warfarin

An evidence-based review of the role of warfarin in stroke prevention in AF is presented below. This is followed by a brief description of the major characteristics of warfarin relevant to anticoagulation therapy in AF.

Efficacy of Warfarin in Primary Prevention of Stroke in AF

Five classic, randomized, controlled clinical trials compared oral warfarin with either control or placebo for the prevention of stroke in patients with nonvalvular AF. These trials include:

FIGURE 13.2 — Long-Term Pharmacologic Stroke Prevention in AF

Long-term pharmacologic strategies for stroke prevention in AF

- Anticoagulants
  - Vitamin K antagonists (warfarin)
  - Novel anticoagulants
    - Direct thrombin inhibitors (eg, dabigatran)
    - Factor Xa inhibitors (eg, rivaroxaban)
- Antiplatelet agents[a]
  - ASA
  - ASA + clopidogrel
- Additional therapies
  - Statins
  - Antihypertension agents (eg, ACEI, ARB)

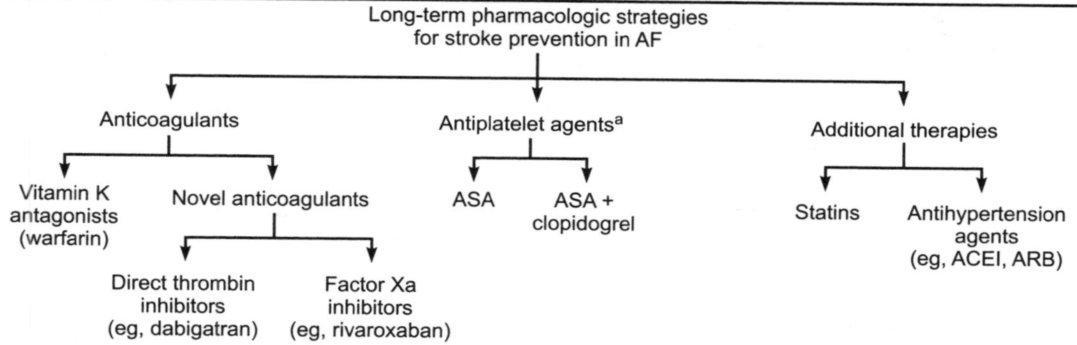

[a] Antiplatelet therapy is recommended for stroke prevention in AF only in low-risk patients and those with absolute contraindication to long-term anticoagulation.

13

- Copenhagen Atrial Fibrillation Aspirin and Anticoagulation (AFASAK)
- Stroke Prevention in Atrial Fibrillation (SPAF-I)
- Boston Area Anticoagulation Trial for Atrial Fibrillation (BAATAF),
- Canadian Atrial Fibrillation Anticoagulation (CAFA)
- Stroke Prevention in Nonrheumatic Atrial Fibrillation (SPINAF).

All of these trials were stopped prematurely because of the demonstrable benefit of oral anticoagulants in preventing ischemic stroke and systemic embolism (CAFA was stopped early because of external evidence of warfarin benefit from other trials). The follow-up period in these trials was generally between 1 to 2 years (the longest was 2.2 years). The mean achieved INR ranged from 2.0 to 2.6 among patients who were assigned to warfarin.

Although differently designed and varying with respect to the intensity of anticoagulation (INR target range 1.4 to 4.5), these studies showed consistent efficacy of adjusted-dose warfarin in the primary prevention of stroke in AF. After unifying clinical definitions, investigators of these primary prevention trials pooled their results in a meta-analysis.

The intention-to-treat analysis of 2461 patients enrolled in these trials showed that patients taking warfarin had an overall 68% RRR in stroke compared with those taking placebo (P <0.001). Annual stroke rate was reduced from 4.5% in control patients to 1.4% in patients assigned to adjusted-dose warfarin.

When patients not taking oral anticoagulation at the time of stroke were excluded (on-treatment analysis), the risk reduction for stroke in patients taking warfarin compared with placebo exceeded 80%. Anticoagulation lowered the all-cause mortality rate by 33% and lowered the combined outcome of stroke, systemic embolism, and death by 48%. Oral anticoagulation was equally effective for preventing strokes of all severities. The majority of strokes in the warfarin arms of these trials occurred in patients who either stopped warfarin or had an INR below the target range. The annual rate of major bleeding with warfarin was reported at 1.3% compared with 1.0% in the control group. These included an annual rate of ICH of 0.3% in warfarin users compared with 0.1% among controls.

The results of these trials have a few limitations. They had a relatively short duration of follow-up compared with clinical practice in which warfarin therapy frequently is prescribed for an extended duration or even lifelong. Additionally, all these landmark trials excluded patients with a high baseline bleeding risk. The average patient's age, a predictor of bleeding risk, at the time of study entry was 69 years old compared with a mean of 75 years in clinical practice. Such limitations could have led to a falsely low number of events and side effects of oral anticoagulation, but are unlikely to have changed the conclusions.

Efficacy of Warfarin in Secondary Prevention of Stroke in AF

The European Atrial Fibrillation Trial (EAFT) was a, secondary prevention trial that compared oral anti-coagulation with ASA or placebo in 439 patients with nonvalvular AF who had a TIA or stroke in the previous 3 months. The mean follow-up period in this trial was 2.3 years and the mean INR among patients who were assigned to warfarin therapy was 2.9. The RRR of stroke with oral anticoagulation was virtually identical to the pooled data from the five primary prevention trials. However, the absolute risk of stroke was higher because of the high-risk status of EAFT patients. The annual rate of stroke in the control patients of EAFT trial was 12% vs 4% in anticoagulated patients. The absolute risk reduction for stroke with oral anticoagulation was greater for secondary prevention (NNT for 1 year to prevent one stroke of 13) than for primary prevention (NNT for 1 year to prevent one stroke of 32).

Efficacy of Low-Intensity Warfarin Alone or In Combination With Antiplatelet Agents

The above mentioned pivotal trials and subsequent data established a therapeutic range of warfarin INR between 2 and 3 and a target of 2.5 to provide the optimal efficacy, ie, stroke prevention, safety, and avoidance of hemorrhagic complications. In an attempt to reduce the risk of bleeding and improve compliance to warfarin, several studies examined the efficacy of low INR intensities or fixed low doses of warfarin with a target INR ≤1.5 (either as monotherapy or in combination with ASA). The most powerful data comes from SPAF III trial.

On the basis of SPAF-I and SPAF-II, the investigators identified five high-risk factors for the subsequent development of stroke in patients with AF. These high-risk features included: females >75 years of age, systolic BP >160 mm Hg, history of recent CHF or fractional shortening <25% on echocardiography (essentially equal to LVEF <45%) and prior TIA or stroke. In the SPAF III trial, high-risk patients were randomized to receive warfarin in a dose sufficient to maintain the INR between 2 to 3 or to receive fixed-dose warfarin of 0.5 to 3.0 mg/day adjusted initially to an INR of 1.2 to 1.5 plus 325 mg ASA per day. Low-risk patients were treated with ASA. This high-risk arm of the trial was terminated early because of an increase in stroke among patients on combination therapy with fixed-dose, low-intensity warfarin. The annual rate of primary events was 7.9% in the fixed low-dose warfarin plus ASA group compared with 1.9% in the dose-adjusted warfarin group. The high stroke rate in the combination-therapy arm of this trial and the high efficacy of adjusted-dose warfarin (the RRR of 74%) suggest that the low-intensity anticoagulation was ineffective in AF patients at a high risk of stroke. Rates of serious bleeding complications were similar in both treatment groups.

Results of SPAF III were further supported by data from pooled analysis of three trials (ASAFAK 2, MIWAF, PATAF) that compared adjusted-dose warfarin (target INR 2 to 3.5) with low or fixed doses of warfarin (mean achieved INR 1.1 to 1.4). This meta-analysis showed a 38% reduction in clinical events for adjusted-dose warfarin (which did not reach statistical significance). Therefore, it is generally accepted that low INR intensity or low fixed-dose warfarin is ineffective in preventing stroke in high-risk patients with AF. Additionally, there is no evidence of a beneficial synergistic effect of low-dose warfarin with ASA for stroke prevention in AF.

Efficacy of Warfarin vs Antiplatelet Therapy for Stroke Prevention in AF

Antiplatelet therapy with ASA alone or a combination of antiplatelet agents is markedly inferior to oral anticoagulation with warfarin. A meta-analysis of 12 trials that compared dose-adjusted warfarin with antiplatelet agents included 11,748 participants who were followed for a mean of 1.5 years. The mean age of the patients in these trials was 70 years. Women represented 38% of patients and 23% had previous stroke or TIA. Therapy with adjusted-dose warfarin was associated with a 37% reduction in strokes compared with antiplatelet therapy alone. The risk of ICH was doubled with adjusted-dose warfarin compared with ASA, although the increase in absolute risk was small (0. 2% per year).

The Birmingham Atrial Fibrillation Treatment of the Aged (BAFTA) study was a randomized, controlled trial of warfarin (INR 2 to 3) vs ASA (75 mg/day) for stroke prevention in elderly patients with AF. In this study, 973 patients (age >75 years, mean age of 82) were followed on average for 2.7 years. The primary end point was fatal or disabling stroke (ischemic or hemorrhagic), ICH, or clinically significant arterial embolism. In this elderly population, patients taking warfarin experienced significantly fewer primary events than patients taking ASA (yearly risk 1.8% vs 3.8%). Warfarin therapy was significantly better than ASA in both overall stroke prevention (RRR of 46%) and the prevention of disabling nonfatal strokes (RRR of 33%). There was no difference in the incidence of hemorrhagic stroke or subdural hemorrhage between the groups. Data from BAFTA study support the use of warfarin over ASA for people >75 years of age who have AF.

Another limitation of ASA therapy compared with warfarin was shown in the analysis of ischemic strokes in a cohort of 13,559 hospitalized patients with nonvalvular AF. Among 596 who had ischemic stroke requiring hospitalization, 32% were receiving warfarin, 27% were treated with ASA, and 42% were receiving neither. The 30-day mortality rate among patients who were taking ASA at the time of the stroke was similar to that among patients who had INR ≤2 while taking warfarin and was

2.5 times greater than those who had an INR ≥2. An INR of 1.5 to 1.9 at admission was associated with a mortality rate similar to that for an INR of <1.5 (18% and 15%, respectively). Patients taking ASA or warfarin with an INR <2 had a 2.6- to 3-fold increase in the severity of the stroke compared with patients who had an INR of ≥2. These data showed that warfarin with an INR ≥2 not only reduced the risk of ischemic stroke but also reduced stroke severity and the risk of death.

The ACTIVE-W trial (Atrial Fibrillation Clopidogrel Trial With Irbesartan for Prevention of Vascular Events) was the largest study comparing antiplatelet agents with warfarin. It was designed to prove that combination therapy of antiplatelet agents, clopidogrel, and ASA (rather than monotherapy with ASA) would be noninferior to oral anticoagulation among patients with AF. A total of 6706 participants eligible for therapy with warfarin were randomized to either clopidogrel (75 mg/day) and ASA (75-100 mg/day) or oral anticoagulant therapy with warfarin, with INR goal of 2 to 3. The primary end point in both trials was a composite outcome, ie, the first occurrence of stroke, non-CNS embolization, MI, or vascular death. The average CHADS risk score among enrolled patients was 2. Prior oral anticoagulation therapy was used in 77% of all patients. Target INR of 2 to 3 was achieved in 64% of patients. The trial was stopped prematurely after a median follow-up of 1.3 years because of a significantly lower annual rate of the primary end point in the warfarin arm (3.9 vs 5.6%, RR 0.69). Patients randomized to warfarin had lower rates of stroke (1.4% per year vs 2.4% per year, RRR of 40%) and non-CNS embolism (0.1% per year vs 0.4% per year). There was no significant difference in MI or vascular death. Overall rate of bleeding was significantly higher in combined antiplatelet group (15.4% vs 13.2% per year). No significant difference in major bleeding (2.4 % vs 2.2% per year) or total mortality (3.8% per year in both groups) was noted.

Major Characteristics of Warfarin Related to Stroke Prevention in AF

Although warfarin is well documented to be highly efficient for stroke prophylaxis in patients with AF, difficulties related to its chronic use lead to underuse of warfarin by physicians and poor patient compliance with therapy. Approximately 70% to 80% of all patients in AF have an indication for continuous oral anticoagulation. Among eligible patients, only approximately 60% overall and only 40% of elderly patients receive warfarin.

Additionally, a recent report from the AFFECTS Registry showed that a considerable portion of high-risk patients did not receive warfarin, and patients considered at no risk of stroke appear to be overprescribed with warfarin. The AFFECTS Registry was designed to assess the treatment patterns of AF among practicing cardiologists in the United States. Although all cardiologists participating in the study had received training with the ACC/AHA/ESC AF guidelines, warfarin use was only 73% and 66% in the rate- and rhythm-control patients with a CHADS2 score of >2, respectively, and approximately 60% and 49% in the rate- and rhythm-control patients with a score of <2, respectively.

Understanding of mechanism of action, interactions, goals of monitoring, and the risks and benefits of oral anticoagulation is crucial for appropriate use of warfarin in AF patients.

Mechanism of Action

The anticoagulation effect of warfarin is mediated through inhibition of the vitamin K-dependent gamma-carboxylation of coagulation factors II, VII, IX, and X. It has a procoagulant effect via inhibition of vitamin K–dependent gamma-carboxylation of naturally occurring inhibitors of coagulation (proteins C and S). It exerts a net anticoagulation action, but a clinically significant thrombogenic effect is possible in certain clinical situations *(see below)*. The prolongation of the prothrombin time (increase in INR) in the first days of therapy occurs due to depression of factor VII (half-life of 4 to 6 hours) but activity of other coagulation factors II, IX, and X remain relatively unchanged (eg, plasma half-life of prothrombin is approximately 3 days). Systemic anticoagulation with heparin or LMWH should overlap for at least 2 to 3 days after therapeutic INR is achieved in patients with acute thrombotic disease.

Pharmacokinetics

Warfarin is a racemic mixture of S-enantiomer and R-enantiomer in approximately equal proportion, however, the former is five times more potent. Warfarin has a biological half-life of approximately 37 hours with a maximum blood concentration in 90 minutes after oral administration. Its peak anticoagulation effect occurs in 36 to 72 hours after administration. Warfarin is strongly protein-bound (primarily to albumin). Only the unbound fraction is biologically active. Any drug which binds to albumin may increase warfarin biological activity. The S-enantiomer is primarily metabolized by the CYP2C9 system and R-enantiomer by CYP1A2 and CYP3A4. Genetic variants or drugs that alter the CYP system may strongly affect warfarin activity.

Loading Doses

A starting dose of approximately 5 mg/day is recommended for most patients. Doses <5 mg/day may be indicated in some subpopulations. These include the elderly, malnourished, patients with heart failure, liver or end-stage kidney disease, postoperative patients, or those with multiple concomitant drug therapy. Doses >5 mg/day can be considered only in selected patients at low risk for bleeding or in patients treated with maintenance doses >5 mg/day. Loading doses >10 mg/day should not be used. Possible concerns with higher loading doses include depletion of protein C and S resulting in a procoagulant state, depletion of factor VII with INR in the desired range without a therapeutic effect, or a supratherapeutic INR with bleeding risk in a patient with a genetic variant with warfarin sensitivity *(see below)*. Current drug labeling suggest lower initial dosing for patients with CYP2C9 and VKORC1 gene polymorphism. However specific drug dosing or mandatory genetic testing prior to initiation of therapy in these patients is not recommended.

Maintenance Doses

These vary significantly based on vitamin K level, nutritional status, liver or GI tract function, or concomitant drug therapy. The doses range from 2 to >10 mg/

day, with the dose adjusted based on the goal INR level. In patients with warfarin resistance, doses that are more than five times higher are frequently required to achieve the same level of anticoagulation. Because of the half-life of warfarin and prothrombin, a change in warfarin dose will not result in a change in the INR level for 2 to 3 days.

Monitoring

A prothrombin time ratio expressed as the INR is the accepted test for monitoring oral anticoagulation therapy with warfarin (INR = patient PT/mean normal PT)[ISI]. ISI or International Sensitivity Index indicates how a particular batch of tissue factor compares with an internationally standardized sample. The goal of successful monitoring is an INR in the desired therapeutic range with avoidance of any time of under- or over-anticoagulation. A baseline INR should be determined before initiation of warfarin and assessed every 2 to 3 days initially. Subsequent dosing should be adjusted in order to achieve a target INR of 2.5 (range: 2 to 3) in patients with AF unless another indication for warfarin is present. Once an INR level is stable for more than 1 to 2 weeks, it may be monitored less frequently (every 2 to 4 weeks). Follow-up in an outpatient anticoagulation clinic appears to offer more time at a therapeutic INR level, better drug-dosing control, and the opportunity for education and assistance with anticoagulation-related issues. Although not feasible for all patients, self-monitoring with small portable devices allows effective and safe anticoagulant dosing. Patients with unexplained unstable INR levels may benefit from a trial of low-dose oral vitamin K, eg, 150 mcg/day. Patients receiving warfarin require regular, detailed assessment on routine follow-up visits (**Table 13**.6). Studies such as ACTIVE A showed an efficacy of warfarin as a function of time in the therapeutic range.

Bleeding Risk

The annual risk of major bleeding on chronic oral anticoagulation in patients with AF is around 3%. The risk of intracerebral hemorrhage is estimated at 0.3% to 0.6%. High-intensity anticoagulation, concomitant use

TABLE 13.6 — Major Elements of Routine Follow-Up on Patients With AF Treated With Warfarin

- INR level checks—ensure patient follow-up on test results within 24 hours
- Compliance with therapy
- Symptoms or signs of bleeding, including melena
- Any changes in medical history
- Any changes in medications/supplements list—emphasis on NSAIDs, antibiotics
- Any major changes in diet/social habits
- Need to interrupt therapy

of other antithrombotic agents, increasing age, and prior history of bleeding are the most powerful predictors of major bleeding. Other generally accepted risk factors for major bleeding include uncontrolled hypertension, history of cerebrovascular disease, anemia, CAD with history of MI, liver or stage III-IV renal failure, high risk of fall, and NSAIDs use. A patient's age impacts not only the risk of bleeding but also the severity of hemorrhage. Elderly patients with hypertension and AF are at increased risk of fatal cerebral hemorrhage. Younger patients may experience mild GI bleeding, frequently with concomitant use of antiplatelet therapy or NSAIDs.

Retroperitoneal hemorrhage in anticoagulated patients may occur even when INR levels are within the therapeutic range, and its risk does not simply depend on degree of anticoagulation. Hematuria in patients taking warfarin is frequently caused by underlying genitourinary pathology. When corrected, oral anticoagulation may be resumed. The best way to estimate bleeding risk in an individual patient is not established. Several algorithms have been postulated such as the HEMORR2HAGES risk index and the recently developed HAS-BLED scoring system. None of them is widely used in clinical practice. A soluble thrombomodulin antigen concentration may become a clinically useful laboratory test to identify AF patients at high risk of bleeding with warfarin therapy. In a recent study from Sweden, an increased level of soluble thrombomodulin was shown to be associated with bleeding complications but not with CV events or all-cause mortality.

Stroke Prevention vs Bleeding Risk

Warfarin has a narrow therapeutic range. Adequate intensity but the lowest anticoagulation to minimize the risk of bleeding risk is a therapeutic goal. An INR range of 2 to 3 (target 2.5) provides maximum protection against ischemic stroke in AF and is recommended for primary and secondary prevention of stroke in non-valvular AF (**Figure 13.3**). Frequently occurring under-treatment (INR range of 1.6 to 2.5) is associated with incomplete efficacy (approximately 80% of that achieved with moderate-intensity anticoagulation) and may be considered only for primary prevention in patients older than 75 years who are at very high risk of bleeding. Once

FIGURE 13.3 — Annualized Incidence of Stroke or Intracranial Hemorrhage According to the INR

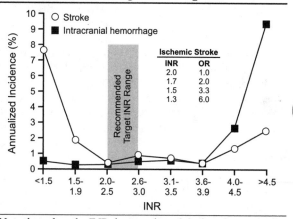

Note that when the INR decreased to <2.0, there is a steep rise in the OR for stroke; but the incidence of ICH remains low and flat (ie, there is no associated decrease in ICH).

Source: Fuster V, et al, eds. *Hurst's The Heart*. 12th ed. New York, NY: The McGraw-Hill Companies, Inc; 2008. Available at http://www .accessmedicine.com. Modified from Hylek EM, et al. *N Engl J Med*. 2003;349(11):1019-1026 and Hylek EM, et al. *N Engl J Med*. 1996;335(8):540-546.

13

the INR is <2, the risk of a stroke becomes exponentially higher. An INR of 1.7 doubles the risk. Once the INR is above 3.5 (which does not enhance the therapeutic efficacy in patients with AF), the risk for bleeding is increased. An INR up to 3.5 (target 3) is acceptable and indicated only for patients who have a mechanical heart valve. The incidence of ICH is flat (0.3 and 0.6 per 100 person-years) when the INR is between 1.5 and approximately 3.5.

Interactions

■ Genetic Polymorphism

Genetic polymorphisms have been associated with altered sensitivity to warfarin. It is estimated that up to 30% of anticoagulated patients with AF have CYP2C9 or VKORC1 gene polymorphism. The CYP2C9 gene is involved in the metabolic clearance of warfarin. The VKORC1 gene is involved in the recycling of vitamin K and is required for gamma carboxylation of vitamin K–dependent coagulation factors. The VKORC1 polymorphism affects drug action. Pharmacogenetic-guided therapy and computer-assisted algorithms are being investigated to improve clinical outcomes of chronic therapy with warfarin. These include multiple variables predicting response to warfarin, such as genetic polymorphism, age, body surface area, and common drug-drug interactions. The genetic testing for detecting variants of the CYP2C9 and VKORC1 genes is commercially available. These may identify patients who are very sensitive to warfarin.

■ Drug Interactions

Drug interactions with warfarin are a major concern in the anticoagulation management of AF patients and are associated with substantial morbidity and mortality. Under-anticoagulation, over-anticoagulation, and increased bleeding not necessarily associated with an elevated INR are well documented. A history of any concomitant drug, over-the-counter medication, herbal, or vitamin supplement intake should be reviewed at the time of each visit. Up to one third of patients anticoagulated with warfarin receive medications that interfere with warfarin effect. Major mechanisms of drug interactions with anticoagulation effect of warfarin include altered platelet function (eg, ASA, clopidogrel), GI tract injury (eg, NSAIDs), change in warfarin metabolism (eg, amiodarone), change in vitamin K metabolism (eg, acetaminophen), or impaired vitamin K synthesis in the GI tract (eg, antibiotics).

The mechanism of increased risk of bleeding with the combination of warfarin and anti-inflammatory agents is complex and involves more than one mechanism *(see above)*. The risk of bleeding appears to be highest with the combination of warfarin and ASA (even at a low dose) followed by the combination of warfarin and NSAIDs. Addition of selective COX-2 inhibitors to warfarin carries the lowest risk among anti-inflammatory drugs, as these agents do not interfere with platelet function. The risk of overanticoagulation with concomitant antibiotic therapy should always be considered prior to initiation of antibiotics in anticoagulated patient with AF. This frequently occurs in the first 3 days of therapy and is strongly increased by clarithromycin, metronidazole, ciprofloxacin, and trimethoprim-sulfamethoxazole (**Table 13.7**).

In a major review of classified warfarin interactions based on the documentation of the data supporting the reported interaction, it concluded that 82% of reported interactions were of poor documentation and 88% were case reports (which were a single case report in 96% of cases). Drug labeling should be used to predict the risk of particular drug interaction with warfarin.

Major classes of agents with proven interaction with warfarin are presented in **Table 13**.7.

▪ *Herbal Dietary Supplements*

Multiple herbs and supplements may have an interaction with warfarin. It is estimated that eight out of 10 of the most popular supplements have an interaction with warfarin and that 35% of the most commonly used 40 herbal and nonherbal supplements can significantly change the INR. Major interactions of warfarin with herbal and dietary supplements are presented in **Table 13.8**.

TABLE 13.7 — Major Warfarin Drug Interaction by Class[a]

| Drug Class | Effect of Warfarin | |
	Increased	Decreased
Antibiotics and antiviral agents	Macrolides Quinolones Amoxicillin/clavulanate Cephalosporins Trimethoprim/sulfamethoxazole Tetracycline Metronidazole Fluconazole and other azoles Isoniazid	Nafcillin Dicloxacillin Griseofulvin Rifampin
Anti-inflammatory agents	NSAIDs COX-2 inhibitors Acetaminophen Interferon	Azathioprine Mesalamine
Cardiovascular drugs	Antiarrhythmics (amiodarone and propafenone) Antiplatelets (ASA, clopidogrel) Statins (lovastatin, simvastatin, fluvastatin) Fibrates Fish oil	Cholestyramine Bosentan

CNS agents	SSRI (fluvastatin, sertraline) Phenytoin Disulfiram	Barbiturates Haloperidol Carbamazepine
GI agents	Cimetidine Omeprazole	Sucralfate
Other	Tamoxifen Anabolic steroids Fluorouracil Allopurinol	Vitamin K Oral contraceptives Antithyroid drugs

[a] Major drug interactions relevant to discussion on stroke prevention with warfarin are only presented.

Data from Holbrook AM, et al. *Arch Intern Med.* 2005;165(10):1095-1106.

13

TABLE 13.8 — Major Interactions of Herbal and Dietary Supplements With Warfarin

Effect of Warfarin	
Increased	**Decreased**
Gingko	Coenzyme Q10
Licorice	St. John's worth
Glucosamine	Soy
Primrose oil	Melatonin
Essential fatty acids	Ginseng
Multiherb products	

■ *Diet*

Profound changes in dietary habits over a short period of time (including alternation in vitamin K intake) may impact the INR level. Maintaining a similar diet while on warfarin therapy should protect a patient from significant diet-induced fluctuations of the INR. An increased consumption of foods high in vitamin K, eg, spinach, lettuce, kiwi, broccoli, liver, avocado, and soy beans, may attenuate warfarin effect. An increase in warfarin effect with moderate consumption of cranberry or grapefruit juice does not appear to be clinically significant. Green tea extract contains significant amounts of vitamin K and can diminish the anticoagulant effect of vitamin K. Only large amounts of brewed green tea may potentially antagonize the effects of warfarin. Acute ethanol ingestion (binge drinking) decreases the metabolism of warfarin and increases the INR. Chronic daily alcohol intake may increase the metabolism of warfarin and decrease the INR.

■ *Hypermetabolism*

Hypermetabolism increases warfarin responsiveness, most likely by increasing the catabolism of the vitamin K–dependent coagulation factors. AF patients with fever or hyperthyroidism are at increased risk of bleeding from anticoagulation with warfarin.

Complications

(For bleeding, see above discussions.)

- *Skin Necrosis*

Skin necrosis is a rare complication of warfarin. It usually occurs 2 to 5 days after the initiation of therapy. It is more common with large loading doses. This presents as an erythematous, well-demarcated lesion with a progressively necrotic center. Pathologic specimen shows thrombi in the microvasculature. This is caused by congenital or acquired deficiencies of protein C or protein S. In these patients, initiation of warfarin therapy leads to a precipitous fall in protein C or S levels before warfarin antithrombotic effect takes place. The resultant procoagulant state triggers thrombosis.

- *Cholesterol Embolization*
  ("purple toe syndrome" or "blue toe syndrome")

Cholesterol embolization is rare. This presents as a dark, purplish discoloration of the plantar and lateral surfaces of the lower extremities. It frequently occurs 3 to 8 weeks after initiation of warfarin.

Other

- *Pregnancy and Lactation*

In patients with AF, oral anticoagulation with warfarin during pregnancy is generally contraindicated. Warfarin is absolutely contraindicated in the first trimester due to its teratogenicity. Warfarin must be used cautiously near term due to the risk of fetal bleeding. UFH, LMWH, or fondaparinux may be used instead.

Cesarean section is generally advised over vaginal delivery in a woman in labor with a therapeutic INR.

Warfarin does not pass into the breast milk and can be safely given to nursing mothers.

- *Sports Activities*

Warfarin carries the increased risk of spontaneous and trauma-induced bleeding. Although moderate physical activity is recommended to reduce CV risk, patients treated with warfarin should not participate in contact sports, eg, basketball or football, or in activities in which there is an increased risk of serious trauma.

13

Newer Anticoagulants

Despite warfarin's well-demonstrated efficacy in prevention of thromboembolism, limitations of this therapy have prompted development of new oral anticoagulation agents. Strategies in the development of new oral anticoagulants focus on blocking coagulation cascade by selective coagulation factor inhibitors, acting preferentially without co-factors, and limiting other drug interactions. The most promising novel oral anticoagulants specifically and directly block the central pathway of the coagulation system either via factor II (thrombin) or factor Xa. Other approaches include factor IXa inhibition or the development of new vitamin K antagonists (eg, Tecarfarin, which is not metabolized via the cytochrome P450 system).

■ Direct Thrombin Inhibitors

Inhibition of thrombin, the final and central constituent of the coagulation cascade, not only blocks conversion of fibrinogen to fibrin but also limits thrombin generation (by feedback activation of factors V, VIII, and IX) and activity of platelets.

DTIs affect both free thrombin and fibrin-bound thrombin. This dual action allows them to not only block thrombin and prevent thrombus formation but also inhibit thrombus growth and expansion. This offers a significant advantage over indirect inhibitors, ie, UFH and LMWH, which inhibit only fibrin-bound thrombin.

The initial data supporting the efficacy of DTI came from studies on ximelagatran, the first novel oral anticoagulant and DTI. Ximelagatran did not require dose adjustment or monitoring and was shown to be noninferior to conventional therapy with vitamin K antagonists; however, it was not approved by the FDA because of concerns about liver toxicity and MI. Results of the studies on ximelagatran provided data for the possible effectiveness of unmonitored chronic anticoagulation in patients with AF and set the stage for development of other novel DTIs. Dabigatran, the first anticoagulant that was shown to be superior to warfarin in the pivotal RE-LY trial, will be discussed below.

Dabigatran Etexilate
Main Characteristics

Dabigatran is a DTI with a high affinity and reversible binding to thrombin. It is a prodrug that is converted to the active metabolite, dabigatran. Low bioavailability (6% to 7%) requires high doses to maintain therapeutic plasma concentrations.

It is rapidly absorbed and reaches peak plasma level in 1.5 to 2 hours after oral administration. Dabigatran has an estimated half life of 14 to 17 hours. Steady-state condition is achieved within 2 to 3 days in healthy subjects and after 1 week in elderly patients. Predictable pharmacokinetics and pharmacodynamics allow fixed dosing without coagulation monitoring. Dabigatran is eliminated mostly by the kidneys. Approximately 80% of the drug is excreted unchanged in the urine. It requires dose adjustment in patients with renal failure. The recommended dosing of dabigatran depends on creatinine clearance:

- CrCl >30 mL/minute: 150 mg dabigatran twice a day
- CrCl 15-30 mL/minute: 75 mg dabigatran twice a day
- CrCl <15 mL/minute: contraindicated.

It appears to be safe in patients with moderate liver disease. Its metabolism is cytochrome P450 independent.

Monitoring for anticoagulation intensity is not possible. Ecarin clotting time (ECT) may be used to estimate anticoagulant activity of dabigatran and bleeding risk in case of emergent surgical intervention. No specific antidote is available to reverse a bleeding event.

13

Dyspepsia and gastritis-like symptoms, which are the most common side effects, occur in 20% of patients. Dyspepsia occurs in 11% of patients and is caused by the formulation of dabigatran. It contains an acid core to enhance intestinal absorption. Optimal bioavailability of dabigatran requires a low pH.

Limited drug-drug interactions have been described to date. Absorption of dabigatran etexilate is reduced 20% to 25% with concurrent use of proton pump inhibitors.

Cotherapy with the P-glycoprotein inducers such as rifampin reduces exposure to dabigatran and should be avoided. P-glycoprotein inhibitors raise dabigatran serum concentrations and may increase risk of bleeding in patients treated with dabigatran. Caution should also be used with the combination of dabigatran with P-glycoprotein inhibitors such as amiodarone, verapamil, quinidine, and ketoconazole.

Interruption of anticoagulation with dabigatran for 1 to 2 days prior to elective surgery in AF patients with CrCl >50 mL/min and for 3 to 5 days in AF patients with CrCl <50 mL/min is recommended.

When switching from parenteral anticoagulant, dabigatran should be started 0 to 2 hours before the next scheduled dose of parenteral anticoagulant (eg, LMWH) or at the time of discontinuation of infusion of parenteral anticoagulant (eg, UFH).

When transition from dabigatran to parenteral anticoagulant therapy is planned, a parenteral anticoagulant should be started 12 hours (patients with CrCl ≥30 mL/min) or 24 hours (patients with CrCl <30 mL/min) after the last dose of dabigatran.

When converting from chronic warfarin anticoagulation, warfarin must be discontinued and the first dose of dabigatran may be started once the INR ≤2.

When switching from dabigatran to warfarin, time of warfarin initiation is based on the patient's CrCl. Warfarin should be started 3 days before discontinuation of dabigatran in patients with CrCl >50 mL/min and 2 days before discontinuation of dabigatran in patients with CrCl between 31 and 50 mL/min. Dosing strategies for patients with CrCl ≤30 mL/min should be individualized. In general, time of overlap therapy with both agents should be minimized.

Dabigatran may elevate INR, and the INR level will better represent warfarin effect after discontinuation of dabigatran for at least 2 days.

RE-LY Trial

The recently published Randomized Evaluation of Long-term Anticoagulant Therapy (RE-LY) study was a landmark phase 3 noninferiority trial of the safety and efficacy of dabigatran etexilate compared with warfarin for stroke prevention in patients with AF. It was the largest AF stroke prevention trial reported to date. In this prospective, randomized, controlled trial of patients with documented AF and at least one risk factor for stroke, two fixed doses of dabigatran (110 mg and 150 mg) were compared with warfarin. The primary study outcome was stroke or systemic embolism, and the primary safety outcome was major hemorrhage. Secondary outcomes included a composite of all stroke, systemic embolism, and death. Other outcomes were MI, PE, TIA, and hospitalization. The primary net clinical benefit outcome was the composite of stroke, systemic embolism, PE, MI, death, or major hemorrhage.

A total of 18,113 patients were recruited from 951 centers in 44 countries. The randomization of study participants was a 1:1:1 ratio, and the baseline patient's characteristics were very similar between the three groups. The mean age of patients was 71 years (63.6% were men) with a mean CHADS2 score of 2.1. Approximately 50% of the participants had received prior long-term oral anticoagulation with vitamin K antagonists. The median follow-up period was 2 years. Patients on warfarin were in the therapeutic range of INR in 64% of the visits. The primary outcome of stroke or systemic embolism (shown as percent per year) was 1.69% in the warfarin group compared with 1.53% in the 110-mg twice-daily dabigatran group ($P < 0.001$ for noninferiority) and 1.11% in the 150-mg twice-daily dabigatran group ($P < 0.001$ for superiority). The rate of nonhemorrhagic stroke was significantly lower in the dabigatran 150-mg arm (0.92%) than in the dabigatran 110-mg (1.34%) or warfarin (1.20%) arms of the study (**Figure 13.4** and **Table 13.9**).

The rate of major bleeding was significantly lower in the dabigatran 110-mg group compared with warfarin (2.71% per year vs 3.36% per year; $P = 0.003$). Patients in the 150-mg dabigatran group had a comparable major bleeding rate compared to warfarin (3.11% per year vs 3.36% per year, $P = 0.31$). The rates of hemorrhagic stroke were lower in both dabigatran groups (0.12% per year and 0.10% per year at 110 mg and 150 mg, respectively) compared with warfarin (0.38% per year). The rate of extracranial hemorrhage was similar in all three groups: 2.67%, 2.51%, and 2.84% with 110-mg dabigatran, 150-mg dabigatran, and warfarin, respectively.

13

FIGURE 13.4 — RE-LY Trial: Cumulative Hazard Rates for the Primary Outcome of Stroke or Systemic Embolism, According to Treatment Group

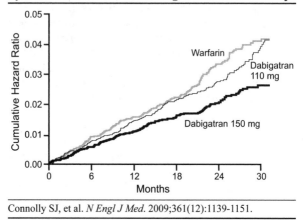

Connolly SJ, et al. *N Engl J Med*. 2009;361(12):1139-1151.

Total bleeding risk (include life-threatening bleeding, intracranial bleeding, and major and minor bleeding) were also significantly higher in the warfarin group than with either of the dabigatran arms of the study.

Based on these results, it was calculated that 357 patients need to be treated with dabigatran at a dose of 150 mg twice daily rather than warfarin to prevent one nonhemorrhagic stroke, and approximately 370 patients need to be treated with either dose of dabigatran rather than warfarin to prevent one hemorrhagic stroke.

It was also estimated that patients randomized to therapy with warfarin in the RE-LY study would need an INR within the therapeutic range approximately 79% of the time (not the 64% achieved in the study) to have a stroke rate as low as that of a patient randomized to 150 mg of dabigatran twice a day.

During 2 years of study, a significant trend for less MIs with warfarin (0.53% per year) compared with dabigatran groups (0.72% per year and 0.74% per year) was observed. Liver function test elevation more than three times the upper limit of normal was observed in approximately 2% in each dabigatran group. This was similar to warfarin.

TABLE 13.9 — Strokes and Systemic Embolism in the RE-LY Study

	Dabigatran (150 mg bid)	Warfarin	HR vs Warfarin (95% CI)
Patients randomized	6076	6022	
Stroke	122	186	0.64 (0.51, 0.81)
Ischemic	103	134	0.75 (0.58, 0.97)
Hemorrhagic	12	45	0.26 (0.14, 0.49)
Systemic embolism	13	21	0.61 (0.30, 1.21)

The efficacy of dabigatran 150 mg twice daily was generally consistent across major subgroups.

Adapted from Connolly SJ, et al. *N Engl J Med*. 2009;361(12):1139-1151.

13

Discontinuation of study medications was higher in both dabigatran groups (21%) compared with the warfarin group (17%), mainly because of GI side effects. Dyspepsia and abdominal pain were common with dabigatran (11.8% in the 110-mg group and 11.3% in the 150-mg group) compared with warfarin (5.8%).

Further subgroup analyses of data from RE-LY focused on the comparison of safety and efficacy of dabigatran on specific population of AF patients. In patients with prior TIA or stroke, there was a significant reduction of hemorrhagic stroke in the 110-mg and 150-mg dabigatran groups compared with warfarin ($P=0.003$ and $P=0.009$, respectively). Stratification of patients based on the CHADS2 score showed an absolute reduction in stroke or systemic embolism with dabigatran therapy as compared with warfarin in the highest CHADS2 score group (3 to 6). Subgroup analysis of patients older than 75 years and with a CrCl of 30 to 50 mL/min found a significant interaction for age and renal function with dabigatran etexilate therapy. The rates of major bleeding with dabigatran etexilate were slightly higher than warfarin in patients older than 75 years (4.09% for warfarin, 4.17% for 110 mg twice daily, 4.81% for 150 mg twice daily). Similar low stroke rates were present on dabigatran and warfarin in the subpopulation of patients undergoing cardioversion.

Based on the results of the RE-LY trial, dabigatran was recently approved by the FDA to reduce the risk of stroke and systemic embolism in patients with nonvalvular AF.

■ Factor Xa Inhibitors

Factor X is situated at the convergence of both extrinsic and intrinsic coagulation pathways. It plays a key role in the coagulation cascade as one molecule of activated factor X can generate >1000 thrombin molecules. Direct factor Xa inhibitors inactivate both prothrombinase-bound and free factor Xa. As such, these molecules have an advantage over indirect inhibitors, which must interact with antithrombin to exert their anticoagulant effects and have limited efficacy to inhibit factor Xa within the prothrombinase complex. One new orally active factor Xa inhibitor (rivaroxaban) has recently been FDA approved to reduce the risk of stroke and systemic embolism in patients with nonvalvular AF. Two others (apixaban and edoxaban) are currently being tested in phase 3 clinical trials. A number of other agents are in less-advanced stages of clinical investigation. Similarly to the new DTIs, novel direct factor Xa inhibitors have a rapid onset of action and a relatively stable pharmacodynamic profile, which obviates the need for initial parenteral anticoagulation or routine monitoring.

Rivaroxaban

Rivaroxaban is an oral direct inhibitor of factor Xa with a competitive and reversible binding to factor Xa. It has high oral bioavailability of 60% to 80% and reaches peak plasma concentrations after approximately 2 to 3 hours. The intestinal absorption of rivaroxaban is not affected by the pH. It achieves higher plasma concentration if administered within 2 hours of food intake. It has a half-life of 7 to 11 hours. One third of the drug is excreted unchanged in the kidney. Approximately one third is metabolized by the liver (primarily via cytochrome P450), and one third is metabolized to inactive metabolites and then excreted by the kidneys. Rivaroxaban is given in a fixed dose once daily but requires dose adjustment in patients with renal insufficiency. The recommended dosing of rivaroxaban depends on creatinine clearance:

- CrCl >50 mL/min: 20 mg orally, once daily with the evening meal
- CrCl 15-50 mL/min: 15 mg orally, once daily with the evening meal
- CrCl <15 mL/min: avoid use.

It has predictable and dose-dependent pharmacokinetic and pharmacodynamic profiles, which are not significantly impacted by age, gender, or body weight.

Co-therapy with potent inhibitors of both cytochrome CYP3A4 and P-glycoprotein pathways (eg, ketoconazole, ritonavir, erythromycin, and clarithromycin) is contraindicated because they may increase rivaroxaban plasma concentrations. Caution should be used with concomitant use of rivaroxaban with drugs that inhibit only the CYP3A4 and P-glycoprotein pathways. Strong inducers of CYP3A4 (eg, rifampicin) decrease rivaroxaban plasma levels and anticoagulation effect.

Selected Clinical Trials

The results of a major clinical trial comparing rivaroxaban with warfarin for the prevention of stroke or systemic embolism in patients with AF have been published. In this trial, Efficacy and Safety of Rivaroxaban for the Prevention of Stroke in Subjects With Non-Valvular Atrial Fibrillation (ROCKET-AF), 14,264 patients with nonvalvular AF and a history of stroke or at least two independent risk factors were randomized to 20 mg daily of rivaroxaban (15 mg daily dose if CrCl 30-49 mL/min) or dose-adjusted warfarin. Among patients enrolled, 90% had a CHADS2 score of 3 or higher (mean score of 3.50). This is higher than in the other trials of new oral anticoagulants. Over half the patients had a prior stroke, TIA, or other embolic event. The mean age was 73 years. The primary efficacy end point was a composite of all-cause stroke and non-CNS embolism. The stroke or new embolism rate was 1.7% in the rivaroxaban group and 2.2% in the warfarin group for 100 patient years ($P <0.001$ for noninferiority) (**Figure 13.5**). The primary safety end point of major and non-major, clinically relevant bleeding occurred in 14.9% in the rivaroxaban group and 14.5 % in the warfarin group ($P=0.44$). Hemorrhagic strokes and fatal bleeding events were significantly less common in the rivaroxaban-treated patients. All-cause mortality and MI incidence were similar in both groups. Among patients with nonvalvular AF and an increased risk for embolic events, rivaroxaban was noninferior to warfarin with a reduced systemic embolic risk without an increased risk of major bleeding.

Rivaroxaban is also being compared with dose-adjusted warfarin in a smaller phase 3 clinical trial being conducted in Japan on 1280 patients.

Apixaban

Apixaban is an oral direct factor Xa inhibitor with reversible binding. The oral bioavailability is approxi-

FIGURE 13.5 — ROCKET-AF: Primary Efficacy Outcome for Stroke and Non-CNS Embolism

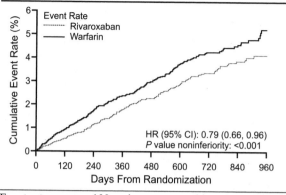

Event rates are per 100 patients-years and based on protocol compliant on treatment population.

Patel MR, et al. *N Engl J Med*. 2011;365:883-891.

mately 50%. It achieves peak plasma levels 2 to 3 hours after oral administration and has a half-life of 9 to 14 hours. It has a fixed twice daily administration.

It is metabolized in the liver via a cytochrome P450-dependent pathway. Approximately 75% of the drug is eliminated by intestinal excretion and 25% via the kidney. Caution should be used with concomitant use of apixaban with drugs which inhibit CYP3A4.

Selected Clinical Trials

In the Apixaban Versus Acetylsalicylic Acid to Prevent Strokes (AVERROES) trial, the safety and effectiveness of apixaban was compared with ASA in AF patients who were intolerant of or unsuitable for warfarin therapy. A total of 5599 patients were randomized to 5 mg of apixaban or 81 to 324 mg of ASA. The primary efficacy outcome was the time from the first dose of the study drug to the first occurrence of ischemic stroke, hemorrhagic stroke, or systemic embolism. The secondary efficacy outcome included the time to the first occurrence of ischemic stroke, hemorrhagic stroke, systemic embolism, MI, or vascular death. The trial was stopped early after a predefined interim analysis revealed a clinically important reduction in stroke and systemic embolism with apixaban. The mean follow-up period was 1.1 years. It had been planned as a 3-year follow-up.

The primary outcome of the trial was the occurrence of stroke on systemic embolism. There were 51 primary outcome events (1.6% per year) in the apixaban group and 113 (7.7% per year) in the aspirin group (P <0.001). Major bleeding was not statistically different between the two groups.

Apixaban for the Prevention of Stroke in Subjects With Atrial Fibrillation (ARISTOTLE) study was a phase 3 randomized, double-blind trial comparing apixaban (5 mg twice daily) with adjusted dose warfarin in AF patients. The primary objective of the study is to determine if apixaban is noninferior to warfarin for reducing the combined end point of stroke (ischemic or hemorrhagic) and systemic embolism in patients with AF with a CHADS2 score ≥1. A total of 18,201 patients have been randomized in ARISTOTLE. The rate of the primary outcome was 1.27% per year in the apixaban group compared with 1.6% per year in the warfarin group (P<0.001 for noninferiority, P=0.01 for superiority). There was less major bleeding in the apixaban group vs the warfarin group (2.13% vs 3.09%, P<0.001) and lower mortality (3.52% vs 3.94%, P<0.047).

Current understanding of advantages and limitations of novel anticoagulants over warfarin is presented in **Table 13.10**. Although two novel anticoagulants are now available and more will become available in the near future, their place in the anticoagulation strategies for AF is not yet established. In the absence of long-term data on large cohorts of patients treated with novel anticoagulants, understanding of benefits and risk of these agents may change. Furthermore, many more drug interactions may be evident in the future. This may impact the safety profile of these agents.

Antiplatelet Therapy for Stroke Prevention in AF

A recent meta-analysis showed that when all randomized comparisons of antiplatelet agents vs placebo are

TABLE 13.10 — Limitations and Advantages of Warfarin and New Anticoagulants for Prevention of Stroke in AF Patients

Agent	Advantages	Disadvantages
Warfarin	Oral administration Antidote (vitamin K)	Unpredictable response Slow onset and offset action Wide clinical experience Multiple drugs and diet interactions Requires routine INR monitoring Narrow therapeutic window
New anticoagulants	Specific coagulation factor target Predictable effect Rapid onset and offset action Less potential for drug interactions? No dietary precautions No coagulation monitoring required Wide therapeutic window	Lack of antidote High cost Long-term safety not clear Inability to monitor for intensity of anticoagulation

Modified from Armaganijan L, et al. *Adv Ther.* 2009;26(12):1058-1071.

13

considered, antiplatelet therapy reduces stroke by 22%. This modest efficacy of ASA does not differ significantly based on the dose and is only mildly improved with addition of another antiplatelet agent.

■ Aspirin vs Placebo

ASA offers only very limited protection against stroke for patients with AF. In fact, using ASA as prophylaxis against stroke in patients who have AF and any additional stroke risk factor is controversial. ASA has proven to be grossly inferior to warfarin in clinical trials and has been recommended only for those patients with risk factors for stroke who cannot take warfarin.

A meta-analysis of seven trials including 3990 participants comparing ASA with placebo showed that ASA was associated with a nonsignificant reduction in the incidence of stroke (19%). When only strokes classified as ischemic were considered, ASA resulted in a 21% reduction in stroke rate. The efficacy of ASA may be higher in some subpopulations of AF patients (eg, hypertension or diabetes) and differs based on the type of stroke (eg, cardioembolic vs noncardioembolic). Cardioembolic strokes are more disabling than noncardioembolic strokes. ASA is more effective in reducing nondisabling strokes (29%) than disabling strokes (13%). Additionally, ASA is reported to lower stroke occurrence by up to 33% in primary prevention studies (in which the stroke rate with placebo averaged 4.5% per year) vs only 11% for secondary prevention trials (in which the stroke rate with placebo averaged 14% per year).

The benefit of ASA in published meta-analyses is derived largely from the results of the SPAF-I trial, which was the only trial to show a statistically significant benefit of ASA for stroke prevention in patients with AF (RRR of 42%). However, because of the disparate nature of the data reported in this trial, this RRR is thought to be unreliable.

Since AF commonly occurs in patients with vascular disease, the effect of ASA on stroke reduction may represent an effect of ASA on prevention of thrombus formation on atherosclerotic plaque rather than an effect on the risk of cardioembolic stroke. This is supported by the observation that thrombi in vascular disease are platelet-rich and may respond to antiplatelet therapy, whereas thrombi in AF are rich in fibrin and, therefore, are more likely to respond to anticoagulation therapy.

■ Combination of Antiplatelet Agents

The combination of ASA and clopidogrel failed to be an equal alternative to warfarin for stroke prevention for AF in the ACTIVE-W trial *(see above)*. However, some patients with AF are not candidates for warfarin anticoagulation. In the subsequent ACTIVE-A study, the combination of ASA and clopidogrel was tested against ASA and placebo in patients with AF at high risk for stroke who were deemed unsuitable for warfarin therapy. The investigators hypothesized that combination therapy would be more effective in preventing vascular complications in patients with AF at high risk for stroke. A total of 7554 patients with AF and at least one risk factor for stroke were enrolled. All received ASA 75 mg to 100 mg daily and were randomized to receive either clopidogrel 75 mg daily or placebo.

The study cohort had a high prevalence of CV risk factors, including hypertension (85%), heart failure (33%), prior stroke (13%), or prior MI (14%). After a median follow-up period of 3.6 years, the combination therapy group showed a significant 11% reduction in the primary composite end point of stroke, MI, systemic embolus, or vascular death (6.8% vs 7.6% per year, RR 0.89). Combination therapy reduced risk of stroke by 28% as compared with ASA alone (2.4% vs 3.3% per year, RR 0.72). These benefits, however, came at a high cost of bleeding complications. The combination of ASA and clopidogrel increased the risk of major bleeding when compared with ASA alone (2.0% vs 1.3% per year, RR 1.57). In particular, adding clopidogrel to ASA increased major extracranial hemorrhage, GI bleeding by 51% and major ICH by 87%.

As such, the decision of dual antiplatelet therapy for stroke prevention of AF appears to be limited only to carefully selected moderate-to-high risk patients who cannot be anticoagulated.

13

■ **Cardioversion of AF**

The risk of thromboembolic event is increased at a time of cardioversion to sinus rhythm. Anticoagulation therapy plays a major role in decreasing this risk. It is estimated that the risk of cardioversion-associated thromboembolism may exceed 5% without anticoagulation. Anticoagulation decreases the risk of cardioversion-associated thromboembolism <1%. Thromboembolic risk depends on the duration of the arrhythmia.

AF of <48 Hours Duration

The likelihood of stroke in patients with AF lasting <48 hours seems low. In a prospective, observational study of 375 patients admitted to the hospital with AF of <48 hours duration, only 0.8% of unanticoagulated subjects had a clinical thromboembolic event.

Since symptoms are unreliable as a marker of the presence or absence of AF, electrocardiographic evidence of AF should be sought to document the duration of arrhythmia. If the true onset of AF is unclear, it should be assumed that the episode lasted >48 hours.

AF Lasting >48 Hours

The risk of thromboembolism with cardioversion of AF begins to increase with episodes lasting >24 to 48 hours. The vast majority of strokes occur after 72 hours of AF. Anticoagulation-based stroke prevention strategies are recommended for AF lasting >48 hours. Further discussion of anticoagulation strategies to decrease this risk applies to restoration of sinus rhythm in AF lasting >48 hours.

Two pathophysiologic mechanisms have been implicated in the increased risk of thromboembolism in the pericardioversion period. First, if left atrial thrombus is present before cardioversion, the recovery of atrial contraction after restoration of NSR may cause dislocation and embolization of existing thrombus. Second, restoration of normal electrical function is not always associated with recovery of normal atrial mechanical function. Atrial "stunning" after cardioversion can last up to 4 weeks after cardioversion. There is an increased risk of clot formation during this period of time. Based on these mechanisms, two goals of the pericardioversion anticoagulation have been identified:

- Lowering risk of preexisting thrombus at the time of cardioversion
- Preventing new thrombus formation postcardioversion.

Lowering Risk of Preexisting Thrombus at the Time of Cardioversion

Two different anticoagulation strategies to decrease risk of pericardioversion embolism are validated and currently recommended: 1) empiric anticoagulation for 3 weeks prior to cardioversion and 2) TEE-guided cardioversion.

Empiric anticoagulation for 3 weeks prior to cardioversion allows organization and potential resolution of preexisting thrombus, as well as prevention of new thrombus formation.

A minimum of 3 weeks of warfarin therapy before cardioversion (target INR of 2.5, range 2 to 3) or LMWH (less validated strategy) is required. It is important to verify a therapeutic effect of warfarin with frequent INR levels before cardioversion. In a retrospective analysis of 1950 patients who underwent 2639 attempts of DC cardioversion, a total of 1932 of cardioversion attempts were performed on patients who had AF >48 hours in duration and who received warfarin for ≥3 weeks prior to procedure. No embolic complication occurred when cardioversion was performed with an INR ≥2.5. Thromboembolism was significantly more common with INR of 1.5 to 2.4 (0.93%). The incidence of embolism after conversion of atrial flutter was similar to that after cardioversion of AF. These data suggest that an INR range between 2.5 and 3.5 may be superior for cardioversion of AF.

TEE-guided cardioversion is the second strategy. As an alternative approach, the decision regarding cardioversion is based on the presence or absence of high-risk features for thromboembolism on TEE. Anticoagulation

13

with heparin is initiated (goal PTT of 60s, range 50s to 70s), followed by TEE. If no thrombus or other high-risk features are seen on TEE, cardioversion is performed. If thrombus is identified, cardioversion is deferred and the patient is therapeutically anticoagulated with warfarin for 3 weeks. TEE is then repeated to document resolution of thrombus prior to cardioversion. Persistence of intracardiac thrombus on repeated TEE is a contraindication to further cardioversion attempts in a majority of cases. Although the presence of spontaneous echocontrast (which represents blood stasis) in the TEE is not a contraindication for cardioversion, dense spontaneous echocontrast with "sludge" in LA or LAA is worrisome and should prompt reconsideration of further anticoagulation prior to cardioversion.

The TEE-guided cardioversion strategy has a few advantages, such as shorter time to cardioversion, shorter total duration of anticoagulation if chronic therapy is not necessary, and possible cost reduction due to a shorter time of therapy and no need for rehospitalization in patients being admitted to the hospital with a paroxysm of AF.

The Assessment of Cardioversion Using Transesophageal Echocardiography (ACUTE) trial compared a conventional strategy (anticoagulation for at least 3 weeks) with the TEE-guided strategy on 1222 patients with AF of >48 hours (mean 13 days) who were undergoing electrical cardioversion. In the TEE-guided arm, patients were anticoagulated with heparin within 24 hours before TEE (inpatient) or with warfarin for 5 days with target INR 2 to 3 (outpatient). If no thrombus was present, TEE was followed by immediate electrical cardioversion. If there was a thrombus (12% of patients), cardioversion was postponed, and patients were anticoagulated with warfarin for 3 weeks. At that time, TEE was repeated to document resolution of thrombus. All patients in the study were anticoagulated for 4 weeks postcardioversion.

After 8 weeks, there was no significant difference between the TEE and conventional groups in the incidence of ischemic stroke (0.6% vs 0.3%) and all embolic events (0.8% vs 0.5%). There was also no statistically significant difference in all-cause mortality (2.4% vs

1%) or cardiac deaths (1.3% vs 0.7%). However, a significantly decreased rate of hemorrhagic events (2.9% vs 5.5%) with the TEE-guided vs conversional strategy was noted, although not associated with a significant difference in the incidence of major bleeding (0.8% vs 1.5%). As expected, TEE-guided strategy was associated with shorter time to cardioversion (3 vs 31 days).

The results of the ACUTE trial suggested that a TEE-guided strategy is a reasonable alternative to a conventional approach, especially in a certain subpopulation of patients with AF, eg, high bleeding risk or potentially hemodynamically unstable. However, this study was statistically underpowered, and it is theoretically possible that the increase in mortality and embolic events associated with the TEE approach could reach statistical significance in a larger trial.

LMWH has been shown to be an alternative to UFH or oral anticoagulation both prior to and after cardioversion. LMWH obviates the need for anticoagulation monitoring, and it may not interfere with the patient's daily activities as much as UFH or warfarin. In a randomized, controlled trial of 496 patients with AF of >48 hours duration, LMWH was compared with UFH plus oral anticoagulation strategy. Of the 496 patients enrolled in the trial, 431 were stratified to TEE-guided cardioversion and 65 to standard empiric anticoagulation followed by cardioversion. In both strategies, patients underwent 4 weeks of anticoagulation postcardioversion. LMWH was found to be noninferior to UFH plus oral anticoagulation in both the standard anticoagulation and TEE-guided treatment arms for the primary end point of preventing embolic events, bleeding complications, and death.

LMWH also appears to be as safe and effective as UFHs when used only as a bridge to oral anticoagulation in patients undergoing TEE-based therapy.

In the ACUTE-II study, 155 patients with AF who were scheduled for TEE were assigned to UFH or enoxaparin prior to cardioversion. Safety outcomes included ischemic stroke, major or minor bleeding, and death over 5 weeks postcardioversion. Length of stay and return to NSR were efficacy measures. There were no significant differences in the safety outcomes between the two strategies. Enoxaparin group had a shorter length of stay (3 vs 4 days), which suggested a better cost effectiveness of this strategy.

As such, TEE-guided approach using LMWH as a bridge to oral anticoagulation appears to be the effective and possibly the most cost-effective anticoagulation strategy in the majority of patients undergoing cardioversion for AF.

Prevention of New Thrombus Formation Postcardioversion

As recovery of atrial mechanical function may lag up to 3 to 4 weeks after restoration of sinus rhythm, all patients after cardioversion of AF lasting >48 hours should undergo at least 4 weeks of therapeutic anticoagulation postcardioversion. Pooled analysis of data from 32 studies (including 4621 patients) examined the timing of embolic events after cardioversion of AF and flutter. Eighty two percent of embolic events occurred within the first 72 hours after restoration of NSR. Importantly, almost all of them (98%) occurred within the first 10 days postcardioversion (**Figure 13.6**). These results underscore the necessity of very strict control of effective anticoagulation in the first few days postcardioversion. In

FIGURE 13.6 — Interval Between Cardioversion and Thromboembolic Events in 92 Patients

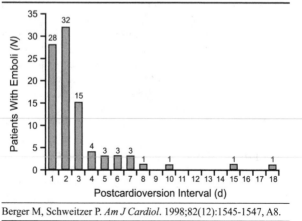

Berger M, Schweitzer P. *Am J Cardiol.* 1998;82(12):1545-1547, A8.

particular, overlapping therapy with heparin (unfractionated or low molecular weight) until the INR level is >2 is recommended. Continuation of anticoagulation beyond 4 weeks should be based on the presence of coexisting risk factors based on the CHADS2 scheme.

Anticoagulation strategies for stroke prevention with cardioversion of AF are summarized in **Figure 13.7**. These strategies will be likely modified once new anticoagulants become available.

■ Anticoagulation After AF Ablation and Cox-Maze Procedure

For discussion of anticoagulation strategies with AF ablation and Cox-Maze procedure, please see *Chapter 10*.

■ Anticoagulation in AF Patients Presenting With Stroke

Patients with AF presenting with thromboembolic stroke are at an increased risk of recurrent stroke, which is estimated as high as 3% to 5 % in the first 2 weeks. However, in the setting of acute cardioembolic stroke, the risk of hemorrhagic transformation and/or ICH is also significantly increased. Imaging studies (CT or MRI) should be performed first to exclude the presence of cerebral hemorrhage and to help estimate the severity of cerebral infarction. The presence of ICH is an absolute contraindication to immediate use of any type of antithrombotic therapy. Uncontrolled hypertension has to be treated prior to initiation of fibrinolytic or antithrombotic therapy in AF patients with stroke or TIA.

In patients who present within 3 hours of the onset of acute ischemic stroke and who meet specific eligibility criteria, the use of thrombolytic therapy significantly reduces long-term disability with no increase in long-term mortality (despite an increased risk of intracerebral hemorrhage and death within the first 7 to 10 days).

The management of anticoagulation in the setting of acute thromboembolic stroke varies in AF patients.

There is no evidence suggesting benefit of immediate use of heparin in patients with AF presenting with thromboembolic stroke, as the risk of hemorrhagic transformation may exceed the benefit of anticoagulation. However,

13

FIGURE 13.7 — Anticoagulation Strategies With Cardioversion of AF

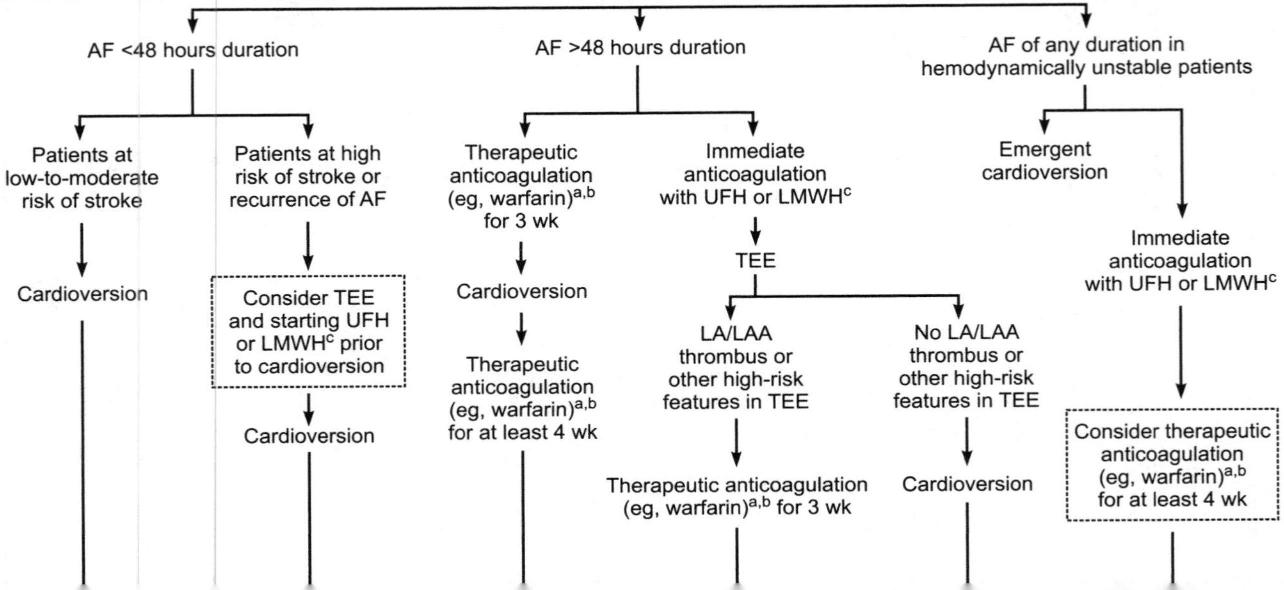

AF <48 hours duration

Patients at low-to-moderate risk of stroke → Cardioversion

Patients at high risk of stroke or recurrence of AF → Consider TEE and starting UFH or LMWH[c] prior to cardioversion → Cardioversion

AF >48 hours duration

Therapeutic anticoagulation (eg, warfarin)[a,b] for 3 wk → Cardioversion → Therapeutic anticoagulation (eg, warfarin)[a,b] for at least 4 wk

Immediate anticoagulation with UFH or LMWH[c] → TEE
- LA/LAA thrombus or other high-risk features in TEE → Therapeutic anticoagulation (eg, warfarin)[a,b] for 3 wk
- No LA/LAA thrombus or other high-risk features in TEE → Cardioversion

AF of any duration in hemodynamically unstable patients

Emergent cardioversion

Immediate anticoagulation with UFH or LMWH[c] → Consider therapeutic anticoagulation (eg, warfarin)[a,b] for at least 4 wk

336

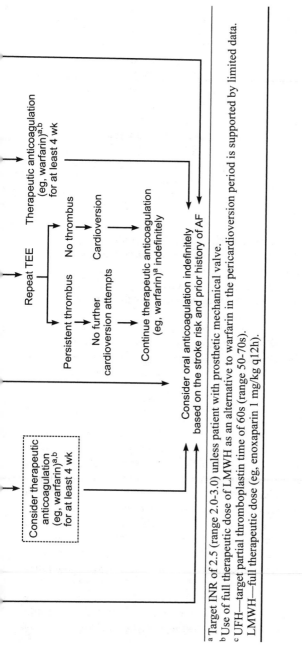

Consider therapeutic anticoagulation (eg, warfarin)[a,b] for at least 4 wk

Therapeutic anticoagulation (eg, warfarin)[a,b] for at least 4 wk

Repeat TEE

Persistent thrombus → No further cardioversion attempts

No thrombus → Cardioversion

Continue therapeutic anticoagulation (eg, warfarin)[a] indefinitely

Consider oral anticoagulation indefinitely based on the stroke risk and prior history of AF

[a] Target INR of 2.5 (range 2.0-3.0) unless patient with prosthetic mechanical valve.

[b] Use of full therapeutic dose of LMWH as an alternative to warfarin in the pericardioversion period is supported by limited data.

[c] UFH—target partial thromboplastin time of 60s (range 50-70s).
LMWH—full therapeutic dose (eg, enoxaparin 1 mg/kg q12h).

13

337

heparin may be considered in patients at high risk of progression of cerebral injury (ongoing stroke with part of the embolus still present in the intracranial segment of the artery, presence of LAA thrombus on TEE, or with prior history of recurrent strokes). Oral anticoagulation with warfarin in the AF patient presenting with a small to moderate stroke may be initiated once the patient is medically and neurologically stable. Warfarin is usually held for 2 weeks in patients with a large cerebral infarction. A follow-up CT scan of the brain before initiation of warfarin is suggested by many experts. AF patients with stroke who are not initially treated with heparin or warfarin are frequently treated with ASA until warfarin is started.

In the AF patient presenting with a TIA, heparin and, subsequently, warfarin should be started as soon as possible after presence of cerebral infarction or hemorrhage is ruled out by imaging studies.

The management of a patient with AF who has been treated with warfarin and presents with a thromboembolic stroke and a therapeutic INR (2 to 3) is controversial. Increasing the therapeutic INR goal to a maximum target of 3 to 3.5 rather than adding an antiplatelet agent is recommended by most experts. LAA closure devices *(see below)* may be a preferred therapy for these patients in the future.

■ Atrial Flutter

Since there is a lack of large, randomized trials on patients solely with atrial flutter (most of the AF trials included a number of patients with atrial flutter), the optimal anticoagulation strategy in atrial flutter alone is not evidence-based. It is suggested that increased embolic risk may mostly affect patients who also have AF. Review of retrospective studies on older patients with atrial flutter revealed that three out of four patients with atrial flutter also had AF. The presence of hypertension, heart failure, and rheumatic heart in a patient with atrial flutter predicted coexisting AF. Although the embolic risk may be somehow lower in atrial flutter than AF, based on the common coexistence of both arrhythmias, current guidelines recommend managing chronic anticoagulation and anticoagulation during cardioversion of atrial flutter in the same manner as AF. As such, the presence of high-risk factors for thromboembolism in patients with a history of atrial flutter warrants chronic oral anticoagulation.

■ Anticoagulation in AF Due to Reversible Causes

AF is very common after cardiac surgery and, without pharmacologic prophylaxis, occurs in 40% of patients after CABG or valve surgery and in 60% of patients undergoing combined bypass and valve surgery. AF usually occurs within the first 5 days of cardiac surgery (peak incidence on day 2). Post-op AF is usually a reversible condition with spontaneous conversion to sinus rhythm much more common than in other settings. Up to 90% of patients restore sinus rhythm in 6 to 8 weeks after surgery. Antithrombotic therapy is frequently withheld for first 48 hours; however, AF lasting >48 hours should prompt therapeutic anticoagulation if bleeding risk after open-heart surgery is acceptable. Oral anticoagulation with warfarin should be continued for 4 weeks following reversion to NSR, especially in patients with risk factors for thromboembolism.

UFH or LMWH is used for anticoagulation of AF in patients with acute MI. Once sinus rhythm is restored, the need for further chronic anticoagulation with warfarin should be assessed based on the patient's stroke risk. Oral anticoagulation is indicated in patients with paroxysmal AF in the setting of a large anterior infarct (regardless of the presence of other risk factors for stroke) and in patients with acute MI who develop persistent AF.

There is an increased body of evidence suggesting that AF associated with hyperthyroidism leads to an increased risk of stroke. Oral anticoagulation with a goal INR of 2 to 3 is recommended in patients with AF associated with hyperthyroidism. The majority of ischemic strokes occur within the first 30 days of presentation. Once euthyroid state is achieved, discontinuation of anticoagulation may be considered in patients who are in sinus rhythm for at least 4 weeks and do not have any other risk for stroke.

Isolated paroxysms of AF commonly occur in acutely ill patients who have no prior history of tachyarrhythmia.

13

Although anticoagulation is frequently deferred in these patients, a paroxysm suggests the electrical substrate for AF. The decision about anticoagulation should be individualized, and the decision for long-term anticoagulation should be considered in patients with other risk factors for stroke. Outpatient monitoring may be considered in patients who had a paroxysm of AF associated with an acute illness since asymptomatic recurrences may indicate the need for long-term anticoagulation.

■ Interruption of Oral Anticoagulation in AF Patients

The average weekly risk for stroke in the absence of oral anticoagulation is very low in the majority of AF patients. As such, according to current ACC/AHA/ESC guidelines, interruption of oral anticoagulation for up to 1 week for surgery (or diagnostic procedure with high risk of bleeding) is acceptable with the exceptions listed below. If interruption of oral anticoagulant therapy is needed for >1 week in AF patients with multiple risk factors for stroke, bridging the interruption with UFH or LMWH therapy is recommended. Bridging with UFH or LMWH may be considered with interruption of oral anticoagulation for <1 week in AF patients with multiple risk factors for stroke, including prior history of stroke or TIA. In AF patients with mechanical heart valves, any interruption of therapy with warfarin leading to insufficient anticoagulation mandates bridging with UFH or LMWH.

■ Anticoagulation for AF in Patients With Coronary Interventions

It is estimated that 20% to 30% of AF patients on chronic anticoagulation with warfarin have CAD and approximately 5% undergo PCI. These patients are temporarily managed with "triple therapy" of ASA and thienopyridines for prevention of stent thrombosis and continuation of warfarin for stroke prevention. Although this strategy appears to be associated with better CV outcomes, it results in more frequent bleeding complications.

The in-hospital incidence of major hemorrhage in patients with ACS treated with PCI and dual antiplatelet therapy without warfarin is approximately 6% to 9%, and the 1-year risk of any bleeding (minor or major) is approximately 15%. Although data on exact risk of bleeding while on triple therapy are lacking, it is estimated that it is associated with at least a 2-fold increased risk.

Warfarin Interruption

Oral anticoagulation may be temporarily stopped prior to PCI in almost all AF patients to prevent bleeding at the site of peripheral arterial puncture, but it should be resumed as soon as possible after the procedure and the dose adjusted to achieve a therapeutic INR.

Current guidelines recommend bridging therapy with UFH or LMWH to protect very high-risk AF patients from thromboembolism due to temporary discontinuation of warfarin. There is lack of data on bridging with other antithrombotic agents (eg, bivalirudin, fondaparinux).

The results of recent studies suggest that uninterrupted anticoagulation with warfarin within the therapeutic INR range (2 to 3) is as effective and could be safer than heparin bridging with PCIs. This strategy may also be superior in patients who undergo a staged PCI procedure.

The use of warfarin within 7 days prior to CABG has been shown to be associated with increased bleeding risk after surgery. Discontinuation of warfarin >1 week prior to CABG and bridging therapy with LMWH or UFH is recommended for high-risk AF patients.

13

Strategies to Decrease Bleeding Risk in Anticoagulated AF Patients Who Require Antiplatelet Therapy

Several strategies are recommended to decrease risk of bleeding in anticoagulated AF patients during and after PCI. A radial approach for PCI is preferred in anticoagulated patients since major bleeding complications are rare with this access site. The use of bare-metal stents is recommended in the majority of anticoagulated patients with AF undergoing PCI. Drug-eluting stents require prolonged dual antiplatelet therapy, which increases the risk of bleeding. As compared with an INR >2.6, INRs kept in a lower range of therapeutic level (2 to 2.5) have been associated with a decreased risk of bleeding in patients on triple therapy and is recommended with any combination of warfarin and antiplatelet therapy.

The dose of the antiplatelet agents should be kept as low as possible. Dose of ASA should be <100 mg daily, and the maintenance dose of clopidogrel should not exceed 75 mg daily. Temporary replacement of warfarin with dual antiplatelet therapy may be considered in AF patients post PCI with a relatively low risk of stroke (CHADS2 score of 1) who are at a high risk of bleeding. Protection with proton pump inhibitors (with the exception of omeprazole due to its possible interaction with clopidogrel) or antihistamine H_2 blockers should be considered in each patient on triple therapy to avoid GI bleeding. General measures to prevent hemorrhage in anticoagulated AF patients, such as aggressive control of the BP and strict avoidance of any other therapies which can increase risk of bleeding (eg, NSAIDs), should always be applied to patients on triple therapy.

Comprehensive data on the safety of newer antiplatelet agents (eg, prasugrel and ticagrelor) in anticoagulated patients with AF are lacking. Furthermore, data on the combination of these agents with warfarin are limited.

Multiple other strategies are being actively investigated to decrease the risk of bleeding in anticoagulated AF patients who require dual antiplatelet therapy after percutaneous interventions with stenting. As an example, in the ongoing WOEST trial (What is the Optimal Antiplatelet and Anticoagulant Therapy in Patients With Oral Anticoagulation and Coronary Stenting), the efficacy and safety of combination of oral anticoagulation and clopidogrel 75 mg daily compared with triple therapy (clopidogrel, oral anticoagulants, and ASA) is being evaluated in AF patients after coronary stenting.

Nonpharmacologic Prevention of Stroke in AF

The efficacy of warfarin stroke prevention in AF is well documented. However, at least 20% of patients with AF have absolute or relative contraindications to chronic warfarin therapy, eg, history of noncompliance, intracranial bleeding, or severe systemic bleeding. Additionally, a number of AF patients who could be treated with warfarin refuse therapy due to the cumbersome regimen and possible side effects. Warfarin is used in only 50% to 60% of eligible patients with AF. Apart from new drug development for stroke prevention, alternative nonpharmacologic therapies have been investigated. Approximately 85% to 90% of strokes in patients with AF are thromboembolic. It is estimated that LAA is a source of thromboembolism in 80% to 85% of patients. As such, surgical and percutaneous approaches to isolate the LAA and hence decrease risk of thrombus formation have been developed.

■ Percutaneous Closure of LAA

LAA occlusion devices delivered via a percutaneous, catheter-based approach have been designed with the goal of permanent stroke prevention in AF without the risk of side effects of anticoagulant therapy. Transcatheter LAA closure in the proximity of its orifice leads to blood stasis and controlled thrombosis with organization and fibrosis of the LAA. As the atrial surface of the LAA closing device is being covered by endocardium, complete isolation of the LAA from the circulation may be achieved. There are presently three devices developed for percutaneous LAA occlusion: the Percutaneous LAA Transcatheter Occlusion (PLAATO), Amplatzer Cardiac Plug, and the Watchman LAA system (**Figure 13.8**). Although each of these systems has some unique characteristics, all of them use IV catheters that cross the intra-atrial septum (through transseptal puncture or a PFO) and deliver the occluder in the LAA under TEE or fluoroscopic guidance (**Figure 13.9**). The learning curve associated with implantation of closure devices is responsible for substantial upfront periprocedural risk. However, this risk appears to be offset by cumulative risk of chronic therapy with warfarin, which may be eventually stopped in the vast majority of patients after implantation of the closure device. None of these devices have been yet approved in the United States.

Watchman Device

The Watchman LAA system is composed of a self-expanding nitinol frame (a nickel titanium alloy), fixation barbs and a polyethylene membrane that covers the LA surface of the device (**Figure 13.8**). Using femoral venous access and transseptal puncture, the device is deployed to the LAA (**Figure 13.9**). TEE is recommended before the procedure (to define LAA anatomy and exclude the presence of thrombus), during the procedure (to guide transseptal puncture, device placement, and exclude residual flow) and postprocedure (to confirm endothialization at 45 days). Other imaging modalities which may supplement TEE in periprocedural monitoring include 3D TEE and intracardiac echocardiography.

As the membrane in the Watchman device is permeable to blood, therapy with warfarin is required post implantation until the device is endothialized (at least 45 days post implant). During the procedure (after transseptal puncture), the patient is anticoagulated with IV heparin to achieve an ACT >200. All patients are treated with both ASA (81 to 325 mg) and clopidogrel (75 mg) daily starting 48 hours prior to procedure. Clopidogrel is then continued for 6 months, and ASA is taken lifelong. Due to possible increased risk of infective endocarditis, antibiotic prophylaxis for 6 months after implantation is recommended.

Embolic Protection in Patients with Atrial Fibrillation (PROTECT-AF) was a pivotal clinical study evaluating efficacy and safety of the Watchman device in patients with AF. In this multicenter, prospective and unblinded noninferiority trial, 707 patients with nonvalvular AF were randomly assigned in a 2:1 ratio to either receive Watchman device plus short-term warfarin therapy (45 days) or chronic anticoagulation therapy with warfarin with target INR of 2 to 3 (control group).

Inclusion criteria allowed enrollment of adult patients with paroxysmal, persistent, or permanent AF and CHADS score ≥1 (approximately two thirds of patients had a CHADS score of 1 to 2) who were otherwise eligible to receive anticoagulation therapy with warfarin. The primary efficacy end point was a composite of the absence of any strokes (ischemic and hemorrhagic), CV and unexplained death, or systemic embolism. The primary safety end point included major bleeding, pericardial effusion, procedure-related stroke,

FIGURE 13.8 — Comparison of Dedicated Left Atrial Appendage Closure Devices

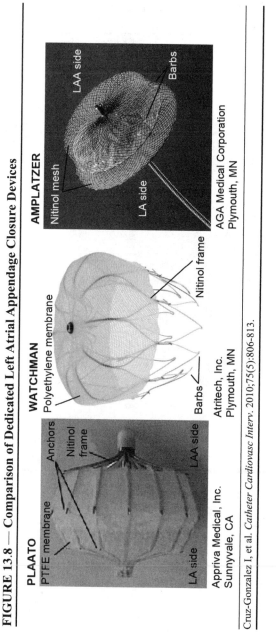

PLAATO
PTFE membrane
Anchors
Nitinol frame
LAA side
LA side
Appriva Medical, Inc.
Sunnyvale, CA

WATCHMAN
Polyethylene membrane
Nitinol frame
Barbs
Atritech, Inc.
Plymouth, MN

AMPLATZER
LAA side
Barbs
Nitinol mesh
LA side
AGA Medical Corporation
Plymouth, MN

Cruz-Gonzalez I, et al. *Catheter Cardiovasc Interv.* 2010;75(5):806-813.

13

FIGURE 13.9 — The Watchman Left Atrial Appendage Closure Device

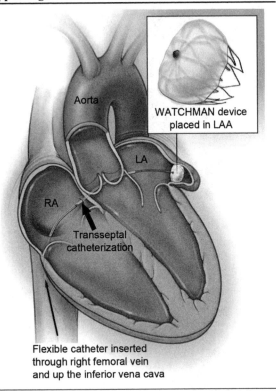

WATCHMAN device placed in LAA

Aorta

LA

RA

Transseptal catheterization

Flexible catheter inserted through right femoral vein and up the inferior vena cava

The device is a self-expanding nitinol structure that is delivered percutaneously with femoral venous access and transseptal technique to the LAA. The device is positioned with the use of angiography and TEE. Implantation is performed in either a cardiac catherization or electrophysiology laboratory with the patient under general anesthesia or conscious sedation.

Maisel WH. *N Engl J Med.* 2009;360(25):2601-2603.

and device embolization. Patients were followed with TEE at 45 days, 6 months, and 1 year, and biannual clinical follow-up to 5 years. After a mean follow-up of 18 months, the primary events were lower in the Watchman group than in the control group (3.0 vs 4.9 events per 100 patient-years respectively, rate ratio 0.62). In particular, there was a 90% reduction in the rate of hemorrhagic stroke in patients assigned to Watchman as compared with the control group (rate ratio 0.09). At 45 days, 86% of patients with an implanted device were able to stop taking warfarin and 92% of patients met TEE criteria for discontinuation of anticoagulation by 6 months.

In this study, LAA closure with the Watchman device with short-term anticoagulation was noninferior to long-term anticoagulation with warfarin, but interpretation of study results carries several limitations.

Device implantation was successful in 91% of all patients in the device group. The primary safety end points were more common in the device group than control (7.4 vs 4.4 events per 100 patient years respectively, rate ratio 1.69). Over 12% of patients in the Watchman group had serious procedural complications. Almost half of them (about 5% of patients) were pericardial effusions requiring drainage or surgery. Acute ischemic stroke due to thromboemboli or air embolus occurred in about 1% of patients. The learning curve required for device implantation resulted in the 50% higher rate of serious pericardial effusion at less-experienced centers. In spite of aggressive periprocedural antithrombotic and antiplatelet therapy, patients in the device group had a higher risk of ischemic stroke than in the control group (2.2% vs 1.6%), with almost half of events occurring in the first month. Over 25% of patients in control group either did not take or discontinued warfarin during the study, and INRs were in the therapeutic range 66% of the time.

Assessment of the appropriate role of devices in clinical practice is also complicated by study design. LAA occlusion devices may benefit AF patients who are at high risk for bleeding with oral anticoagulation. However, since short-term aggressive periprocedural anticoagulation and long-term antiplatelet therapy are needed with implantation of the Watchman device, these patients were excluded from the study. Additionally, about 33% of patients in Watchman group had a CHADS2 score of 1 and were candidates for only ASA according to current ACC/AHA/ESC Guidelines.

Amplatzer Cardiac Plug

In a small study, the Amplatzer Septal Occluder, initially developed for atrial septal defect closure, was successfully tested for LAA closure. Based on these promising results and taking advantage of low thrombogenicity of the Amplatzer devices, the manufacturer developed the Amplatzer Cardiac Plug (ACP) as a dedicated LAA occlusion system. It is made up from nitinol mesh with a polyester fabric and composed of a distal lobe and a proximal disk connected by a central waist (**Figure 13.8**). The distal lobe conforms to the inner wall of the LAA, and the proximal disk covers the orifice of the LAA. A central waist works as an articulate responsible for positional adjustment and allowing the disc to self-orient to the left atrial wall. The ACP occludes the LAA with full cross-sectional coverage. If necessary, the ACP has the capability to be retrieved, re-deployed, or replaced. More than 200 ACPs have been implanted worldwide. Two device embolizations and two pericardial effusions requiring drainage were reported. The Cardiac Plug European Registry is a prospective, open-label, postmarket registry of 100 AF patients in eight centers. Patients are treated with low-dose ASA for 6 months and clopidogrel 75 mg for 1 month with a follow-up with TEE at 1 and 6 months post procedure. Appropriate endocarditis prophylaxis is also recommended. The results of the Registry are expected in late 2010. The Amplatzer cardiac plug is not yet available in the United States, but a clinical trial to evaluate the efficacy and safety for stroke prevention in AF recently began.

Surgical Techniques

LAA amputation or ligation can be safely performed during cardiac surgery, sometimes as a part of Cox-Maze procedure for AF. Minimally invasive LAA ligation through a thoracoscopic approach has also been developed.

Based on results of a small series of studies which suggested that these techniques can reduce the risk of stroke, exclusion of LAA at the time of mitral valve surgery is frequently performed in centers with expertise in this procedure. Furthermore, current 2006 ACC/AHA guidelines on valvular disease recommend LAA amputation in certain patients undergoing mitral valve surgery. However, data from transesophageal studies in patients who underwent surgical exclusion of LAA showed a high rate of incomplete occlusion. This was responsible for a risk of thrombus formation and thromboembolic events. TEE studies report only about a 55% to 65% long-term successful rate of LAA exclusion (including stapling, ligation, or amputation). Amputation was more effective than ligation. Presently, there are insufficient data to recommend surgical LAA exclusion for prevention of thrombus formation. If the procedure is carried out, the presence of complete exclusion should be followed with serial TEE. Heart failure may be a concern when removing the left or both appendages, since up to 30% of atrial natriuretic factor, a regulator of volume status, is produced in the atrial appendages.

13

SUGGESTED READING

ACTIVE Investigators, Connolly SJ, Pogue J, Hart RG, et al. Effect of clopidogrel added to aspirin in patients with atrial fibrillation. *N Engl J Med*. 2009;360(20):2066-2078.

ACTIVE Writing Group of the ACTIVE Investigators, Connolly S, Pogue J, Hart R, et al. Clopidogrel plus aspirin versus oral anticoagulation for atrial fibrillation in the Atrial fibrillation Clopidogrel Trial with Irbesartan for prevention of Vascular Events (ACTIVE W): a randomised controlled trial. *Lancet*. 2006;367(9526):1903-1912.

Adjusted-dose warfarin versus low-intensity, fixed-dose warfarin plus aspirin for high-risk patients with atrial fibrillation: Stroke Prevention in Atrial Fibrillation III randomised clinical trial. *Lancet*. 1996;348(9028):633-638.

Ahrens I, Lip GY, Peter K. New oral anticoagulant drugs in cardiovascular disease. *Thromb Haemost*. 2010;104(1):49-60.

Armaganijan L, Eikelboom J, Healey JS, Morillo CA. New pharmacotherapy for stroke prevention in atrial fibrillation: Update 2010. *Adv Ther*. 2009;26(12):1058-1071.

Black IW, Hopkins AP, Lee LC, Walsh WF. Evaluation of transesophageal echocardiography before cardioversion of atrial fibrillation and flutter in nonanticoagulated patients. *Am Heart J*. 1993;126(2):375-381.

Connolly SJ, Eikelboom J, Joyner C, et al; AVERROES Steering Committee and Investigators. Apixaban in patients with atrial fibrillation. *N Engl J Med*. 2011;364(9):806-817.

Connolly SJ, Ezekowitz MD, Yusuf S, et al; RE-LY Steering Committee and Investigators. Dabigatran versus warfarin in patients with atrial fibrillation. *N Engl J Med*. 2009;361(12):1139-1151.

Connolly SJ, Laupacis A, Gent M, Roberts RS, Cairns JA, Joyner C. Canadian Atrial Fibrillation Anticoagulation (CAFA) Study. *J Am Coll Cardiol*. 1991;18(2):349-355.

Cooper NJ, Sutton AJ, Lu G, Khunti K. Mixed comparison of stroke prevention treatments in individuals with nonrheumatic atrial fibrillation. *Arch Intern Med*. 2006;166(12):1269-1275.

Cruz-Gonzalez I, Yan BP, Lam YY. Left atrial appendage exclusion: state-of-the-art. *Catheter Cardiovasc Interv*. 2010;75(5):806-813.

Dawson AG, Asopa S, Dunning J. Should patients undergoing cardiac surgery with atrial fibrillation have left atrial appendage exclusion? *Interact Cardiovasc Thorac Surg*. 2010;10(2):306-311.

Ezekowitz MD, Bridgers SL, James KE, et al. Warfarin in the prevention of stroke associated with nonrheumatic atrial fibrillation. Veterans Affairs Stroke Prevention in Nonrheumatic Atrial Fibrillation Investigators. *N Engl J Med*. 1992;327(20):1406-1412.

Fang MC, Go AS, Chang Y, Borowsky L, Pomernacki NK, Singer DE; ATRIA Study Group. Comparison of risk stratification schemes to predict thromboembolism in people with nonvalvular atrial fibrillation. *J Am Coll Cardiol.* 2008;51(8):810-815.

Fuster V, Rydén LE, Cannom DS, et al; American College of Cardiology/American Heart Association Task Force on Practice Guidelines; European Society of Cardiology Committee for Practice Guidelines; European Heart Rhythm Association; Heart Rhythm Society. ACC/AHA/ESC 2006 Guidelines for the Management of Patients with Atrial Fibrillation: a report of the American College of Cardiology/American Heart Association Task Force on Practice Guidelines and the European Society of Cardiology Committee for Practice Guidelines (Writing Committee to Revise the 2001 Guidelines for the Management of Patients With Atrial Fibrillation): developed in collaboration with the European Heart Rhythm Association and the Heart Rhythm Society. *Circulation.* 2006;114(7):e257-3354.

Gage BF, Waterman AD, Shannon W, Boechler M, Rich MW, Radford MJ. Validation of clinical classification schemes for predicting stroke: results from the National Registry of Atrial Fibrillation. *JAMA.* 2001;285(22):2864-2870.

Gage BF. Can we rely on RE-LY? *N Engl J Med.* 2009;361(12):1200-1202.

Gallagher MM, Hennessy BJ, Edvardsson N, et al. Embolic complications of direct current cardioversion of atrial arrhythmias: association with low intensity of anticoagulation at the time of cardioversion. *J Am Coll Cardiol.* 2002;40(5):926-933.

Go AS, Hylek EM, Chang Y, Phillips KA, Henault LE, Capra AM, Jensvold NG, Selby JV, Singer DE. Anticoagulation therapy for stroke prevention in atrial fibrillation: how well do randomized trials translate into clinical practice? *JAMA.* 2003;290(20):2685-2692.

Granger CB, Alexander JH, McMurray JJ, et al; ARISTOTLE Committees and Investigators. Apixaban versus warfarin in patients with atrial fibrillation. *N Engl J Med.* 2011;365(11):981-992.

Gulløv AL, Koefoed BG, Petersen P, et al. Fixed minidose warfarin and aspirin alone and in combination vs adjusted-dose warfarin for stroke prevention in atrial fibrillation: Second Copenhagen Atrial Fibrillation, Aspirin, and Anticoagulation Study. *Arch Intern Med.* 1998;158(14):1513-1521.

Harenberg J. New anticoagulants in atrial fibrillation. *Semin Thromb Hemost.* 2009;35(6):574-585.

Hart RG, Pearce LA, Aguilar MI. Meta-analysis: antithrombotic therapy to prevent stroke in patients who have nonvalvular atrial fibrillation. *Ann Intern Med.* 2007;146(12):857-867.

13

Heppell RM, Berkin KE, McLenachan JM, Davies JA. Haemostatic and haemodynamic abnormalities associated with left atrial thrombosis in non-rheumatic atrial fibrillation. *Heart*. 1997;77(5):407-411.

Holbrook AM, Pereira JA, Labiris R, et al. Systematic overview of warfarin and its drug and food interactions. *Arch Intern Med*. 2005;165(10):1095-1106.

Holmes DR, Reddy VY, Turi ZG, et al; PROTECT AF Investigators. Percutaneous closure of the left atrial appendage versus warfarin therapy for prevention of stroke in patients with atrial fibrillation: a randomised non-inferiority trial. *Lancet*. 2009;374(9689):534-542.

Hylek EM, Go AS, Chang Y, et al. Effect of intensity of oral antico-agulation on stroke severity and mortality in atrial fibrillation. *N Engl J Med*. 2003;349(11):1019-1026.

Hylek EM, Skates SJ, Sheehan MA, Singer DE. An analysis of the low-est effective intensity of prophylactic anticoagulation for patients with nonrheumatic atrial fibrillation. *N Engl J Med*. 1996;335(8):540-546.

Khattab A, Meier B. Transcatheter devices for left atrial appendage occlusion. *Cardiovasc Med*. 2010;13(4):130-134.

Khoo CW, Lip GY. Insights from the dabigatran versus warfarin in pa-tients with atrial fibrillation (RE-LY) trial. *Expert Opin Pharmacother*. 2010;11(4):685-687.

Kinch JW, Davidoff R. Prevention of embolic events after cardioversion of atrial fibrillation. Current and evolving strategies. *Arch Intern Med*. 1995;155(13):1353-1360.

Klein AL, Grimm RA, Jasper SE, et al; ACUTE Steering and Publi-cations Committee for the ACUTE Investigators. Efficacy of trans-esophageal echocardiography-guided cardioversion of patients with atrial fibrillation at 6 months: a randomized controlled trial. *Am Heart J*. 2006;151(2):380-389.

Klein AL, Grimm RA, Murray RD, et al; Assessment of Cardioversion Using Transesophageal Echocardiography Investigators. Use of trans-esophageal echocardiography to guide cardioversion in patients with atrial fibrillation. *N Engl J Med*. 2001;344(19):1411-1420.

Kowey PR, Reiffel JA, Myerburg R, et al; AFFECTS Scientific Advi-sory Committee and Investigators. Warfarin and aspirin use in atrial fi-brillation among practicing cardiologist (from the AFFECTS Registry). *Am J Cardiol*. 2010;105(8):1130-1134.

Lip GY, Huber K, Andreotti F, et al; Consensus Document of European Society of Cardiology Working Group on Thrombosis. Antithrombotic management of atrial fibrillation patients presenting with acute coronary syndrome and/or undergoing coronary stenting: executive summary—a Consensus Document of the European Society of Cardiology Working Group on Thrombosis, endorsed by the European Heart Rhythm Association (EHRA) and the European Association of Percutaneous Cardio-vascular Interventions (EAPCI). *Eur Heart J.* 2010;31(11):1311-1318.

Lip GY, Lim HS. Atrial fibrillation and stroke prevention. *Lancet Neurol.* 2007;6(11):981-993.

Lip GY, Nieuwlaat R, Pisters R, Lane DA, Crijns HJ. Refining clinical risk stratification for predicting stroke and thromboembolism in atrial fibrillation using a novel risk factor-based approach: the euro heart survey on atrial fibrillation. *Chest.* 2010;137(2):263-272.

Lloyd-Jones DM, Wang TJ, Leip EP, et al. Lifetime risk for development of atrial fibrillation: the Framingham Heart Study. *Circulation.* 2004;110(9):1042-1046.

Maisel WH. Left atrial appendage occlusion—closure or just the beginning? *N Engl J Med.* 2009;360(25):2601-2603.

Manning WJ, Arnsdorf MF. Anticoagulation prior to and after restoration of sinus rhythm in atrial fibrillation. In: *UpToDate.* Estes NA, Saperia GM. Waltham, MA: UpToDate; 2010.

Manning WJ, Hart RG. Risk of embolization in atrial fibrillation. In: *UpToDate.* Zimetbaum PJ, Kasner SE, Saperia BM, eds. Waltham, MA: UpToDate; 2010.

Manning WJ, Singer SE, Lip GYH, Hart RG. Antithrombotic therapy to prevent embolization in nonvalvular atrial fibrillation. In: *UpToDate.* Zimetbaum PJ, Kasner SE, Saperia GM, eds. Waltham, MA: UpToDate; 2010.

Mant J, Hobbs FD, Fletcher K, et al; BAFTA investigators; Midland Research Practices Network (MidReC). Warfarin versus aspirin for stroke prevention in an elderly community population with atrial fibrillation (the Birmingham Atrial Fibrillation Treatment of the Aged Study, BAFTA): a randomised controlled trial. *Lancet.* 2007;370(9586):493-503.

Menke J, Lüthje L, Kastrup A, Larsen J. Thromboembolism in atrial fibrillation. *Am J Cardiol.* 2010;105(4):502-510.

Patel MR, Mahaffey KW, Garg J, et al; ROCKET AF Investigators. Rivaroxaban versus warfarin in nonvalvular atrial fibrillation. *N Engl J Med.* 2011;365(10):883-891.

Petersen P, Boysen G, Godtfredsen J, Andersen ED, Andersen B. Placebo-controlled, randomised trial of warfarin and aspirin for prevention of thromboembolic complications in chronic atrial fibrillation. The Copenhagen AFASAK study. *Lancet.* 1989;1(8631):175-179.

Risk factors for stroke and efficacy of antithrombotic therapy in atrial fibrillation. Analysis of pooled data from five randomized controlled trials. *Arch Intern Med.* 1994;154(13):1449-1457.

13

Sarafoff N, Schomig A, Holes DR Jr. Triple antithrombotic therapy in patient with cardiovascular disease. In: *UpToDate*. Cannon CP, Cutlip D, Saperia GM, eds. Waltham, MA: UpToDate; 2010.

Singer DE, Albers GW, Dalen JE, et al; American College of Chest Physicians. Antithrombotic therapy in atrial fibrillation: American College of Chest Physicians Evidence-Based Clinical Practice Guidelines (8th Edition). *Chest*. 2008;133(6 suppl):546S-592S.

Singer DE, Chang Y, Fang MC, et al. The net clinical benefit of warfarin anticoagulation in atrial fibrillation. *Ann Intern Med*. 2009;151(5):297-305.

Stroke Prevention in Atrial Fibrillation Study. Final results. *Circulation*. 1991;84(2):527-539.

The effect of low-dose warfarin on the risk of stroke in patients with nonrheumatic atrial fibrillation. The Boston Area Anticoagulation Trial for Atrial Fibrillation Investigators. *N Engl J Med*. 1990;323(22):1505-1511.

Valentine KA, Hull RD. Therapeutic use of warfarin. In: *UpToDate*. Leung LLK, Landaw SA, eds. Waltham, MA: UpToDate; 2010.

van Walraven C, Hart RG, Singer DE, et al. Oral anticoagulants vs aspirin in nonvalvular atrial fibrillation: an individual patient meta-analysis. *JAMA*. 2002;288(19):2441-2448.

Waldo AL. Anticoagulation: stroke prevention in patients with atrial fibrillation. *Cardiol Clin*. 2009;27(1):125-135, ix.

Wang TJ, Massaro JM, Levy D, et al. A risk score for predicting stroke or death in individuals with new-onset atrial fibrillation in the community: the Framingham Heart Study. *JAMA*. 2003;290(8):1049-1056.

Wann LS, Curtis AB, Ellenbogen KA, et al. 2011 ACC/AHA/HRS focused update on the management of patients with atrial fibrillation (update on dabigatran): a report of the American College of Cardiology Foundation/American Heart Association Task Force on practice guidelines. *J Am Coll Cardiol*. 2011;57(11):1330-1337.

Warfarin versus aspirin for prevention of thromboembolism in atrial fibrillation: Stroke Prevention in Atrial Fibrillation II Study. *Lancet*. 1994;343(8899):687-691.

Watson T, Shantsila E, Lip GY. Mechanisms of thrombogenesis in atrial fibrillation: Virchow's triad revisited. *Lancet*. 2009;373(9658):155-166.

Weitz JI. New oral anticoagulants in development. *Thromb Haemost*. 2010;103(1):62-70.

You JJ, Singer DE, Howard PA, et al; American College of Chest Physicians. Antithrombotic therapy for atrial fibrillation: Antithrombotic Therapy and Prevention of Thrombosis, 9th ed: American College of Chest Physicians Evidence-Based Clinical Practice Guidelines. *Chest*. 2012;141(suppl 2):e531S-e575S.

14 Case Studies

Case 1: Lone Atrial Fibrillation

A 45-year-old male presents to the emergency department (ED) with a 2-hour history of palpitations. He awakened from an afternoon nap with this symptom. He has no associated symptoms. His medical history is remarkable for two prior episodes of AF, 3 and 5 years ago. He carries a diagnosis of paroxysmal lone AF. He takes no medications. A prior echocardiogram was within normal limits except for mild left atrial enlargement. His physical exam is remarkable for an irregular pulse at a rate of 130 BPM. His BP was 110/70 mm Hg. Laboratory data are all within normal limits. An ECG shows no abnormalities other than the AF.

■ Question 1: Is the patient a candidate for acute cardioversion?

Yes. The patient has an acute onset of symptomatic AF. He must be able to identify, within reasonable certainty, the timing of onset. This duration should be <24 to 48 hours.

Thromboembolic risk would be increased if:

- Duration is >48 hours
- AF has been occurring on an asymptomatic basis such that the duration has been longer than suspected.

■ Question 2: Is TEE required prior to cardioversion?

Not in this case. TEE should be done precardioversion if there is a concern about a left atrial appendage thrombus that could present an embolic risk. The presence of such a thrombus would preclude proceeding with the cardioversion. Since this patient's AF is only of 2 hours' duration, a left atrial–appendage thrombus would be unlikely.

The other situation where TEE would not be required precardioversion is in a patient with a therapeutic INR with warfarin use for >3 weeks. In such a case, the thromboembolic risk is low.

The patient's wife was present in the ED. She expressed reluctance about her husband undergoing conscious sedation for electrical cardioversion.

■ Question 3: Can acute pharmacologic cardioversion be carried out?

Yes. The most commonly used drug for acute pharmacologic cardioversion is ibutilide. This drug is generally well tolerated but does present a risk of acute QT prolongation and TdP. Ibutilide should not be given to patients who are already taking certain other AADs since this markedly increases the risk of TdP. Close telemetry observation is required for at least 4 to 6 hours after administration of ibutilide. Ibutilide is more effective at terminating atrial flutter. Use of an investigational drug, vernakalant, has been successful in termination of short-duration AF. This drug is still under clinical investigation.

Other drugs could be given for acute cardioversion, including:
- Oral administration of 300 mg flecainide
- Oral administration of 600 mg propafenone
- IV administration of 7 to 15 mg/1 kg body weight of procainamide
- IV amiodarone 150-mg bolus over 10 minutes (may repeat once), followed by 1 mg/minute for 6 hours and then 0.5 mg/minute
- IV vernakalant 3 mg/kg IV over 10 minutes; if cardioversion fails in 15 minutes, IV bolus may be repeated at 2 mg/kg over 10 minutes (currently available in the European Union; is under investigation in the United States).

If a pharmacologic attempt at cardioversion is unsuccessful, electrical cardioversion can be performed. The patient should be fasting for 8 hours to reduce aspiration risk. A synchronized cardioversion should be used to reduce risk of ventricular fibrillation. A biphasic shock of 200 J could be given.

The patient overruled his wife and decided to undergo electrical cardioversion. This was successful. NSR at a rate of 60 was restored.

■ Question 4: How should this patient be managed long-term?

His wife inquired about AF ablation. Although quite symptomatic, the infrequent nature of the episodes would make an ablation procedure a less-desirable treatment option at this point. Similarly, daily maintenance-preventive therapy would be inappropriate because of the infrequency of the episodes.

This patient may be a candidate to use a medication such as flecainide 300 mg or propafenone 600 mg on an as-needed (pill-in-a-pocket) basis for an acute attack. To be such a candidate, the patient should first receive this specific treatment in an in-hospital telemetry setting to observe the response. A decision regarding long-term therapy would be delayed until it is determined how often the patient has recurrences.

Case 2: Asymptomatic Elderly Person Presenting With New-Onset AF

A 78-year-old male presents to the office for a routine follow-up visit. He is noted to have an irregular pulse at 90 BPM. ECG shows AF with an age-indeterminate inferior wall infarction. The AF is new since an office visit with his internist 1 month ago. The patient denies palpitations or any other symptoms. His medical history is remarkable for an inferior wall infarction 15 years ago. His LVEF was calculated at 40% on a postexercise gated SPECT nuclear scan 1 year ago. This test was negative for ischemia. He has a history of hypertension and dyslipidemia. His medications include aspirin, metoprolol succinate, losartan, and atorvastatin. He had a bothersome cough with use of enalapril. His physical exam is remarkable for a BP of 110/70 mm Hg, an irregular pulse of 90 BPM, and a Grade I/VI apical systolic murmur.

- **Question 1: Does this patient require hospitalization?**

No. The patient is hemodynamically stable and is not symptomatic. The pulse rate is only mildly increased.

- **Question 2: Is warfarin therapy indicated?**

Yes. The patient has a CHADS2 score of 2, ie, including a history of hypertension and age >75 years. He has mild-to-moderate left ventricular dysfunction but no history of CHF, and his LVEF is >35%. His yearly stroke risk is about 4% without treatment. Since he has no contraindications to warfarin, the benefits would outweigh the risks for this gentleman. Dabigatran would be an option as an alternative to warfarin.

- **Question 3: What other evaluation is indicated?**

Please refer to the evaluation of new-onset AF in *Chapter 6*.

An echocardiogram should be done to reassess LV function and wall motion abnormalities. Left atrial size and pulmonary pressures can be assessed.

Blood tests, including TSH, electrolytes, CBC, and liver/renal function, should be checked. Ambulatory monitoring was done to assess the patient's variability in pulse rate with AF. Near-syncopal symptoms can be caused by bradycardia or prolonged pauses (>3 seconds), particularly if they occur during wakeful hours. Poor stamina, easy fatigability, and dyspnea on exertion could be caused by excessively rapid heart rates, particularly at lower levels of exertion.

- **Question 4: Should restoration of NSR be attempted and, if so, when?**

The answer to this question is controversial. Many believe that all patients deserve at least one attempt at restoration to NSR. In this elderly, asymptomatic man, a reasonable option is rate control with therapeutic anticoagulation.

Certainly, the option of cardioversion should be discussed with the patient and family. In this discussion, several points should be emphasized:

- Long-term anticoagulation will likely still be required, even if the cardioversion is successful.
- Cardioversion, either electrical or pharmacologic, does not guarantee maintenance of sinus rhythm. Long-term therapy with AADs will likely be required.
- Since the onset of his AF is unknown, any attempt at cardioversion would require antecedent, either:
  - TEE to exclude left atrial thrombus with peri-cardioversion anticoagulation, or
  - Documented therapeutic INR for a minimum of 3 to 4 weeks precardioversion.

Since he has an auto-controlled rate, he has conduction disease. If he is cardioverted, his sinus rate is likely to be slow and he might then need a pacer—better to be in rate-controlled AF if he is experiencing no symptoms from it.

After this discussion, the patient opted for a rate-control strategy. He began long-term warfarin therapy with periodic INR assessment. Initial outpatient telemetry demonstrated a rapid ventricular rate, and his metoprolol succinate dose was increased from 50 to 100 mg a day. Repeat telemetry showed average pulse rate of 60 BPM, no pauses >2 seconds, and appropriate acceleration of pulse rate with activity. He remains asymptomatic in follow-up.

Case 3: AF Post–CABG

A 77-year-old man presented 1 week ago to another hospital with a non–ST-segment elevation MI. He had noted several hours of chest pain associated with new anterior T-wave inversions. He had a troponin rise to 1.4 ng/mL. His medical history was remarkable for hypertension, untreated hypercholesterolemia, and a one pack per day smoking history. Family history was remarkable for sudden cardiac death in his father at age 52. His physical exam was unremarkable. He was transferred to our facility after an episode of postinfarction angina. Cardiac catheterization showed mild inferior wall hypokinesis with overall preserved LV systolic function, an occluded proximal dominant right coronary artery with the visualization of this vessel via left-to-right collateral flow, an 80% proximal left anterior descending stenosis, and a 90% stenosis of a large obtuse marginal branch of circumflex. He underwent off-pump coronary bypass surgery. He had a left internal mammary artery graft placed to his left anterior descending vessel, right internal mammary graft to his right coronary artery, and a radial graft to an obtuse marginal branch of the circumflex artery.

His postoperative medications included aspirin, clopidogrel, atorvastatin, ramipril, and metoprolol succinate. On day 3, while in the telemetry unit, the patient developed AF with a rapid ventricular rate of 140 BPM. The patient noted palpitations and mild dyspnea. His other vital signs remained stable with a BP of 120/60 mm Hg and a respiratory rate of 20. He was afebrile. There was no evidence of HF, jugular venous distention, rales, or S3 gallop. He had decreased breath sounds at both lung bases secondary to postoperative atelectasis. His pulse oximetry was 92% on room air. A repeat ECG was unchanged except for the AF. Electrolytes were normal.

■ Question 1: What are the risk factors for postoperative AF?

Risks for postoperative AF include old age (>70 years considered to be high risk), male sex, prior history of AF, hypertension, obesity, COPD, left atrial enlargement, and decreased LVEF.

■ Question 2: How can post-op AF be prevented in patients at risk?

The efficacy of β-blockers in lowering the incidence of AF post-op has been demonstrated in several trials. β-Blockers should be administered perioperatively (in patients without contraindications) to reduce the incidence of AF after CABG. There is no clear benefit of IV β-blockers over oral formulations.

Amiodarone and other AADs also may work prophylactically—it is not clear whether they are really better than a β-blocker alone, and it is not clear whether their risk is warranted in most patients.

Recent evidence also suggests a role for statin and steroids in reducing postoperative AF. In the case of steroid use, the potential for adverse effects (eg, wound healing, infection) may outweigh the benefit of attempting to prevent this usually self-limited condition.

■ **Question 3: How should this patient be managed?**

Multiple treatment options are reasonable. The patient was acutely converted using an amiodarone bolus of 150 mg followed by an infusion of 1 mg/minute for 6 hours, then 0.5 mg/minute for another 18 hours. The amiodarone was then switched to an oral loading dose of 400 mg twice daily, and metoprolol succinate was increased to 100 mg orally daily. He had a second episode of AF on day 5. This episode lasted 60 minutes and was rate-controlled.

■ **Question 4: Is anticoagulation needed here?**

Yes. The patient was begun on a warfarin protocol. Thromboembolic events are reported complications in this setting, ie, AF post–CABG. Because of the initial concomitant use of amiodarone, the warfarin dosing was reduced. Dronedarone does not potentiate warfarin effect as does amiodarone, but its use in the post–CABG population has not been studied.

■ **Question 5: How long should the amiodarone and warfarin be continued?**

These would both be continued for about 8 weeks postoperatively. If recurrent episodes continue, a longer duration of therapy may be required. Generally, the pericardial inflammation and other factors that precipitate AF subside by about 8 weeks. Ongoing episodes >8 weeks postsurgery suggest that the patient may have other reasons predisposing to AF and may require lifelong treatment.

Case 4: AF With Hyperthyroidism

This 85-year-old woman presented with a complaint of fevers, chills, urinary frequency, dysuria, nausea, and vomiting. She was admitted to another hospital with a presumed diagnosis of urosepsis and was started on antibiotics and fluids. She then developed HF along with a positive troponin rise, not associated with new ECG changes. Patient had a chronic left bundle branch block. The patient was transferred to us for further evaluation and treatment.

She was given aspirin and low-dose β-blocker therapy for her positive cardiac enzymes. She was started on an IV infusion of furosemide for her HF. Upon transfer, she was noted to have an increased respiratory rate and respiratory insufficiency, and was intubated for acute respiratory failure.

During her ICU stay, the patient developed AF with a rapid ventricular response. Blood work showed a suppressed TSH level. She was seen by an endocrinologist and diagnosed with hyperthyroidism.

The patient underwent coronary arteriography during the hospital stay. This study again showed luminal irregularities similar to those in a study several years before.

■ Question 1: Can the patient's hyperthyroidism be treated with β-blocker therapy alone?

No. The patient requires specific treatment for the hyperthyroid condition. β-Blockers were administered to control the ventricular rate. She then spontaneously converted back to sinus rhythm. She was given methimazole 5 mg twice daily with adequate control of her hyperthyroidism. The decision was made to postpone I-131 ablation because of the contrast dye that she had received for her coronary arteriography due to the concern that this might exacerbate her hyperthyroidism.

■ Question 2: Does the patient need urgent cardioversion to restore NSR?

No. The management of AF associated with hyperthyroidism requires direct treatment of the excessive thyroid state. Within 6 weeks of becoming euthyroid, 60% of patients have a spontaneous conversion to NSR. β-Blocker therapy alone is often inadequate to restore and maintain sinus rhythm but is used effectively to control the ventricular response.

■ **Question 3**: **What is the most important determinant of persistence of AF in hyperthyroid patients?**

AF remains more prevalent in treated patients with hyperthyroidism even after restoration of a euthyroid state. The duration of AF and advanced age are the most important prognostic factors for persistence of AF in patients with hyperthyroidism. In patients who do not convert to NSR after becoming euthyroid, cardioversion should be considered.

■ **Question 4**: **Does the patient require anticoagulation for AF due to hyperthyroidism?**

Yes. This patient would require anticoagulation for the AF associated with hyperthyroidism. This patient was given IV heparin therapy, then warfarin therapy.

■ **Question 5**: **Should be patient placed on amiodarone?**

No. Amiodarone would not be a good choice in a patient with thyroid dysfunction.

Case 5: AF in Patient With Stent Placement

A 76-year-old man presents with an ACS, ie, 3 hours of substernal chest distress with radiation to his left shoulder. He had no associated symptoms or preceding chest distress.

His medical history is remarkable for persistent AF, hypertension, and dyslipidemia. He had presented 5 years ago with a transient ischemic attack manifested by right lower facial weakness and right-hand incoordination. He was noted to be in AF with a controlled ventricular rate at that time. A head CT scan showed a localized hypodensity in the left parietal cortex compatible with an area of infarction. He was anticoagulated and has been on warfarin since that time. There is no history of diabetes. He had a cholecystectomy 15 years ago. He smoked one pack per day of cigarettes for 35 years but stopped 20 years ago.

14

His only medications are lisinopril 20 mg daily and warfarin with dosage adjusted based on INR. He had also been prescribed simvastatin 20 mg daily but had "run out" of this medication 2 months ago. He also had been taking a daily aspirin but stopped several months ago.

Family history is remarkable for his mother dying with an MI at age 78 and a brother having a coronary stent placed at age 67.

Review of systems is unremarkable.

Physical exam shows an elderly white male in moderate distress with chest pain. His BP is 120/80 mm Hg. His pulse is 80 BPM with AF. He has no evidence of jugular venous distention or signs of CHF.

An ECG shows AF with a controlled ventricular rate and new anterior T-wave inversions in V2 to V5. Troponin was 1.2 pg/mL on presentation and rose to 5.8 pg/mL. Chest x-ray and other lab results are normal. INR is therapeutic at 2.1 on admission.

The patient received aspirin, enoxaparin, a loading dose of clopidogrel, metoprolol tartrate, and IV nitroglycerin. He became painfree shortly after hospitalization. His warfarin was stopped, but the lisinopril and simvastatin were continued.

He was taken to cardiac catheterization 2 days later. INR had fallen to 1.3. Coronary arteriography showed an 80% stenosis of the left anterior descending artery after a first septal perforating branch. An obtuse marginal of circumflex had a 30% stenosis. The right coronary artery had only luminal irregularities. He underwent successful placement of a drug-eluting stent to the left anterior descending artery.

■ **Question 1**: **Should he be kept off warfarin while taking aspirin and clopidogrel**?

The patient's CHADS2 score is 4. This represents a higher stroke risk of approximately 8% to 9% per year without therapy.

In the ACTIVE-A arm of ACTIVE (Atrial Fibrillation Clopidogrel Trial With Irbesartan for Prevention of Vascular Events), patients were enrolled who were thought not to be candidates for warfarin. The mean CHADS2 score was low at 2. Patients who received the combination of aspirin (70-100 mg daily) and clopidogrel did show a reduction in the rate of ischemic stroke (however, this combination was inferior to warfarin). Major bleeding occurred at an increased rate with the combination therapy.

In this patient with a CHADS2 score of 4, the warfarin dose should be resumed.

■ **Question 2**: **Should a dose adjustment be made with the triple therapy of aspirin, clopidogrel, and warfarin?**

ACC/AHA Guidelines permit the use of triple therapy if a patient has indications for both antiplatelet and antithrombotic therapy as this patient does.

In such a case, the increased risk of bleeding must be weighed against the increased risk of stent thrombosis or thromboembolic events without such therapy. The guidelines discuss a lower dose of warfarin, ie, aim for an INR of 2 to 2.5 rather than 2 to 3 (Class IIb, level of evidence C). Aspirin dosing of 75 to 81 mg daily is recommended, although this dose change must be weighed against the risk of DES thrombosis. Clopidogrel dosing is unchanged.

■ **Question 3**: **How long should the triple therapy be continued?**

With the DES and presentation with an ACS, clopidogrel should be continued for at least 1 year. The patient should be maintained on aspirin 75 to 81 mg daily and warfarin to maintain the INR goal of 2 to 3 lifelong after clopidogrel has been discontinued.

Dabigatran would be an acceptable alternative to warfarin in this patient. Data for dabigatran use with ASA and clopidogrel are not available at present.

14

15 Abbreviations/Acronyms

A to Z	Aggrastat to Zocor [trial]
A4	Atrial Fibrillation Ablation Versus Antiarrhythmic Drugs [trial]
AAD	antiarrhythmic drug
ACC	American College of Cardiology
ACCF	American College of Cardiology Foundation
ACE	angiotensin-converting enzyme
ACEI	angiotensin-converting enzyme inhibitor
ACLS	advanced cardiac life support
ACP	Amplatzer Cardiac Plug
ACS	acute coronary syndrome
ACT	Atrial Arrhythmia Conversion Trial
ACTIVE	Atrial Fibrillation Clopidogrel Trial With Irbesartan for Prevention of Vascular Events
ACUTE	Assessment of Cardioversion Using Transesophageal Echocardiography [trial]
ADHF	acute decompensated heart failure
ADONIS	American-Australian-African Trial with Dronedarone in Atrial Fibrillation or Flutter Patients for the Maintenance of Sinus Rhythm
ADT	antiarrhythmic drug therapy
AF	atrial fibrillation
AFASAK	Atrial Fibrillation Aspirin and Anticoagulation [study]
AF-CHF	Rhythm Control versus Rate Control for Atrial Fibrillation in Heart Failure [trial]
AFFIRM	Atrial Fibrillation Follow-up Investigation of Rhythm Management [trial]
AFI	Atrial Fibrillation Investigators
AHA	American Heart Association
ANDROMEDA	Antiarrhythmic Trial With Dronedarone in Moderate-to-Severe Congestive Heart Failure Evaluating Morbidity Decrease
ANP	atrial natriuretic peptide
AP	action potential
APAF	Ablation for Paroxysmal Atrial Fibrillation [trial]
ARB	angiotensin receptor blocker

ARDS	adult respiratory distress syndrome
ARISTOTLE	Apixaban for the Prevention of Stroke in Subjects With Atrial Fibrillation [trial]
ARMYDA3	Atorvastatin for Reduction of Myocardial Dysrhythmia After Cardiac Surgery [study]
AS	aortic stenosis
ASA	acetylsalicylic acid (aspirin)
ASD	atrial septal defect
ATHENA	Assess the Efficacy of Dronedarone for the Prevention of Cardiovascular Hospitalization or Death From Any Cause in Patients With Atrial Fibrillation/Atrial Flutter [trial]
ATRIA	Anticoagulation and Risk Factors in Atrial Fibrillation [study]
AV	atrioventricular
AVERROES	Apixaban Versus Acetylsalicylic Acid to Prevent Strokes [trial]
AVN-VS	atrioventricular-nodal vagal stimulation
BAATAF	Boston Area Anticoagulation Trial for Atrial Fibrillation
BAFTA	Birmingham Atrial Fibrillation Treatment of the Aged [study]
BB	β-blocker
bid	twice daily
BMI	body mass index
BNP	B-type natriuretic peptide
BP	blood pressure
BPM	beats per minute
CABANA	Catheter Ablation Versus Anti-arrhythmic Drug Therapy for Atrial Fibrillation [trial]
CABG	coronary artery bypass graft
CACAF	Catheter Ablation for the Cure of Atrial Fibrillation [trial]
CAD	coronary artery disease
CAFA	Canadian Atrial Fibrillation Anticoagulation [study]
CAPP	Captopril Prevention Project
CARAF	Cocktail Attenuation of Rotational Ablation Flow Effects [study]
CAST	Cardiac Arrhythmia Suppression Trial
CCB	calcium channel blocker
CHADS	congestive heart failure, hypertension, age >75, diabetic, and history of stroke [score]
CHARM	Candesartan in Heart Failure: Assessment of Reduction in Mortality and Morbidity [trial]

15

ERATO	Efficacy and Safety of Dronedarone for the Control of Ventricular Rate [trial]
ESC	European Society of Cardiology
ESPS	European Stroke Prevention Study
EURIDIS	European Trial in Atrial Fibrillation or Flutter Patients Receiving Dronedarone for the Maintenance of Sinus Rhythm
FDA	Food and Drug Administration
g	gram
GFR	glomerular filtration rate
GI	gastrointestinal
h	hour(s)
HAS-BLED	Hypertension, Abnormal renal/liver function, Stroke, Bleeding history or predisposition, Labile INR, Elderly (>65), Drugs/alcohol concomitantly
HCM	hypertrophic cardiomyopathy
HDL	high-density lipoprotein
HEMORR2HAGES	Hepatic or renal failure, Ethanol abuse, Malignancy, Older (age over 75), Reduce platelet count or function, 2 points for Rebleeding risk, Hypertension (uncontrolled), Anemia, Genetic factors, Excessive fall risk (including neurodegenerative and psychiatric disorders) and history of Stroke
HF	heart failure
HOT CAFE	How to Treat Chronic Atrial Fibrillation
HR	hazard ratio
HRS	Heart Rhythm Society
HTN	hypertension
IAD	implantable atrial defibrillator
ICa	calcium current
ICD	implantable cardioverter defibrillator
ICH	intracranial hemorrhage
ICU	intensive care unit
IK1	inward rectifier current
IKACh	acetylcholine-regulated potassium current
IKr	rapid delayed-rectifier potassium current
IKs	slow delayed-rectifier potassium current
IKur	ultrarapid delayed-rectifier potassium current
INa	sodium current
INR	international normalized ratio
IRAF	immediate recurrence of atrial fibrillation
Ito	transient outward current
IV	intravenous
IVC	inferior vena cava
J	joules

J-RHYTHM	Japanese Rhythm Management Trial for Atrial Fibrillation
K	potassium
LA	left atrium
LAA	left atrial appendage
LFTs	liver function tests
LIFE	Losartan Intervention For End Point Reduction in Hypertension [trial]
LIPV	left inferior pulmonary vein
LMWH	low molecular weight heparin
LSPV	left superior pulmonary vein
LV	left ventricular
LVEDP	left ventricular end diastolic pressure
LVEF	left ventricular ejection fraction
LVH	left ventricular hypertrophy
MAT	multifocal atrial tachycardia
Mg	magnesium
mg	milligram
MI	myocardial infarction
min	minute(s)
MIWAF	Minidose Warfarin in Atrial Fibrillation
mo	month(s)
MOST	Mode Selection Trial
MRA	magnetic resonance angiogram
MRI	magnetic resonance imagine
msec	millisecond(s)
mV	millivolt(s)
NAC	N-acetylcysteine
NASPEAF	National Study for Primary Prevention of Embolism in Non-Rheumatic Atrial Fibrillation
NICE	National Institute for Health and Clinical Excellence
NNT	number needed to treat
NO	nitrous oxide
No.	number
NSAID	nonsteroidal anti-inflammatory drug
NSR	normal sinus rhythm
NYHA	New York Heart Association
ONTARGET	Ongoing Telmisartan Alone in Combination with Ramipril Global Endpoint Trial
OR	odds ratio
OSA	obstructive sleep apnea
PABA CHF	Ablation for Paroxysmal Atrial Fibrillation; Pulmonary Vein Atrium Isolation Versus AV-Nodal Ablation and Bi-Ventricular Pacing for Patients With Congestive Heart Failure [trial]

15

PAC	premature atrial contraction
PAF	Paroxysmal Atrial Fibrillation [trial]
PAI-1	plasminogen activator inhibitor 1
PATAF	Primary Prevention of Arterial Thromboembolism in Nonrheumatic Atrial Fibrillation [trial]
PAVE	Left Ventricular-Based Cardiac Stimulation Post AV Nodal Ablation Evaluation
PBO	placebo
PCI	percutaneous coronary intervention
PDGF	platelet-derived growth factor
PE	pulmonary embolus
PIAF	Pharmacological Intervention in Atrial Fibrillation [trial]
PLAATO	Percutaneous LAA Transcatheter Occlusion
PO	by mouth
PPM	permanent pacemaker
PR	pulse rate
PROTECT-AF	Embolic Protection in Patients with Atrial Fibrillation [trial]
PROVE-IT	Pravastatin or Atorvastatin Evaluation and Infection Therapy [trial]
PTT	partial thromboplastin time
PUFA	polyunsaturated fatty acids
PV	pulmonary vein
PVC	premature ventricular contraction
PVD	peripheral vascular disease
PVI	pulmonary vein isolation
QoL	quality of life
QRS	part of electro-cardiographic wave representing ventricular depolarization
QT	time between beginning of QRS complex and end of T-wave
QTc	length of time it takes electrical system in heart to repolarize, adjusted for heart rate
RA	right atrium
RAA	right atrial appendage
RAAFT	Radiofrequency Ablation of Atrial Fibrillation Trial
RAAS	renin-angiotensin-aldosterone system
RACE II	Rate Control Efficacy in Permanent Atrial Fibrillation: A Comparison Between Lenient Versus Strict Rate Control II
RACE	Rate Control Versus Electrical Cardioversion for Persistent Atrial Fibrillation [trial]

RAFT	Rythmol Atrial Fibrillation Trial
RE-LY	Randomized Evaluation of Long-term Anticoagulant Therapy
RF	radiofrequency
RFA	radiofrequency ablation
RHD	rheumatic heart disease
RIKS-HIA	Registry of Information and Knowledge About Swedish Heart Intensive Care Admissions
RIPV	right inferior pulmonary vein
ROCKET-AF	Efficacy and Safety of Rivaroxaban for the Prevention of Stroke in Subjects With Non-Valvular Atrial Fibrillation [trial]
RR	relative risk
R-R	the time elapsing between two consecutive R waves in the electrocardiogram
RRR	relative risk reduction
RSPV	right superior pulmonary vein
RV	right ventricular
SA	sinoatrial
SAFE-T	Sotalol Amiodarone Atrial Fibrillation Efficacy Trial
SAFIRE-D	Symptomatic Atrial Fibrillation Investigation Research on Dofetilide [trial]
SAVEPace	Search AV Extension and Managed Ventricular Pacing for Promoting Atrio-Ventricular Conduction [trial]
sec	second(s)
SNP	single-nucleotide polymorphism
SOLVD	Studies of Left Ventricular Dysfunction
SPAF	Stroke Prevention in Atrial Fibrillation [trial]
SPINAF	Stroke Prevention in Nonrheumatic Atrial Fibrillation [trial]
SR	sinus rhythm
SSRI	selective serotonin reuptake inhibitor
STAF	Strategies of Treatment of Atrial Fibrillation [trial]
STOP-2	Swedish Trial in Old Patients with Hypertension-2
STOP-AF	Sustained Treatment of Paroxysmal Atrial Fibrillation [trial]
SVC	superior vena cava
SVT	supraventricular tachycardia
TdP	torsades de pointes
TE	thromboembolism
TEE	transesophageal echocardiography
TGF-β	transforming growth factor beta

15

TIA	transient ischemic attack
TIMI	Thrombolysis in Myocardial Infarction [trial]
TRACE	Trandolapril Cardiac Evaluation [study]
TRANSCEND	Telmisartan Randomized Assessment Study in ACE Intolerant Subjects With Cardiovascular Disease [trial]
TSH	thyroid-stimulating hormone
TTE	transthoracic echocardiography
UFH	unfractionated heparin
US	ultrasound
Val-HeFT	Valsartan Heart Failure Trial
VALUE	Valsartan Antihypertensive Long-term Use Evaluation
VF	ventricular fibrillation
wk	week(s)
WPW	Wolf-Parkinson-White (syndrome)
VT	ventricular tachycardia
vWF	von Willebrand factor
y	year

INDEX

Note: AF stands for atrial fibrillation.
Page numbers in *italics* indicate figures.
Page numbers followed by a "t" indicate tables.
Clinical trials and studies are indexed under the acronym of the name.

16

16

16

16

16

16

16

16

16

16

16

16

16